W9-CDU-515

Industry and Underdevelopment

The Industrialization of Mexico,
1890-1940

Industry and Underdevelopment

The Industrialization of Mexico, 1890-1940

STEPHEN H. HABER

Stanford University Press, Stanford, California

1989

Stanford University Press
Stanford, California
© 1989 by the Board of Trustees of the
Leland Stanford Junior University
Printed in the United States of America

CIP data appear at the end of the book

Burgess

HC

135

.H17

1989

c.3

For My Parents, Joan and Kermit Haber,
who first introduced me to Mexico

Acknowledgments

GRANTS TO CARRY OUT the archival research for this study
came from the Fulbright Research Grant Program (1982–83), the
Columbia University Council on Research in the Social Sciences
Summer Grant Program (1986), and the Arthur H. Cole Grant-
in-Aid Program of the Economic History Association (1986).
Much of the initial analysis of the data and writing was done at
the Center for U.S.–Mexican Studies at the University of California, San Diego, during my stay as a Visiting Research Fellow
there in 1983–84. Further write-up support and computer assistance were provided in 1986–87 by the UCLA Program on Mexico through its U.S.–Mexico Social, Economic, and Technology
Relations Project, which is funded by the William and Flora
Hewlett Foundation.

Research in Mexico was carried out at the Archivo General de
la Nación, the Biblioteca Nacional, the Hermeroteca Nacional,
the Biblioteca Miguel Lerdo de Tejada, the Archivo General del
Estado de Nuevo León, the Biblioteca del Instituto Nacional de
Antropología e Historia, the Biblioteca del Banco de México, the
Biblioteca de Nacional Financiera, the Biblioteca de la Secretaría
de Programación y Presupuesto, the Biblioteca Daniel Cosío
Villegas at the Colegio de México, the Biblioteca de la Bolsa
Mexicana de Valores, and the Library of the American Chamber
of Commerce in Mexico. I would like to express my appreciation
to the directors and staffs of all these institutions. A special
word of thanks is owed to Enrique Cervantes at the Ramo de
Trabajo del Archivo General de la Nación, Juan Manuel Herrera
at the Ramo de Gobernación del Archivo General de la Nación,
and Elvia Barbarena, Director of the Biblioteca del Banco de

México, for making rare and uncatalogued materials available to me.

In Mexico numerous individuals gave their time and expertise. Without their counsel and help this study would have been a much more arduous task. I would especially like to thank John M. Bruton of the American Chamber of Commerce in Mexico, Felipe García Beraza of the Instituto Mexicano-Norteamericano de Relaciones Culturales, José Hinojosa Petit of Fábricas Monterrey, Hans Lenz of Las Fábricas de Papel Loreto y Peña Pobre, Carlos Prieto of Fundidora Monterrey, Agustín del Río of Vidriera Monterrey, and Gerardo Valdéz Ramírez of the Consejo Coordinador Empresarial. Marcia Grant, Harry B. Iceland, and Araceli Suárez of the Fulbright Program in Mexico facilitated my research in innumerable ways. Rose Robertson de Portilla and Felipe Moira Robertson generously allowed me access to their family papers.

In the United States several friends provided much-needed technical advice on accounting methods. CPAs Joseph C. Lamagna and Jack Campbell endured my endless village-idiot questions about depreciation schedules, memorandum accounts, and stock dividends. David Lomita took time from his busy schedule to hunt down financial data in the Library of Congress that I was unable to obtain in Mexico.

Early drafts of chapters were skillfully typed by Lycette Irving. Lisa Sue Abrams typed many of the revisions. Research assistance was provided by Diana Derycz, who worked under deadline pressure with uncommonly good humor.

Many scholars have contributed to the preparation of this book. Kenneth L. Sokoloff, James W. Wilkie, and Mary A. Yeager, teachers and friends, encouraged my interest in Mexican economic history, counseled me on research design and presentation, read the manuscript, and provided many kinds of support over the years. Clark W. Reynolds suggested the case-study approach, linked me up with other scholars working on the period, and provided much useful advice along the way. Enrique Cárdenas Sánchez generously shared his ideas, expertise, and research with me. Jeffrey L. Bortz, John H. Coatsworth, Stanley L. Engerman, Herbert S. Klein, Richard Salvucci, and John D. Wirth read and critiqued the entire manuscript—some of them more than once. I would also like to thank the referee from Stanford University Press for his comments.

In addition, numerous scholars read various parts of the manuscript or earlier papers and made many helpful suggestions. I would especially like to acknowledge León Bendesky, Woodrow Borah, Frederick Bowser, Barry Carr, Wayne Cornelius, Paul David, Sergio de la Peña, Michael Edelstein, Gustavo Garza, Gary Gereffi, Adolfo Gilly, Victor Godínez Zúñiga, William Lazonick, Carlos Malamud Rikles, Dana Markiewicz, Juan Molinar Horcasitas, Michael Monteón, the late Marie Musgrave de Portilla, Larry Neal, Leandro Prados de la Escosura, Richard Roberts, Alex Saragoza, Richard Sutch, Barbara A. Tenenbaum, Gabriel Tortella Cáceres, René Villarreal, Eugene White, Gavin Wright, and the late Donald Wyman. Finally, thanks are due to Peter F. Klarén, who first sparked my interest in Latin American history and set a challenging example of intellectual integrity.

A special word of thanks goes to my wife, Marsy, who traveled with me to Mexico, read and critiqued chapters, and kept me on track along the way. Her love and support made this study easier to complete and worth doing in the first place.

S.H.H.

Contents

Abbreviations   xv

1. Introduction   1

2. The Political-Economic Environment   12

3. The Imperatives of the Market, Technology,
   and Labor   27

4. The Structure of Production   44

5. Finance and Entrepreneurship   63

6. The Strategy of the Firm   84

7. Profits   103

8. The Revolution and Its Aftermath, 1910–1925   122

9. The Crash, 1926–1932   150

10. Recovery and Growth, 1933–1940   171

11. Conclusions   190

   Notes   203
   Bibliography   217
   Index   231

Tables

3.1	Utilization of Installed Capacity in the Cement and Steel Industries, 1903–1910	33
3.2	Production, Importation, and Consumption of Cement, 1906–1911	41
4.1	Mexican Cigarette Production, 1898–1911	49
4.2	El Buen Tono Sales, 1894–1909	51
4.3	Cervecería Cuauhtemoc Sales, 1892–1910	53
5.1	Debt-Equity Ratios, Selected Manufacturing Companies, 1901–1913	65
5.2	Investment Portfolio of Thomas Braniff in 1905, by Functional Category	78
5.3	Investments of Thomas Braniff in Manufacturing, 1905	79
7.1	Estimated Rates of Return on Capital Stock, 1902–1910	110
7.2	Yields on Common Stock, Selected Manufacturing Companies, 1896–1910	113
7.3	Yields on Common Stock, Composite Values, 1896–1910	114
7.4	Real Dividends, Selected Manufacturing Companies, 1895–1910	115

7.5 Average Yields on Industrial Stocks Compared to Government Bonds and Banco Nacional de México Stock, 1901–1910 — 118

7.6 Real Returns to Investors, 1902–1910 — 120

8.1 Cotton Textile Industry, Main Economic Indicators, 1895–1925 — 125

8.2 Cervecería Cuauhtemoc Sales, 1911–1925 — 126

8.3 Utilization of Installed Capacity in the Cement and Steel Industries, 1911–1925 — 127

8.4 Estimated Rates of Return on Capital Stock, 1911–1925 — 128

8.5 Yields on Common Stock, Selected Manufacturing Companies, 1911–1925 — 129

8.6 Yields on Common Stock, Composite Values, 1911–1925 — 130

8.7 Dividend Earnings, Selected Manufacturing Companies, 1911–1925 — 131

8.8 Estimated Value of Physical Plant, Fundidora Monterrey, CIDOSA, El Buen Tono, 1903–1925 — 142

8.9 Real Return to Investors, 1918–1925 — 145

8.10 Real Dividend Earnings, Selected Manufacturing Companies, 1911–1925 — 146

8.11 Capital Stock, Ratio of Market to Book Values, Fundidora Monterrey, CIDOSA, El Buen Tono, 1902–1925 — 148

9.1 Cotton Textile Industry, Main Economic Indicators, 1925–1932 — 158

9.2 Estimated Rates of Return on Capital Stock, 1926–1932 — 160

9.3 Real Dividend Earnings, Selected Manufacturing Companies, 1926–1932 — 161

9.4   Beer Production, National and Cervecería
      Cuauhtemoc, 1924–1932   163

9.5   Utilization of Installed Capacity in the Cement
      and Steel Industries, 1926–1932   165

9.6   Estimated Value of Physical Plant, Fundidora
      Monterrey, CIDOSA, El Buen Tono,
      1924–1932   167

9.7   Capital Stock, Ratio of Market to Book Values,
      Fundidora Monterrey, CIDOSA, El Buen
      Tono, 1926–1932   168

9.8   Real Return to Investors, 1926–1932   169

10.1 Utilization of Installed Capacity in the Cement
      and Steel Industries, 1933–1938   177

10.2 Estimated Rates of Return on Capital Stock,
      1933–1937   178

10.3 Real Dividend Earnings, Selected Manufactur-
      ing Companies, 1933–1938   179

10.4 Beer Production, National and Cervecería
      Cuauhtemoc, 1933–1940   180

10.5 Cotton Textile Industry, Main Economic In-
      dicators, 1933–1940   181

10.6 Real Return to Investors, 1933–1938   183

10.7 Estimated Value of Physical Plant, Fundidora
      Monterrey, CIDOSA, El Buen Tono,
      1933–1937   185

10.8 Capital Stock, Ratio of Market to Book Values,
      Fundidora Monterrey, CIDOSA, El Buen
      Tono, 1932–1937   186

11.1 Real Return to Investors, 1902–1938   195

Abbreviations

The following abbreviations are used in the Tables and the Notes:

AGENL   Archivo General del Estado de Nuevo León. Numbers following citation denote box, file, and document number.

AGNT   Archivo General de La Nación, Ramo de Trabajo. Numbers following citation denote box, file, and document number.

Amcham   *Journal of the American Chamber of Commerce of Mexico.*

BCM   Banco Central Mexicano, *Las sociedades anónimas de México, año I* (Mexico City, 1908).

BFM   *Boletín Financiero y Minero* (Mexico City financial weekly).

EM   *El Economista Mexicano* (Mexico City financial weekly).

FI   *El Fomento Industrial* (Mexico City financial weekly).

FM   Compañía Fundidora de Fierro y Acero de Monterrey.

FMIA   Compañía Fundidora de Fierro y Acero de Monterrey. Informe Anual.

MI   *México Industrial* (Mexico City financial weekly).

MYB   *The Mexican Yearbook* (London: McCorquodale and Company, 1908–14).

SM   *La Semana Mercantil* (Mexico City financial weekly).

Industry and Underdevelopment

The Industrialization of Mexico,
1890-1940

ONE

Introduction

SINCE THE SUMMER of 1982, when Mexican treasury minister Jesús Silva Herzog declared a moratorium on the repayment of his government's external debt, Mexico's economic crisis has become progressively more severe. As I was finishing this book in 1987, national economic growth had been at a standstill for five years: in per capita terms it fell by better than 2.5 percent per year. The downward spiral of the economy caused a serious deterioration in wages and living standards. Between 1982 and 1987 the real wages of working people fell by approximately 50 percent, with concomitant drops in levels of nutrition, housing, and other basic needs. What many Mexican families once considered staples—eggs, meat, milk—were now considered luxuries. Much of the nation's manufacturing plant lay idle because consumer demand was not high enough to support its operation. The Mexican peso, long one of the world's most stable currencies, fell to a minute fraction of its former value. In early 1982 it traded for 22.5 to the dollar; by the end of the year it had fallen to 148, and it continued to lose 50 percent of its value per year ever since. By the summer of 1987 it traded for 1,500 to the dollar.

Oil, which former President José López Portillo perceived as Mexico's ticket to the developed world, has proved to be a bust. Mexico spent almost as much money on imported capital goods, technology, exploration, and infrastructural investments as it realized in oil revenues. With petroleum prices seriously depressed, and with no indication that market conditions will improve over the medium term, it is extremely doubtful that Mexico will be able to finance its way out of the crisis through the exportation of oil.

Oddly enough, in 1979, just three years prior to Silva Herzog's declaration of a moratorium, the Mexican economy was being touted, in both the popular and the academic press, as a major success story. With each new loan negotiated and with each new rise in world oil prices, the outlook for Mexico looked increasingly bright. Mexico's continued economic growth, according to the prevailing wisdom, was bound to lessen the country's dependence on the United States and make it more nearly America's equal. Until everything came apart in 1982, it seemed that the combination of petroleum and foreign credit could accomplish anything.

It should have surprised no one that the Mexican "miracle" fell apart as quickly as it did. The Mexican economy was an unhealthy one; the same foreign loans and petroleum exports that most analysts viewed so positively were in fact an indication that the economy was in deep trouble. Indeed, national economic growth became almost totally dependent on these two items (three quarters of all export earnings in 1982 were from petroleum sales). Mexico, unable to control either interest rates or the price of oil, pegged its future to these risky and uncertain sources of growth because its manufacturing sector, long the motor of its economic expansion, could no longer drive the economy. At the core of Mexico's economic difficulties lay an industrial base that could neither compete in foreign markets nor grow at a rate rapid enough to fuel continued economic growth; in 1982 manufacturing made up 20 percent of Gross Domestic Product (GDP) but only 3 percent of merchandise exports. Unwilling to face the political repercussions of a slowdown in the economy, the Mexican government turned to petroleum and to Wall Street.

The problems of Mexican industry were myriad. Dependent upon government protection and subsidies, developing almost none of its own technology, producing relatively high-cost, low-quality goods by archaic, inflexible production methods, Mexican industry was able to grow to a point. By the mid-1970's, however, this inward-looking style of industrialization had exhausted most of its possibilities. The long wave of innovation, investment, and profits that had yielded impressive results since the 1940's was now winding down under the weight of the very institutions and arrangements that had permitted the earlier growth to occur.

What were these institutions and arrangements? Why did Mexican industry develop the way it did, with production oriented almost entirely to the home market, protected behind a wall of government subsidies, tariffs, and import quotas? Similarly, why was production organized in such an inflexible, noncompetitive fashion? Why did oligopolies and monopolies dominate the manufacture of most goods? Moreover, why did these firms employ inappropriate technology imported from other countries, and why did Mexico not develop and produce its own capital goods? Above all, how did the political and economic organization of Mexico combine with exogenous factors related to the "lateness" of Mexican industrialization to form this peculiar industrial structure?

For answers to these questions about economic organization, we turn not to Mexico's recent period of decline, but to the period in which the basic structures of modern Mexican industry were established. This study, therefore, is concerned with the first wave of modern Mexican industrialization, which extended from the 1890's to the 1930's. This was the period in which Mexican manufacturing moved out of the artisanal shop and into the factory, when production for local and regional markets began to give way to production for the national market, and when family-owned and family-run firms were replaced by publicly held joint-stock corporations. During this first wave of large-scale industrialization, the production of a wide range of industrial staples, including steel, cement, beer, cotton textiles, paper, glass, dynamite, soap, and cigarettes, came to be dominated by large, vertically integrated firms that utilized mass production techniques to satisfy the mass market.

These firms, all founded between 1890 and 1910, served as the backbone of Mexican industry after 1940 when the implicit protection provided by the Second World War set off a second round of industrial expansion. In fact, many of them are among Mexico's present-day industrial giants. Examples are the Vidriera Monterrey glass works, today the nucleus of the Grupo Vitro industrial conglomerate; the Moctezuma and Cuauhtemoc breweries, which together with the Cervecería Modelo totally control the Mexican beer market; and the Fundidora Monterrey steel works, which until it was liquidated in 1986 was part of the government steel consortium, Sidermex. Other examples can be found in the cement, cotton textile, and paper industries. It is on the epoch in which manufacturing became big business in Mexico that this study focuses.

During the early phase of industrialization, patterns of entrepreneurial behavior and industrial organization were established that were not conducive to long-term, balanced economic growth. From its very beginning, Mexican manufacturing was characterized by the inability to export, the need for protection from foreign competition, an almost total dependence on imported technology, and an extraordinarily high degree of market concentration. Thus, many of the contemporary "problems" of Mexican manufacturing are not new, but date from the very inception of large-scale industry in Mexico.

Mexican industry developed in this manner because of the contradictions and limitations inherent in the rapid industrialization of an underdeveloped economy. These economic constraints, which are outlined in Chapter 3, conditioned Mexican industrialization in three crucial ways. First, the relatively small size and depth of the Mexican market compared to the productive capacity of its imported manufacturing plant meant that the rate of capacity utilization in many industries was extremely low. This in turn meant that manufacturing during this early phase of industrialization was not particularly profitable unless a firm had a high degree of control over the market. The net result, as discussed in detail in Chapter 4, was that Mexican industry came to be controlled by oligopolies and monopolies. Given the scale of production implicit in Mexico's imported plant, only a few large firms could survive.

If Mexico had been able to export some of these manufactures, the problem of excess installed capacity and the noncompetitive market structure to which it gave rise could have been alleviated. But, given fierce competition in the international market and the transitional nature of the Mexican economy, this was not a possibility. As early as 1902 Mexican industrialists tried to export, but to no avail. In fact, they had a difficult time holding their own in the domestic market against foreign imports and were continually forced to ask the government for increased levels of protection.

Here Mexico's emerging industrialists were further hampered by the second major constraint to successful, rapid industrialization: the productivity of Mexican labor was far lower than that of workers in the advanced industrial countries. As had been the case in Europe in the early nineteenth century, Mexican workers actively resisted the routinization and discipline of the factory system during the early phase of industrialization. Factory operatives therefore worked far fewer machines per worker and produced far less per hour than did their British or U.S. counterparts. The result of this lower productivity was that Mexico's lower wage levels could not be translated into a competitive advantage in the international market.

The third major constraint to Mexico's early industrialization was the relatively high cost of imported capital goods compared to the ability of Mexico's financial sector to mobilize capital. The financing of Mexican industrialization fell to a relatively small clique of merchant-financiers who, because of their backgrounds in commerce and money-lending, were more adept at rigging the market and manipulating government policy than at streamlining production methods or innovating new processes or techniques. This both reinforced the manufacturing sector's tendency toward oligopoly and monopoly production and further encouraged a style of industrialization dependent on government protection and subsidies. This subject is taken up in detail in Chapter 5.

The shape that a nation's industrial structure takes is not entirely the product of abstract social and economic forces but is also the outcome of human agency. Mexico's emerging industrial entrepreneurs, with government support, consciously set out to discourage competition through the formation of monopolies, oligopolies, and rigged markets. How they did this is the subject of Chapter 6.

Underlying this structure of production and entrepreneurship was a generally low and uncertain level of profitability. Contrary to much of the popular mythology about the Porfiriato,* Mexican manufacturing companies of that era—even some of the monopolies—lost money as often as they made it. In fact, although the rate of profit picked up after the Revolution, manufacturing in Mexico was over the long run an extremely risky and often unremunerative enterprise. It was precisely because of this low level of profitability that the rate of growth of the manufacturing sector was so slow and that Mexican industry took such a peculiar form. This is demonstrated in Chapter 7, in which I provide a set of estimates of the financial returns to investors and accounting rates of profit for Mexico's most important manufacturing companies.

Mexican entrepreneurs did not go into manufacturing blindly. They recognized that the structure of the Mexican economy imposed certain restrictions on their enterprises. They hoped, however, that the process of economic growth would eventually rectify the imbalances that made many of their enterprises perennial money losers. That is, they invested ahead of the economy, anticipating healthier returns over the long run, and subsidized the low marginal returns from manufacturing with profits from other investments, such as commerce, urban real estate speculation, agriculture, and mining. This, as Chapter 2 demonstrates, was not an unreasonable strategy in view of the rapid rate of growth of the Mexican economy during the 1880's and 1890's. Mexico's future looked bright, and there was reason to believe that investments in manufacturing would pay off handsomely.

In this they were sadly mistaken, as Chapter 8 discusses in detail. Rather than rectifying structural imbalances in the economy, the process of economic growth set off a revolution. Although this did not imply the destruction of Mexico's manufacturing plants, as many scholars have erroneously believed, the combined shock of the financial crash of 1907–8 and the overthrow of the Porfirian state in 1910 created a crisis of confidence among Mexican industrialists that discouraged new investment

---

*The Porfiriato is the period 1876–1910, during which Porfirio Díaz ruled Mexico. He stepped down from the presidency only once, 1880–84, when Manuel González, one of his cronies, served as president.

in plant and equipment for the next two decades. In fact, after 1907 the process of industrialization, in a certain sense, began to reverse itself. New machinery was seldom purchased, few new enterprises were founded, and entrepreneurs grew increasingly cautious.

The contraction in manufacturing investment became even more severe as the result of a nationwide depression from 1925 to 1932, a subject that is discussed in Chapter 9. When market conditions finally improved by the latter part of the 1930's, much of the nation's manufacturing plant dated from before the Revolution of 1910. It was this industrial plant, along with scattered new industries founded in the early 1920's and late 1930's, that served as the backbone of the rapid industrial expansion of the 1940's and 1950's, made possible by the implicit protection of the Second World War. This period of renewed growth is discussed in Chapter 10. Chapter 11 then summarizes the argument and presents the general conclusions of the work.

This study is concerned predominantly with questions of industrial structure and organization and with the historical factors that gave rise to this ordering of production. It is not intended as an overall survey of the history of Mexican manufacturing. For this reason it covers only the first wave of modern Mexican industrialization, from 1890 through the 1930's.

I do not cover the period prior to 1890 because Mexican manufacturing was then restricted to a few industries that functioned only on a regional scale. Prior to the 1890's the only industry that utilized the factory system on a large scale was cotton textiles, and even in this line of production there were still a number of firms that more closely resembled artisanal shops than modern factories. Moreover, the organization of industrial enterprises between the two periods was entirely different. Prior to the 1890's firms were owned and administered by individual entrepreneurs, or at most, two or three partners. With the expansion of the scale and range of enterprises after the 1890's, the financing and administration of firms changed totally. Joint-stock companies were formed to finance the mammoth enterprises of the Porfiriato, and these enterprises were no longer run by the individuals who owned them. Instead, there were salaried managers. Above all, during the 1890's Mexican manufacturing moved into a whole new wave of technology and began to produce a far wider variety of fairly complex goods. By the turn of the century Mexico was utilizing large-scale production methods to produce steel, cement, dynamite, glycerine, newsprint, and fine cotton cloth—industries that had not existed at all prior to the 1890's.

This study also does not address the period after 1940. This is for two reasons. First, there is already a voluminous literature on Mexican industry since the Second World War. Second, I view that period as essentially an elaboration and consolidation of the process that took place between 1890 and 1940.

In some ways Mexico's post–1940 industrialization was different from that which occurred during the Porfiriato. A new entrepreneurial group led the economy, the government played a larger role in fomenting and financing growth, and the working class was now controlled through methods far more subtle than those used during the Porfiriato. Above all, Mexican industry was far bigger after the Second World War than before and now led national economic growth.

The fundamental patterns of organization and structure were, however, much the same from one period to the next. Mexican industrialists faced the same kind of constraints after 1940 as before, and this meant that business was carried out in much the same way. Mexican manufacturing continued to be confined to the home market and to need government protection and subsidization. Oligopolistic production still predominated, with a few firms carving up the lion's share of the market. Similarly, Mexican industry remained technologically dependent, drawing on imported capital goods from the advanced industrial countries. In fact, in the 1980's, close to one hundred years after modern Mexican industrialization got under way, Mexico still lacks a well developed capital goods industry.

This study concentrates on structural and organizational questions for two reasons. First, the path of industrialization that Mexico has followed over the last century has in large part determined the development of the nation's polity and society. In fact, in the years since 1940 the Partido Revolucionario Institucional (PRI) has built a political consensus around national industrial growth and has used it to help legitimate one-party rule. Indeed, part of the success of the PRI in maintaining control for so long has been its ability to portray itself as a "modernizing" party, which has created jobs for workers and profits for manufacturers.

Second, studying the organization and structure of Mexican industry is highly instructive in understanding the industrial development of other less-developed countries. The process of state building and internal market growth—both reactions to the expansion of the export economy during this period—which set off a wave of industrial expansion in Mexico, occurred throughout the less-developed world. In addition, these other countries faced many of the same technological, labor, and financial constraints that Mexico faced. Where those countries actively pushed a policy of industrial expansion, the results were much the same. Brazil, for example, underwent a similar process of economic growth, which produced an industrial structure much like Mexico's.[1]

Because structural considerations take center stage in this study, other issues, such as government policy or the formation of the working class, are discussed only to the extent that they impinge on this central concern. Readers interested primarily in these other subjects will be disappointed to find that neither one receives a chapter of its own. Other scholars, however, have already studied both of these important issues at length.[2]

The period covered in this work has been little studied by scholars. Almost all of the literature on Mexican manufacturing has focused on the period since 1940. The relative lack of attention to Mexico's early industrialization is a function of the fact that almost all of the studies written to date are based upon macro-level, official sources. That is, they have been written from government reports, industrial censuses, surveys, and other published data, which do not become plentiful until the postwar period. The extant literature often gives the impression, therefore, that Mexican industry miraculously appeared out of thin air in the 1940's when the government began to publish statistics about it. As Clark Reynolds has pointed out, however, there was nothing miraculous about Mexico's post-1940 industrial growth: the industrialization process actually began in earnest during the late nineteenth century. Much of the boom during the Second World War was actually due to the running of Mexico's already installed plant around the clock.[3]

Because it is based upon firm-level sources, this study is able to go beyond the conventional literature. Instead of relying on official government publications, it utilizes primary source materials from individual firms and individual entrepreneurs. These sources include corporate annual reports, the correspondence of industrialists and labor unions with government agencies, corporate accounts, and stock market records. These firm-level sources are supplemented by data from the industrial and commercial directories of the time, tax records and registers compiled by the Ministry of the Treasury, the reports of foreign commercial attachés and consuls, and the Mexican financial press. Oral history interviews with Mexican industrialists further complement the written sources.

The method employed is to look at individual firms and individual industries, and to use these case studies to derive generalizations about the structure and development of Mexican manufacturing. It therefore differs fundamentally from the method of previous studies of Mexican industry written from the vantage point of aggregate census categories, which lump all firms and industries together.

Because I proceed in this fashion, this study addresses questions that have been neglected in the literature to date. First, it addresses the question of the origins of Mexico's manufacturing plant prior to the Second World War: When was it built? What kind of technology was employed? How were production and distribution organized? How did particular industries fare during the Revolution and the Great Depression? Second, it addresses a whole range of questions related to the social and political history of Mexican industrialization: Who were the investors in early Mexican manufacturing enterprises, and where did they get their capital? What was the relationship between these industrialists and the state? By what means did the government encourage these manufacturers, and what did it get in return? Finally, the method employed in this study permits the examination of quantitative questions: How profitable was early Mexican manufacturing? What was the rate of capacity utilization? What effect did the Mexican Revolution and the Great Depression have on capital markets and investor confidence?

There are limits to the case study approach, however, which should be mentioned at the outset. Because of the nature of the sources, it was not possible to cover every line of manufacturing. Because firm-level data for several important industries, shoes and boots being a case in point, are relatively scarce, this study focuses predominantly on the steel, cement, glass, paper, wool textile, cotton textile, beer, soap, glycerine and dynamite, and cigarette industries. The data are likewise uneven in their coverage. For some firms it was possible to put together complete series on profits, capital stock, expenditures on new investment, debt-equity ratios, output, sales, and the like. For others, it was possible to construct series on only a few of these variables. Most serious was the lack of price data. Thus, constructing a formal and comprehensive model of the manufacturing sector was not feasible. The industries that left the most complete records, and which therefore comprise the greater part of my data base, tend to be the larger, more successful companies. Smaller enterprises, or those that went out of business fairly early in their development, tend not to figure as prominently in the sources. Thus the case study approach creates a natural bias toward larger, more successful enterprises.

But even with this inherent bias in the data our story is not one of unbridled success. Rather, the image that emerges from the sources is one of truncated and uneven growth. It is the story of an industrialization process unable to overcome the limitations imposed by an underdeveloped economy—limitations that Mexico in the 1980's continues to face.

TWO

The Political-Economic Environment

BEGINNING IN THE 1870's, Mexico became more fully integrated into the world market. A nation heretofore characterized by a segmented and backward economy was becoming transformed into a protean, capitalist economy with increasingly unified markets and accelerated rates of economic growth. Along with these changes in the productive sphere came similar changes in the political sphere. The transformation of the economy required changes in the country's political organization. From the 1820's, when independence was achieved, until the 1870's the Mexican state had been weak and ineffective, unable either to defend itself from internal and external attacks or to create an environment propitious to the long-run accumulation of capital on a national scale. Beginning in the 1870's, with the rise of Porfirio Díaz, the state began to grow stronger, continually increasing the authority and power of the central government at the expense of the regional *caciques* who until then had held sway.

The engine driving this whole process of political and economic transformation was the inflow of capital from Europe and the United States. After 1870 capital, and capitalists, flowed into the nation, draining and retimbering the mines, spurring the growth of haciendas and plantations, and financing the whirlwind construction of a national railway system. By 1910, according to the available estimates, foreigners had invested close to $2 billion in Mexico's railroads, mines, and a variety of other undertakings, a sum that accounted for between 67 and 73 percent of total invested capital in the country.[1]

The key area into which foreign capital flowed was the transport sector. Unlike the United States, England, or the other already industrialized countries, whose cities were connected by coastal traffic, rivers, or canal systems, Mexico's water transport was confined to the pre-Columbian canal system constructed by the Aztecs around the area of Mexico City.[2] Mexico's lack of navigable rivers and its mountainous topography required that most traffic move overland, either by wheeled vehicle or by mule train. During the sixteenth and seventeenth centuries the Spaniards had constructed an impressive highway system, which was designed to accommodate the heavy, two-wheeled *carros* that were used to transport silver from the mines in the Bajío and imported manufactures from the port city of Veracruz to Mexico City. By the nineteenth century this system, neglected for over a century and badly in need of repair, served as the sole means of long-distance transport. Although there had been a revival of the mining industry during the eighteenth century, it did not occasion increased expenditures on the highway system. In that same period the internal and external conflicts of the Spanish Crown served as a sieve through which the wealth of the empire poured. Little money was available for the improvement or maintenance of the rapidly deteriorating roads. Thus, by the nineteenth century only a single roadway existed that was suitable for wheeled traffic along its entire length. Even on this highway, which ran from Mexico City to Chihuahua via Zacatecas and Durango, mule trains outnumbered wheeled traffic.[3]

After independence the condition of the roadways continued to deteriorate. In the incessant conflicts throughout the nineteenth century between the central government and regional political bosses who wanted to maintain their political and economic autonomy, the latter regularly tore up and otherwise refused to repair the roads that ran into their enclaves.[4] During the 1850's the Mexican government began to repair the highways, but the general lack of funds dictated that its efforts be limited to the maintenance of a few well-traveled routes. This program was continued and expanded during the French Intervention (1862–67) and the Restored Republic (1867–76), but the lack of resources paralyzed road work for years at a time. By

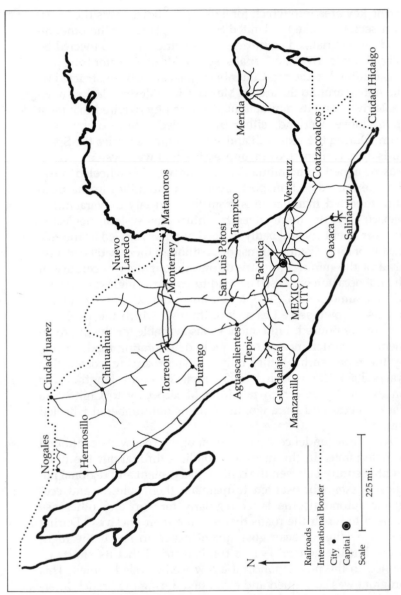

The Mexican Rail System in 1910. Based on map in Ortiz Hernán 1974:144.

1876, when Porfirio Díaz seized power, half of all federal highways were suitable only for beasts of burden. Others were so narrow and broken that they could be passed only by pedestrian traffic.[5]

Railroads, which would have alleviated the transport problem, were not constructed for the same reasons that affected highway maintenance. Federal funds were nowhere near sufficient to launch a railroad program. Even without sponsoring major infrastructure projects the governments of the mid-nineteenth century were continually broke. Foreign investment could have been used to build a rail system, but none of the regimes from 1821 to 1876 had much luck in enticing foreign capitalists into financing such a venture. Mexico's first rail line, from Mexico City to Veracruz, was not completed until 1873. In fact, in 1877 Mexico possessed not more than 640 kilometers of track, of which 114 employed mules rather than steam engines as their source of motive power.[6]

Beginning in 1880 the inflow of foreign capital changed this situation. In that year two major concessions to build trunk lines from Mexico City to the U.S. border were awarded to competing groups of American investors. Mexico's rail grid expanded rapidly thereafter. In 1873 Mexico possessed only 572 kilometers of track; by 1883 it had over 5,000. The network expanded to over 10,000 kilometers by 1893, and to 16,000 in 1903. In 1910, just before the Revolution broke out, the Mexican rail system boasted over 19,000 kilometers of track. These figures account only for track laid under federal concession. In addition, commuter and feeder lines constructed under state or municipal concessions accounted for an additional 7,810 kilometers of track.[7]

Though the system was laid out without any central plan, the Díaz government generally awarding concessions on an ad hoc basis, the ultimate effect was that a fairly well-integrated grid developed. The primary purpose of the railways was to move raw materials to the coast or to the northern border for export to foreign markets, but the sheer number of feeder lines eventually gave rise to an interconnected grid that linked internal markets as well as the mining areas and the ports. By the turn of the century most of the major cities were connected to one another by rail (see map).

The effect of this railroad boom on the rest of the economy was extraordinary. Transport costs fell precipitously, stimulating the revival of the mines, furthering the expansion of commercial agriculture, and uniting the internal market. According to the conservative estimates of John Coatsworth, freight rates fell from 10 cents per ton kilometer (using wagon transport) in 1878 to 2.3 cents per ton kilometer (using railroads) in 1910. If Mexico had tried to move the volume of freight transported by the railroads in 1910 using the next best available technology, that is, wagon transport, the cost would have increased between five and ten times.[8] To give a concrete example: the cost of shipping a ton of cotton textiles the roughly 130 miles from Mexico City to Querétaro declined from $61 in 1877 to $3 in 1910.[9]

The fall in transport costs redounded throughout the economy as commercial producers expanded their output to serve the now vastly wider markets they faced. Among the industries whose growth was stimulated by the construction of railroads, perhaps the most important was mining. Throughout the colonial period the engine driving the economy of New Spain had been the mines. The silver mines of Zacatecas, Guanajuato, and San Luis Potosí were part of a dynamic extractive economy that not only directly employed tens of thousands of workers, but also created derived demand effects as well. In order to satisfy the mining sector's demand for food, equipment, clothing, and all manner of intermediate inputs, the rest of the economy reacted. Large stock-raising enterprises sprang up in northern Mexico to produce beef, tallow, and leather. Haciendas and small farms in the Bajío expanded in order to feed the mining center's populations. Local weavers produced cloth for the work force, and artisans constructed the necessary tools and mechanical devices. The flourishing commerce that grew out of this activity enriched Mexico City's merchants, who served both as suppliers of the mines and as important financial intermediaries. In short, the Mexican economy was led by the mining sector throughout the colonial period. With periodic booms in production the rest of the economy expanded. During harsher times for the mines, the economy contracted.

During the early nineteenth century the mining sector experienced a severe decline. Throughout the period from Independence to the Porfiriato most of Mexico's major mines lay in ruin, their revival requiring that huge sums be invested in retimbering and draining. Foreign companies, mostly from England, stepped in to finance these operations, but their efforts met with little success. Apparently underestimating the obstacles, they sank huge sums into reviving the mines, only to become frustrated at their losses due to inadequate transport and low grade ores.

Though a comprehensive history of mining in nineteenth-century Mexico is still to be written, we may conclude that the critical factor was transport.[10] Even getting the necessary machinery to the mines proved to be a near-impossible task. For example, it took the Real del Monte company almost a year to transport the equipment it needed to renovate its mines in Hidalgo from the seacoast. That is, a 350-mile journey (Veracruz to Pachuca) took almost 12 months.[11] Delays of this sort not only drove up the cost of equipment—for example, imported textile machinery often doubled in cost by the time it reached Mexico City—they also created even greater risk and uncertainty in meeting production schedules.[12] Transporting the ore to the coast must have been compounded by equally serious problems.

Given the transport and other problems facing the industry, it is not surprising that most of the foreign companies abandoned Mexico's mines as unprofitable. Of the seven companies formed between 1821 and 1825 to exploit Mexico's silver mines, only one survived into the 1850's. Mexico's level of silver production in 1810 was not matched again until the 1870's.[13] The situation in nonprecious metals was no doubt even worse than it was in silver production. The high weight-to-price ratio of most industrial metals (zinc, copper, and the like) made the lack of inexpensive transport an even larger obstacle than it was in the production of precious metals such as silver.

Beginning in the 1880's the combination of falling transport costs and the availability of capital to invest in mineral exploration and exploitation revitalized the mining sector. Between 1880 and 1890 foreign investors undertook three major projects: Sierra Mojada in Coahuila, Batopilas in Chihuahua, and El Boleo in Baja California. There were also major investments in the smelting of ore, the Guggenheim's American Smelting and Refining Company being the most important investor in this line of activity. Silver production climbed from 606,037 metric tons in fiscal 1877–78 to 2.3 million metric tons in 1910–11. During the same period, gold production climbed from scarcely over 1,000 metric tons to 37,112 metric tons. Overall, precious metal output increased fivefold between 1877 and 1911, while industrial metal production (copper, lead, zinc, and like minerals) increased by three times between 1893 and 1911.[14]

A similar process was under way in petroleum production. As was the case with railroads and mining, the expansion of the oil industry was the result of the inflow of foreign capital. As foreign companies pumped money into the exploration and exploitation of Mexico's oil resources, Mexico pumped increasingly larger quantities of oil into the world market. Petroleum production grew from scarcely over 5,000 barrels in fiscal 1900–1901 to over eight million barrels in 1910–11. In no year during that ten-year period did Mexico's oil output fail to increase.[15]

The movement of capital into Mexico also spurred the growth of the agricultural sector. In part, the expansion of commercial agriculture was a response to that of the mines, oil fields, and railroads: the armies of workers toiling in these operations had to be fed. Thus the demand for abundant, inexpensive food-stuffs increased, and it could not be satisfied by peasant agriculture. This was not, however, the only impetus behind the transformation of rural Mexico. There was also the development of an export-oriented agriculture that produced raw materials for the advanced industrial countries. Most significant here was the growth of the cotton industry in the La Laguna area in the north and the development of the sisal industry in Yucatán.

Whether the commercialization of agriculture was directed toward the internal market or toward export markets, the ultimate effect on the peasantry was the same: the peasants lost their lands. The transformation of the relations of production in the agricultural sector was uneven. In some areas, particularly those farthest from large haciendas, the peasantry was successful in defending its lands. In others, especially in central Mexico, the transformation was more complete.

As had occurred in England during the seventeenth and eighteenth centuries, a series of legal acts aimed at eliminating communally held property transformed the organization of peasant agriculture. The intention of the Liberal governments of the 1850's and 1870's was not only to attack the Church, as many scholars have argued, but to undo the peasantry, which in their eyes was an equally large impediment to "progress" and "modernization." Juárez and the other Liberal reformers of the mid-nineteenth century sought to create a class of yeoman farmers in Mexico that would serve as the basis for a stable and forward-looking economy and polity. That which stood in the way of this political-economic project—that which was retrograde and backward looking, that which was mired in the past, in short that which interfered with the creation of a modern, capitalist state in Mexico—had to be swept aside. That this project entailed vast human costs was not deemed particularly important.

The attack upon Indian communal lands, which began in the 1850's, accelerated after 1870 when the construction of the railroads and the inflow of foreign capital set off increased speculation in rural real estate. New laws were passed that assaulted private property in the Indian villages, not just the communal lands. In 1883 and again in 1893 the government passed legislation enabling land companies to survey "unused national lands," receiving one-third of the lands surveyed in compensation for the expenses incurred in surveying them.

These laws were used as a pretext for the rich and powerful to accumulate enormous estates at the expense of the poor. Imperfect titles could be denounced and the owners forced off the land. This meant essentially that most of the properties owned by the peasantry could be legally confiscated by the government and then sold to private interests, minus the one-third taken by the surveying company, unless the owners could present proof of ownership dating back to a primordial deed emanating from the Spanish Crown. Between 1883 and 1892, 38.2 million hectares of land were surveyed, two-thirds of which eventually wound up in private hands. All told, between 1876 and 1910 one-fifth of the national territory was transferred to private ownership. Though the data on land tenure for this period are rough, and comparisons difficult, they suggest a loss between 1854 and 1910 of perhaps 50 percent or more of communal lands. According to data from the 1910 population census, 82 percent of Indian communities had been incorporated into haciendas, and about half the rural population lived permanently on large properties.[16] This figure probably overestimates the percentage of Indian communities subsumed into haciendas, since the census takers had an easier time censusing haciendas than they did remote, rural villages. Even if it is off by a factor of two, which is most likely the case, the figure still implies that a substantial transformation occurred in land tenure patterns during the Porfiriato.

The Mexican peasantry did not passively accept these changes. In addition to setting off a boom in rural real estate speculation, the arrival of the railroad in an area also set off a wave of Indian rebellions,[17] which in turn were frequently met by the government with a repression unprecedented in its brutality. In response to resistance among the Yaqui Indians of Sonora, for example, the Díaz government carted them off like slaves to work in the henequen plantations of Yucatán, where most of them soon died of tropical diseases.

The creation of a rapidly growing wage-earning class in Mexico during the late nineteenth century was therefore as much the result of violence as it was of the growth of the economy and the wage-paying jobs it created. People left their villages for the cities not only because they were interested in advancing economically or because they sought to escape the monotony of rural life; they were forced to do so.

The result of all these changes in the organization of production and distribution was that the economy once again began to grow. According to Coatsworth's estimates, per capita national income (expressed in 1950 U.S. dollars) fell throughout the early part of the nineteenth century, from $73 in 1800 to $56 in 1845, and to $49 in 1860. In the 1870's this downward spiral was reversed. Per capita income increased to $62 by 1877 and continued growing, to $91 in 1895 and $132 by 1910.[18]

The inflow of capital not only brought about basic structural changes in the economy; it also produced concomitant changes in Mexico's political structures. Indeed, the two phenomena were organically linked: without creating change in the political sphere, the transformation of the economy could have gone only so far.

Prior to the rise of Porfirio Díaz, the Mexican state was weak and disorganized. The central government exercised little control over the provincial areas, which operated with almost complete autonomy. Indeed, national politics between 1821 and 1876 were characterized by a succession of provincial caudillos to power. In the 55 years between Independence and the Porfiriato, the presidency changed hands 75 times. For every constitutional president there were four interim, provisional, or irregular presidents. One military figure, Antonio López de Santa Ana, occupied the presidential chair on 11 different occasions.

The weakness of the central government vis-à-vis the provinces during this period was underlined by the existence of a system of internal tariffs similar to that which existed in Germany prior to the *Zollverein*. The tariffs, called the *alcabala*, were levied whenever goods crossed from one state into another. This not only provided the individual states with a good deal of fiscal, and therefore political, autonomy, but it also served as an impediment to the development of a national market and a national economy.

The lack of central government control was manifested in another impediment to the formation of a national economy: the government could not safeguard commerce along the main highways. Banditry was widespread. By mid-century, brigandage was so commonplace that the National Congress could not meet because the representatives feared traveling from their home districts to Mexico City on the nation's bandit-infested roads. Though no global data are available on the frequency of highway robberies, Paul Vanderwood's qualitative data indicate that most travelers expected to be robbed at least once on a long journey. The available quantitative data mirror this judgment. In one single day in 1861, for example, the stagecoach from Mexico City to Puebla was robbed three times.[19] During one 15-day period in 1865 there were four major robberies along the highway from Orizaba, Veracruz, to Mexico City, an average of one every four days.[20] The Mexico City *Independencia*, summing up this situation, proclaimed that it was "a scandal the way bandits infest the roads. What the government is thinking about we do not know, but the bandits rampage with impunity."[21]

What the government evidently was thinking about was that the army, which was supposed to be defending the national interest by fighting the bandits, was not doing its job. Lacking the resources to build a professional army subordinate to its interests, the central government had to rely upon a corrupt, opportunistic military establishment little better than the bandits it was supposed to be fighting. As Vanderwood has observed:

They [Mexico's military leaders] had no allegiance to the national government and regularly pronounced against it not only for promotion but to loot on a march to nowhere across a rural sector or to steal a payroll assigned to their troops. . . . Army generals got rich during disturbances, so they kept banditry alive to justify their campaigns. In fact, they themselves robbed like bandits: horses and food from campesinos, money and weapons from hacendados. The local authority who called on the army to dispel trouble chanced much worse from the soldiers. So the officials learned to work with the bandits, who were hardly more scrupulous.[22]

All this began to change during the 1880's and 1890's. The inflow of foreign capital gave the central government the resources to curtail banditry, to break the power of Mexico's regional political bosses, and to bring to an end the incessant political coups and insurrections that had plagued the nation throughout the century.

The vehicle for this political change was Porfirio Díaz, a Liberal army commander who seized power in 1876 and ruled Mexico, either directly or indirectly, for the next 34 years. During this time he dedicated himself and the power of the state to the expansion of the economy—at whatever cost. Indeed, the entire political-economic project of the Díaz regime was to create the necessary conditions and incentives for capitalist enterprise in Mexico. As Clifton Kroeber has put it, "To him [Díaz] and his supporters it was the creation of wealth that was urgent. All the other fine things—an educated populace, a democratic polity, and a commonwealth as civilized as those of Europe—would follow inevitably from the appearance of enough prosperity, enough wealth."[23]

Díaz surrounded himself with a brain trust of Positivists and Social Darwinists who furnished his government with the ideology and intellectual justification it needed in order to believe in itself and in its program. Influenced by the ideas of Herbert Spencer and Auguste Comte, the *Científicos*, as this group of intellectuals, bureaucrats, and professionals was called, emphasized that government policy should be carried out according to the rules of "science." That is, they believed that society should be governed along scientific laws, and that there were social as well as natural sciences that governed the order of the world.[24] Essentially they held that in the arena of social policy the government should take a laissez-faire stance: for the good of the social organism as a whole, the strong in society should wipe out the weak. As José Y. Limantour, Díaz's minister of the treasury, put it in 1901, "The weak, the unprepared, those who lack the tools in order to emerge victorious against evolution, must perish and leave the struggle to the more powerful." It was, as Rodney Anderson has noted, a "convenient, 'scientific' justification for the ruthless exercise of power."[25]

This pseudo-scientific policy was invoked selectively. While the Díaz government conveniently forgot about laissez-faire economic policies when it came to government subsidies, tax breaks, and tariff protection for the enterprises of the rich, it stringently adhered to "scientific laws" when it dealt with the working class, the peasantry, or other groups that lacked wealth or power. To cite but one example, when the Confederación Obrera de las Fábricas del Valle de México asked the government for aid in resolving a labor dispute, Matías Romero, Limantour's predecessor as secretary of the treasury, responded that the law forbade the government from doing so. "Labor," he pronounced, "is under the unavoidable natural laws of supply and demand."[26] It was selective justice such as this that prompted the writing of popular ballads with lyrics like these: "Only he who has money enjoys the guarantees of the law, only the rich get the advantages of the peace."[27]

In general, the aim of the Díaz government was to create the internal political and economic conditions that would continue to attract the foreign capital that would modernize Mexico. This inflow of capital in turn provided the financial resources that permitted the continued expansion and consolidation of the central government. Under the lemma of "Order and Progress" the Díaz regime moved to eliminate the political opposition, break the power of the regional caudillos, curtail banditry, and prevent the organization of the working class. Order was to be provided by the federal government, often at bayonet point. The "progress" part of the equation would be brought about by the infusion of foreign capital into the economy. This was, therefore, a reflexive process. Just as Díaz needed to attract foreign capital in order to fuel the growth of federal government power, foreign capitalists understood that it was in their interest that a strong, centralized government be created that could instill and inspire popular loyalty and maintain order and stability.[28]

The Díaz regime, unlike earlier governments, had the resources to exercise political hegemony over the provinces. The expansion of the mines, commercial agriculture, railroads, and the petroleum industry provided the government with a much larger tax base. Total federal government revenues, adjusted for inflation, grew from just over 26 million pesos in fiscal year 1876–77 to over 85 million pesos in 1906–7 (both in 1900 pesos).[29] The central government now had the resources to create a professionalized federal army and to expand the paramilitary rural guard that President Juárez had created in 1861. Moreover, it could rapidly move these forces on the national railways to areas where its authority was challenged. The projection of this power brought about a decline in banditry along the federal highways. More important, it brought the provinces under the control of the central government, a development that was underlined by the elimination of the alcabala in 1896.

All of this, as Vanderwood has pointed out, took some doing. Díaz's program met with great resistance from the quasi-military strongmen who ruled provincial Mexico. Recognizing the rapid growth of the economy and the possibilities it afforded to those who played ball with Díaz, however, they agreed to cooperate with the central government. Mexico's regional caciques did not necessarily capitulate to the hegemony of Mexico City. Rather, they agreed to cooperate because they believed they had more to gain through partnership than through autonomy. Over time, the central government increasingly gained control.[30]

Crucial to the rise of the centralizing state was the ability to stifle challenges to the existing distribution of wealth and power. Indeed, it was the explicit policy of the Díaz government to actively oppose the creation of an organized working class. Even Justo Sierra, Díaz's minister of public instruction and fine arts, took it upon himself to drive home the government's message that militant labor movements would be met by armed force. Speaking to the National Congress of Tobacco Workers in 1906, Sierra warned the assembled workers that in the event of a strike the government would respond with "all its resources, all its political organization, all its army, all its authority, on the side of even a single worker who wants to work."[31]

The Díaz government followed up these threats of force with the army and the Rural Guard—the *Rurales*, as they were commonly called. Díaz did not induct known bandits into the Rurales, as is commonly believed, but neither did he try to clean up their image for being cutthroats. On the one hand, the Rurales provided protection for internal commerce, guarding shipments of ore and other goods. On the other hand, they served as insurance to investors that their property would be safeguarded and their profits protected. Both the Rurales and the army were often used to put down strikes. The most famous case was the Río Blanco textile strike of 1907, in which scores of workers were gunned down by federal troops.[32]

From the point of view of the Porfirian elite these economic and political changes created the conditions necessary to foment large-scale industrial investment. They controlled a state that would both support their endeavors and keep the working class under control. At the same time, the creation of that expanding wage-earning work force and the development of the national railroad system meant that the internal market was growing rapidly. The expansion of commerce, both internal and external, was fueling the process of capital accumulation: Mexico's merchants were growing increasingly wealthy, commanding capital that could be invested in all manner of economic activities. Most important, Mexico's capitalists believed that the process of economic growth that the country had been experiencing since the 1880's was going to continue. Influenced by the neo-positivist notions of progress then popular throughout Latin America, and convinced that the Díaz dictatorship was going to convert Mexico into a "modern" nation, they were willing to sink their fortunes into industrial ventures. Success, for them and for

Mexico, seemed inevitable. To their way of thinking, it was of little importance that the economy was not yet ready for many of the industries they were founding. The rest of the economy, they reasoned, would soon catch up. When it did, those who had had the foresight to invest early would be in a very favorable position. In this judgment they were sadly mistaken.

THREE

The Imperatives of the Market, Technology, and Labor

ONE OF THE requisites of large-scale industrialization is a market that can absorb the vast quantities that a modern manufacturing plant is capable of producing. Modern capitalism requires not only highly efficient production, but also a well-developed consumer market. The two are inseparable.

By the mid-1890's such a market was, in a certain sense, coming into existence in Mexico. In 1895 Mexico had a population of 12.6 million, of whom 4.8 million were in the labor force. Even if we discount the population engaged in agriculture as being probably too poor to serve as much of a source of demand, there were still close to two million workers engaged in mining, manufacturing, petroleum production, commerce, transport, and other services. This was a nearly threefold increase in the size of the wage-earning sector since 1861.[1] Assuming that each of these workers supported roughly 1.5 other people,* then the total number of consumers whose money incomes were large enough to purchase manufactured goods was close to five million. The expansion of the railway network, along with the suppression of the alcabala and banditry, was uniting this population into a single, national market.

The depth of this market did, however, have certain limits. It was not the same kind of market that industrialists in the United States, England, or other advanced industrial countries faced: it was a market in transition to modernity.

*This ratio was derived from the 1895 census by comparing the total population with the number economically active.

Mexico was still predominantly rural. In 1910, even after a thirty-year period of relatively rapid economic growth and urbanization, 71 percent of Mexico's population still lived in communities of less than 2,500 inhabitants.[2] Sizable segments of the population continued to function outside the market economy, producing for their own subsistence through traditional peasant agriculture. Even in areas where haciendas had swallowed up Indian communities, this did not imply that all of the dislocated peasants became wage workers; sharecropping and rental arrangements still tended to predominate. Although the peasantry had lost control of its lands, it continued to exist. Many areas of the country had not yet been integrated into the national rail transport system, large sections of the south and long stretches along the Pacific Coast remaining outside the rail grid.

Most important, the vast majority of the population was quite poor. The range of manufactured products they could be expected to consume was therefore restricted. No figures are available on average wage rates, but data on minimum wages can provide a rough idea as to just how poorly paid most of the Mexican population was. During the first decade of the twentieth century the average minimum wage in agriculture, which employed 62 percent of the work force, was 37 centavos a day (roughly 19 cents U.S.). The minimum wage for manufacturing workers, who made up 12 percent of the work force, was about 24 percent higher, at 46 centavos, or 23 cents U.S., per day.[3] In fact, the income of the average worker was so low that the consumption of cotton cloth was highly sensitive to fluctuations in the price of corn, which along with beans and chiles made up the largest part of the diet of Mexico's working class. As León Signoret, one of Mexico's most prominent financiers and textile industrialists, noted in 1904, in years of bad corn harvests, when the price of this important staple rose, Mexico's working class could not afford to purchase cotton cloth, thereby setting off a crisis in the textile industry.[4] Analyzing this problem in 1909, Andrés Molina Enríquez, one of the most important social thinkers of the Porfiriato, noted that the nation's small farmers and ranchers had an extremely low capacity to consume industrial goods. The country's Indian groups, according to him, were "in an even more unhappy situation. Their capacity to consume is practically nil."[5]

Quantitative evidence for Mexico's skewed income and occupational structure is provided by a study of the changing class structure of Mexico from 1895 to 1970.[6] In it James W. Wilkie and Paul D. Wilkins estimate that in 1895 over 90 percent of the population fell into what they define as the lower class: menial laborers with low incomes. Nothing even approximating a middle class existed, save for a few bureaucrats and professionals. Wilkie and Wilkins place the size of this group at just under 8 percent of the population. At the same time, a small group of financiers, merchants, and hacendados (estimated at just over 1 percent of the population) controlled the lion's share of national income and wealth. This latter group had an extremely high propensity to consume fine, imported goods from Europe. It purchased little in the way of domestic manufactures. As Molina Enríquez put it:

The foreigners and creoles who are the owners of our textile factories do not use the cloth that their factories produce. For the most part their clothing is of European cloth; they wear European or American-made hats, and walk on American-manufactured shoes. They ride in European or American carriages, and they decorate their houses with European art. In short, they prefer everything foreign to everything that is Mexican, including their taste in paintings, literature, and music.[7]

The result was that in terms of the market for consumer goods, Mexican industry was almost entirely dependent upon producing for the working class, whose incomes did not permit them to consume much beyond inexpensive consumer non-durables like coarse cotton cloth, cigarettes, soap, beer, and other low-cost items. Manufacturers therefore faced a very insecure and limited consumer goods market.

Since the engine of growth of the Mexican economy was foreign direct investment in the export sector, there was also demand for manufactures that could be employed in moving exports from their point of production to the exterior of the country. Thus, there existed a market for steel rails for railroads and steel structural shapes and cement for port construction, mining projects, and other activities related to primary product production and transport.

This intermediate goods market was not articulated, however, with that for consumer goods. Undoubtedly, small artisanal shops in industries like leather-working supplied manufacturers with incidental items such as belting for their European- and U.S-made machinery. In terms of heavy industry, with the exceptions of the glass bottle and newsprint industries, Mexico's producer goods industries did not manufacture intermediate inputs for the consumer goods sector, which imported almost all of its capital goods and intermediate inputs from Europe and the United States. The market for domestically produced intermediate goods was therefore even more shallow than for consumer goods, as it was almost completely dependent upon a few large, export-oriented mining, petroleum, and transport companies and the government for its sustenance. The problem of a limited market was thereby rendered even more serious for producers of intermediate goods than for those who produced consumer goods.

This uneven and limited market had to combine with a relatively sophisticated and expensive imported technological base. Mexico historically had imported technology from Europe. It never developed an engineering, machine tool, or capital goods industry of its own. Throughout the colonial period, for example, most of the machinery employed in the mining sector came from Europe. Much the same was true in the post-colonial era. The Mexican railroads, for example, were designed and built by foreign technicians employing foreign technology, because Mexico had none of the necessary engineering know-how. Similarly, Mexico's big mining and petroleum concerns of the Porfiriato were run with technology borrowed from the advanced industrial countries.

Manufacturing technology also had to be imported. By the time Mexican industrialization got under way in the 1890's, a one-hundred-year backlog of manufacturing technology existed. From the point of view of individual entrepreneurs, it made little sense to repeat the long process of trial, error, and experimentation that had gone into the development of that technology; it was less costly to import it. Thus, almost none of the technology employed in Mexico's new steel mills, cement factories, beer breweries, or other large industrial establishments was developed in Mexico. The blast furnaces and rolling mills came from the United States, the high-speed cigarette machinery from France, the paper-making machinery from Switzerland, the textile looms, spindles, and other equipment from England, Belgium, the United States, or Germany.

Although this certainly sped up the process of early industrialization, this imported technology was inappropriate to the shallow and limited Mexican market. It had been designed to meet the needs of the mass production / mass consumption economies of the United States and Europe. Engineered for large-batch production, it was far too big for the Mexican market. In order to industrialize rapidly, Mexico was therefore forced to combine the productive apparatus of a mass consumption economy with a market incapable of absorbing the quantity of goods that plant could produce. The result was a severe problem of excess installed capacity.

This problem was most serious in intermediate goods production. In the cement industry, for example, between 1906 and 1911 Mexico's three big manufacturers produced on average at only 43 percent of their capacity. In some years during the Porfiriato, capacity utilization was as low as 30 percent. Until the late 1920's Mexico's cement industry generally ran at less than 50 percent of capacity. Because high fixed costs had to be spread over a small amount of output, the industry's unit costs of production were higher than they would have been had the industry run at capacity. Underutilization also created a serious engineering problem for the industry. Cement plants are designed to be run around the clock; if the refractory bricks that line the furnaces of a cement factory are alternately cooled and heated, which occurs if the plant cannot be run full and steady, they crack, and their replacement is both costly and time-consuming. Thus, in the cement industry there were sizable diseconomies to running at less than full capacity.

One of the curious features about the data on the cement industry is that they indicate that installed capacity was expanding even while the utilization of existing capacity was extremely low. This peculiar situation is explained by the fact that cement manufacturers did not compete on a national basis. The high cost of transporting cement, coupled with its low price, meant that it could be sold only within a 250-kilometer radius of its point of production. The cement industry was therefore segmented into regional markets, with individual firms holding monopolies in their respective areas. In order to expand their market, firms had to erect new production facilities in new regions of the country. Thus, capacity continued expanding right up until 1910 even though the rate of utilization of the existing plants was extremely low.

In the steel industry the situation was even worse. Although there was only one major producer, Fundidora Monterrey, the industry was hampered by its inability to utilize all the expensive equipment it had imported from the United States. From 1903, when Fundidora Monterrey's mill came on line, to the end of the Porfiriato the average utilization of the company's blast furnace, which is used to convert iron ore and coal to pig iron, the first step in the production of steel, was only 30 percent. In fact, until 1929 Fundidora Monterrey never ran its blast furnace at more than 50 percent of capacity for two consecutive years (see Table 3.1).

Integrated steel mills, like cement factories, are designed to be run full and steady. Blast furnaces cannot be run intermittently or at less than capacity. Shutting down the furnace prevents the mill from achieving the economies of scale it was designed to take advantage of, thereby pushing up unit costs of production; also, as in the cement industry, it can cause extensive damage to the furnace linings. In the late nineteenth century repairing "blowouts" usually involved repairs costing from $5,000 to $10,000. In addition, sometimes several weeks were required to ease the furnace back into production. There are also significant economies of speed in integrated steel operations. By the 1890's mills were designed so that molten pig iron could be converted into steel and then into rails or billets without reheating. That is, there had to be a continuous flow of output from the blast furnace to the Bessemer converters to the rolling mills. Not being able to run full and steady meant that pig iron had to be cooled, stockpiled, and then reheated to be converted into steel, and this added substantially to the cost of the product.[8]

In consumer goods, capacity utilization was probably not so serious a problem. The market for consumer goods was much

TABLE 3.1
Utilization of Installed Capacity in the Cement and Steel Industries,
1903–1910

(000 metric tons)

Year	Cement industry			Steel industry[a]		
	Capacity	Output	Utilization[b]	Capacity	Output	Utilization[b]
1903	—	—	—	110	22	20%
1904	—	—	—	110	36	33
1905	—	—	—	110	4	4
1906	66	20	30	110	25	23
1907	66	30	45	110	16	15
1908	66	40	61	110	17	15
1909	86	50	58	110	59	54
1910	151	60	40	110	45	41

SOURCES: Cement industry, unpublished data from the Cámara Nacional de Cemento. Fundidora Monterrey, calculated from *FMIA*, 1900–1911.

[a]Data are for the Fundidora Monterrey steel company, which was the only integrated producer in Mexico. Blast furnace capacity and output are used as a proxy for the total productive capacity of the plant, since it is the blast furnace that provides the first step in the reduction of iron ore to steel. A Banco de México study suggests that the blast furnace capacity was actually higher—133,000 metric tons per year—which would produce even lower capacity utilization rates. I have estimated yearly productive capacity from information on daily productive capacity contained in the company's annual reports. This estimate of 110,000 metric tons per year is probably more realistic.

[b]Production divided by installed capacity, expressed as a percent.

larger than that for producer goods and, furthermore, in many consumer goods industries the capital equipment was not indivisible, as it was in the cement and steel industries. That is, producers did not necessarily have to purchase more capacity than they needed. Theoretically, in industries like cotton textiles manufacturers could simply have bought the number of carders, spindles, and looms that were necessary.

Even in the consumer goods industry, however, there was most probably a capacity utilization problem. The scarcity of consistent data makes it impossible to estimate capacity utilization rates in these industries accurately, but reports from manufacturers and analyses conducted by the Mexican financial press on the cotton textile manufacture, the largest and most developed of the consumer goods industries, indicate that the industry could not run at capacity.[9] In competing for control of the market at the turn of the century, Mexico's major textile mills began to switch to the recently developed, high-velocity, auto-

matic looms, which had first been put into use in the United
States in the 1890's. If the entire Mexican cotton textile industry
had then been run at capacity, the market could not have absorbed all the output. Indeed, throughout the period crises of
"overproduction" occurred on a fairly regular basis: at least
twice during the latter part of the Porfiriato, in 1901–2 and again
in 1907–8. Throughout the years of the Revolution (1910–17)
and the 1920's the problem was endemic.

As a result, a large part of Mexican industry was structurally
inefficient from its beginning. Foreign-produced capital goods
led to low levels of capacity utilization, with concomitantly high
unit costs. In industries with sizable economies of speed, like
steel rails or newsprint, unit costs of production were pushed
even higher because Mexican manufacturers could not run their
plants full and steady. Finally, in at least some industries, the
inability to run at capacity created expensive engineering and
maintenance problems.

In addition to these structural constraints, imported capital
goods also meant that Mexican industrialists had higher start-up
costs than did industrialists in the advanced industrial economies. Not only did they have to pay for the foreign-produced
machinery; they also had to set aside funds to cover the cost of
transport, insurance in transit, and the salaries of the foreign
technical personnel who set up the plant. In the cotton textile
industry, for example, which imported most of its machinery
from Great Britain, these added expenses pushed up the final
cost of erecting a mill in Mexico by 59 percent. According to
Gregory Clark's calculations, the cost of erecting a mill was
$12.72 per spindle in Great Britain in 1910, but $19.72 per spindle
in Mexico.[10] All of these costs had to be recovered, which bid up
the price of the final goods even further.

Exacerbating an already bad situation was the fact that the
productivity of Mexican labor was lower than in the advanced
industrial countries, and this pushed up the cost of final goods
even higher. The Mexican industrial working class had its social
roots in the peasantry; many workers were only recently off the
farm; some moved back and forth between the factory and the
field. They therefore worked with the rhythm of a peasantry,

not of an industrial proletariat. For this reason Mexican industrialists did not have the same degree of control over labor as did
their counterparts in the United States, England, or Germany.
Though they could force workers to work long hours, which in
fact they did—the average length of the workday prior to the
Revolution was approximately 12 hours—they could not instill
in them the attitudes and values that are essential to the development of industrial discipline. Like European industrialists in
the late eighteenth and early nineteenth centuries, Mexican factory owners regularly complained about the "laziness" of their
work force and their inability to force the workers to submit to
routinized work.[11]

Workers openly resisted employers' attempts to change traditional work habits in order to increase productivity or achieve
greater discipline on the shop floor. To cite one example, during
the 1890's the workers of the San Antonio Abad textile mill
struck because the mill's manager refused to allow them to continue the long-standing practice of bringing pulque (a mildly in-
toxicating alcoholic beverage made from the maguey plant) to
the mill for their lunch.[12] There were even occasions when entire
shifts of textile workers abandoned their machines in order to
attend a fiesta at a nearby hacienda or barrio. One of the most
remarkable of these episodes occurred in 1923 in the San Lorenzo cotton textile mill in the state of Veracruz. From 7:00 A.M.
on Tuesday, May 15, until 4:00 P.M. the following day, the entire
work force—796 workers, in two shifts—failed to report for
work, choosing instead to participate in a fiesta at the nearby
Hacienda Encinas.[13]

Quantitative evidence of the low productivity of Mexican labor compared with that of U.S. or English workers is supplied
by Gregory Clark's cross-national study of the cotton textile
industry in 1910. In the weaving department of Mexico's mills
each worker operated on average 2.5 looms, whereas his British
counterpart worked 3.8, and workers in New England operated
8.0. In the spinning department of the mills the results were
relatively similar: in Mexico 540 ring spindles per worker, compared with 625 for British workers and 902 for New England
workers. When reduced to a single measure of staffing levels—

loom equivalents per worker—the data indicate that Mexican textile mills employed almost twice as many workers per machine as did British mills, and over two-and-one-half times as many workers per machine as did New England mills.[14] What is more, these measures probably overestimate the efficiency of Mexican workers relative to those in Britain or New England because they do not account for differences in output per machine, which were probably significant.

The low productivity of Mexican workers in the textile industry was largely the result of workers' resistance to running more machines than they had historically been accustomed to. The transition to automatic looms, therefore, did not bring about as great an increase in labor productivity in Mexico as it did in the United States. According to W. A. Graham-Clark, who carried out the investigation of Mexico's textile mills for the U.S. Bureau of Foreign and Domestic Commerce in 1910, "the Mexican workers are very conservative, and as they have been accustomed to running two to four looms, usually not over three, it has as yet been found impossible to persuade them to run any large number of automatic looms."[15]

Given Mexico's large, redundant labor force, one might expect that industrial discipline would have been easy to enforce. Recalcitrant workers could easily have been replaced. In fact, the contrary was the case: although there was a large body of unskilled laborers clamoring for jobs, there was a severe shortage of skilled workers like weavers, glass blowers, and foundrymen, and it was they who were essential to the running of Mexican industry. Skilled industrial workers were therefore able to command relatively high wages and had a good deal of leverage in their relations with their employers. As *La Unión* of Monterrey put it in an 1899 article, "The severe lack of workers who understand the operation of the different machines that are being employed with the growth of our businesses is becoming more and more notable every day. Some businesses have never gotten off the ground because of this."[16]

La Unión went on to note that in some classes of skilled work there were so few Mexican workers that foreigners had to be contracted from abroad. In the glass bottle industry, for example, the country's first major factory, the Monterrey-based

Fábrica de Vidrios y Cristales, had to import its entire skilled work force. All 54 of its skilled glassblowers, foremen, and other technical personnel were brought over by the company from Germany. Conflicts with this highly independent work force, along with problems stemming from the uneven quality of the raw materials, forced the factory to close down only nine months after it opened in 1903. The problem of the lack of a skilled work force was not overcome until 1909 when automated glass bottle-making machinery was introduced.[17] The case was much the same in the dynamite industry, where skilled workers had to be imported from France and Italy.[18] Similarly, European and U.S. workers predominated in the highly skilled positions in the steel, beer, cement, and cotton textile industries.[19]

In short, Mexican manufactures cost more to produce than similar goods produced in the advanced industrial countries: their start-up costs were higher, they were unable to take advantage of the economies of scale and economies of speed of their imported machinery, and the productivity of their work forces was lower.

To an extent these disadvantages would have been offset by lower labor costs in Mexico. Though little research has been done on wages in Porfirian Mexico and international comparisons are difficult because of differences in exchange rates and work weeks, comparative data from the cotton industry indicate that on average Mexican textile workers earned roughly half of what British workers did and less than one-third of what New England workers did. It is clearly not the case, however, that lower wages made up for lower labor productivity and for higher capital and operating costs. In the cotton textile industry, for example, Mexican manufacturers conservatively calculated that foreign competitors could undersell them by roughly 10 percent. This is in rough agreement with Clark's calculations that in Mexico the cost of production of cloth was 19 percent higher than in Great Britain.[20] In less labor-intensive industries, like beer brewing, glass making, steel, and chemicals, the savings from lower wages would have been even smaller than they were in the textile industry. In addition, it may well not have been the case that wage rates in these industries were lower than in the advanced industrial economies because of the severe shortage of qualified skilled personnel to man the machinery. The fact that most of the highly skilled workers in these industries were contracted from abroad would, in fact, indicate that wages were competitive with those in Europe and the United States.

Mexican manufactures therefore found it difficult to compete in the home market against foreign manufactures without the protection and support of the government. Almost all of Mexico's major industries received some sort of tariff protection or federal subsidy. Beginning in the late 1880's import duties on manufactures jumped markedly. One Mexican financial publication calculated that with the new tariff schedule and the costs of transport and marketing a piece of cloth produced in England trebled in price by the time it reached Mexico.[21] Throughout the Porfiriato, tariffs continued to climb, the schedules being revised upwards in 1892, 1893, 1896, and 1906, causing one U.S. commercial agent to report in 1909 that "the Mexican tariff on cotton goods is the highest in the world [*sic*], being exceeded only by those of Russia and Brazil. In some classes of cloth the duty amounts to three times the value of the goods abroad."[22]

In addition to protective tariffs, most of the country's major manufacturing enterprises operated under some kind of federal concession, which gave them tax-exempt status for a period of between 7 and 30 years. In 1893 the government declared that all new industries capitalized in excess of 250,000 pesos were exempt from direct federal taxes and from customs duties on the machinery and other materials needed to erect their factories. The required minimum capitalization was lowered to 100,000 pesos in 1898.[23] A few enterprises were able to do even better than this in their negotiations with the Díaz government. It sometimes granted firms the sole right to operate under a federal concession. In these instances, then, only one firm could receive tax-exempt status within that particular product line, giving it a sizable advantage over would-be competitors. In many cases, this tax exemption applied to domestic production taxes and to duties on intermediate and capital goods imports as well. In effect, in order to foment industrialization in an extremely difficult environment, the government was setting up officially sanctioned and subsidized monopolies.

Had Mexico been able to export the surplus products that it could not consume at home, the capacity utilization and unit cost problem would have been solved. Production for the export market would have utilized the excess capacity and allowed the industries to take advantage of economies of scale and of speed, thereby driving down unit costs of production and eliminating part of the need for government protection and subsidization.

Mexican industrialists tried to pursue this strategy. It was not the case, as many scholars have assumed, that Mexico's industrialists were not interested in exporting. In fact, as early as 1902 the nation's most prominent merchants and manufacturers got the federal government to underwrite a fact-finding trip to South America to see if Mexico could market its industrial goods there. From October 1902 until May 1903 the group traveled to Brazil, Uruguay, Argentina, Chile, and Peru in search of markets for Mexico's excess industrial production. What they found, much to their surprise and unhappiness, was that Mexican goods were not competitive in the international market for several reasons.[24]

First, Mexico had no merchant marine and therefore could not move its goods to foreign markets without the use of foreign shipping companies, which had little interest in the project. Because most of Mexico's population has historically lived in the center of the country, in the plateau that lies between the Sierra Madre Oriental and the Sierra Madre Occidental, communication via coastal or riverine transport was never important. As a result, Mexico had no shipbuilding or seafaring tradition. The problems that the fact-finding group encountered in getting from Mexico to South America illustrate how serious an impediment this was. Because they could not book passage directly from Mexico to any major South American port, they had to travel first to the United States and then to England and from there board a steamer for Brazil. One of the first things, therefore, that the Mexican industrial group tried to accomplish was to interest European steamship companies in establishing regular freight routes between Mexico and South America. Even with the promise of subsidies from the Mexican government, however, they found European shippers little interested in doing so, since the Mexican group could give them no idea of how often the ships would have to run or how much they would most likely carry.[25]

Second, even if Mexico had been able to ship its goods to foreign markets, its internal transport costs were still high, in spite of having fallen since the advent of the railroad. Its industry, meanwhile, had developed near the major population centers, in the interior of the country. As the *Avisador Comercial de Havana* put it in 1901: "Freight rates on the Mexican railroads are high. How, then, can merchandise be shipped to the coast at an advantageous price? How can they [Mexican manufacturers] compete in foreign markets with products similar to those of other countries if within their own borders they have incredibly high freight rates?"[26]

For this reason, in Mexico's coastal areas foreign products often had an advantage over Mexican-produced goods, especially if those goods had a high bulk-to-price ratio. Such was the case, for example, in the cement industry. In the important port city of Tampico, a major user of cement, it was cheaper to buy cement manufactured in England and shipped by ocean from Liverpool than to purchase it from a Mexican producer several hundred miles away, who shipped by rail.[27] In fact, railway freight charges were so great that cement became too expensive to employ beyond a distance of 250 kilometers. Therefore, even though the Mexican cement industry had the productive capacity to fill all of the nation's demand for cement, it never took more than 47 percent of the market during the Porfiriato (see Table 3.2). This further exacerbated the capacity utilization problem because it meant that cement manufacturers had to continually open new plants in different areas of the country even though the utilization of their already installed plant was abysmally low (see Table 3.1, above).[28] In short, a successful export program would therefore have required that production take place at the ports, not in the interior.

Third, competition in international markets during this period was quite fierce. Producers in the United States and Europe were tenaciously defending their dominance of the world market through aggressive dumping and discounting. In the case of steel, for example, the United States Steel Corporation tried to suppress new competition by selling its products below cost.

TABLE 3.2
Production, Importation, and Consumption of Cement, 1906–1911
(Metric tons)

Year	Imports[a]	Production[b]	Consumption[c]	Domestic share of consumption[d]
1906	98,142	20,000	118,142	17%
1907	96,872	30,000	126,872	24
1908	132,099	40,000	172,099	23
1909	55,392	50,000	105,392	47
1910	73,357	60,000	133,357	45
1911	62,483	50,000	112,483	44

SOURCES: Production data from Table 3.1. Import data from *MYB 1909–10*: 412; *MYB 1913*: 87; Rojas Alonso 1967.
[a]Fiscal years.
[b]Calendar years.
[c]Imports plus domestic production, based on the reasonable assumption that all production was consumed during the year it was produced. This is fairly typical of the cement industry, where the low price-to-volume ratio of the product makes the stockpiling of inventory highly uneconomical.
[d]Domestic production divided by apparent consumption.

It even tried to give Mexico's new steel company, Fundidora Monterrey, a run for its money in Fundidora's own backyard. A Mexican financial press analysis of U.S. Steel's pricing policy in Mexico in 1904 revealed that the American company was selling at less than 50 percent of its costs of production, transport, and marketing, an analysis that was later used by Fundidora Monterrey to get an increase in tariff protection.[29]

Fourth, exporters in Europe and the United States had access to a large, well-integrated banking system that allowed them to provide long-term credit to their South American customers on very favorable terms. In fact, they often accepted raw materials in lieu of cash as payment for the interest and principal they were owed on goods they had shipped. Given the underdeveloped state of Mexico's banking and financial institutions (see Chapter 5), this put Mexican exporters at a sizable disadvantage since interest rates were generally higher in Mexico than in the United States or in Europe.[30] Even if credit could have been arranged, Mexican merchants—as they themselves pointed out—could not have accepted raw materials instead of cash as payment inasmuch as the raw materials being exported from South America were the exact same products that Mexico was exporting to the United States and to Europe. Mexico therefore had no use for them.

Fifth, Mexican manufacturers had a difficult time entering the export market because they had little to offer other Latin American countries that those countries did not already have. The technology that Mexico had purchased in the United States and Europe had also been purchased by other Latin American nations. When the Mexican fact-finding contingent arrived in Brazil, which they expected would be a large market for Mexican textiles, they were shocked to find that Brazil had a textile industry of its own and did not need to import Mexican products. A similar thing happened in Cuba, where Mexican manufacturers hoped to sell beer. Not only did they find that U.S. producers were already all over the island hawking their products, but they also found that Cuba had a national beer industry of its own.[31]

Finally, as if to add insult to injury, the fact-finding group found that, like Mexican producers, industrialists throughout South America had secured protective tariffs for their enterprises in order to exclude foreign competitors.[32] Just as Mexico's manufacturers had protected their industries from less expensive foreign products, South America's industrialists, especially the Brazilians, had pressured their governments to erect high tariff barriers on manufactured goods. This put Mexican products at an even greater disadvantage in these markets.

Confronted with these problems and limitations, the Mexican contingent returned home defeated, without bothering to stop in Central America as originally planned. Writing in the financial weekly *El Economista Mexicano*, León Signoret, one of Mexico's most important merchants and industrialists and the principal organizer of the trade mission, summed up Mexico's possibilities in the export of manufactures: "Given the prevailing circumstances, Mexico should renounce the idea of exporting to South America as a way of benefiting its industry."[33]

Mexican industry, then, for the time being, was confined to the home market. Not until the 1980's, when the structure and rationale of the nation's economic system have been called into question, would the idea of exporting manufactures once again become popular. Thus, during the entire first wave of industrialization, Mexico was stuck with more capacity than it could use. The only solution would be for a few giant firms to carve up the market between them. Only by this means could they discourage new plants from coming on line and stiffen their control of pricing and production. To this end there would have to be a total reorganization of the structure of production and distribution in Mexican industry.

FOUR

The Structure of Production

IF MEXICO'S internal market was too small for the scale of its industrial plant, and if Mexican manufacturers could not export their surplus, how were they to get around the problem of excess capacity? In many industries oligopoly and monopoly production became the rule. A manufacturing sector previously characterized by small, family-owned and family-run firms producing for local and regional markets became increasingly characterized by large, capital-intensive, vertically integrated firms producing for the national market. This transformation held true across product lines and across regions. From cement to steel, from textiles to beer, large corporations that exercised monopoly or oligopoly control of the market began to appear, pushing aside the smaller regional producers that had historically been the mainstay of Mexican industry. This chapter outlines the degree and nature of this change. Chapter 6 discusses the strategies firms used in order to achieve control of the market.

Within any given product line a few extremely large firms controlled the lion's share of the market. In steel, glass, soap, paper, and dynamite production single firms held monopolies or near-monopolies. Cigarette manufacturing was dominated by two horizontally integrated giants; in beer and cement, three big firms carved up each market. Even in the cotton textile industry, which is usually characterized by near-perfect competition, two firms claimed roughly 20 percent of total national production and almost all of the production of fine, high-quality goods.

In no other area was the transformation from small, regional producers to a single, large, national producer as pronounced as in the steel industry. Throughout the nineteenth century, iron and steel production was carried out in small foundries that produced a limited range of finished products and employed the most archaic production techniques. An 1853 census of existing iron and steel foundries listed five, only one of which employed more than 100 workers. Median mill size was 14 employees.[1]

All this changed in 1900 with the founding of the Compañía Fundidora de Fierro y Acero de México, S.A. (Fundidora Monterrey), which was big business from the start. The subscribed capital of the firm was 10 million pesos (about $5 million), making it in terms of capitalization the second largest manufacturing enterprise in Mexico—the Compañía Industrial de Orizaba, the nation's largest cotton textile conglomerate, was first—and the thirtieth largest corporation of any type.[2] Unlike the small foundries that had preceded it, Fundidora Monterrey was a totally integrated operation, handling all phases of steel production, from the mining of the ore to the rolling of finished products. Moreover, Fundidora Monterrey's equipment was a far cry from the antiquated technology utilized by its predecessors. Iron ore was reduced to pig iron in a Massick and Crook–type blast furnace capable of handling 1,000 tons of ore per day, with an output of approximately 350 tons of pig iron; and three Siemens-Martin open-hearth furnaces, with a daily capacity of 35 tons each, and one Bessemer converter refined the pig into steel ingots. The firm also owned all the necessary rolling mills, cranes, locomotives, and other machinery to turn out a variety of finished steel products.[3] It owned, in addition, valuable ore- and coal-bearing properties throughout Mexico and held 20 percent of the stock of the Compañía Explotadora de Concessiones de Muzquiz, a coal-mining company.[4] When the mill was running at full blast, over 2,000 workers toiled around the clock in its various departments.

Fundidora Monterrey, unlike its predecessors in iron and steel manufacturing, was thus not an owner-run operation with an informal chain of command and a nonspecialized, flexible work force. It was a modern corporation with a hierarchical management structure and a specialized, nonflexible work force of several thousand that performed routinized tasks in a mass-production setting. That is, the firm had a central administration that coordinated the efforts of over twenty functionally specialized departments.

The only other steel firm in Mexico, the Consolidated Rolling Mills and Foundries Company, better known as La Consolidada, was a complementary operation to Fundidora Monterrey. It bought pig iron from Fundidora and produced specialty steel alloys and castings that the larger firm was not equipped to produce. La Consolidada was not an integrated operation, nor did it compete in the same product lines as Fundidora Monterrey. Of the nation's domestically produced steel, it accounted for but 5 percent, Fundidora Monterrey taking the rest.[5] Fundidora Monterrey did, on the other hand, face sizable competition from foreign producers. Essentially the company locked up the market for structural shapes and steel rails, while it competed in the market for steel ingots and conceded the market for tubing, sheeting, and other flat-rolled products.[6]

Paper production also was dominated by one company. The Compañía de las Fábricas de Papel de San Rafael y Anexas controlled the nation's entire production of newsprint, the paper product with the largest market in Mexico, and virtually controlled the domestic production of other classes of paper goods. Founded in 1890, San Rafael y Anexas ran two mills, both in the state of México. Like Fundidora Monterrey, it was a totally integrated operation: it owned and operated its own haciendas, where the trees were grown, ran its own mechanical wood pulp plant, generated its own hydroelectric power, and operated its own railroad. The total number of workers in all these operations is unknown, but in its two paper mills alone it employed roughly 2,000 operatives. The total paid-in capital of this giant firm was 7 million pesos.[7]

San Rafael's strategy, like Fundidora Monterrey's, was to concentrate on the product lines in which it had the largest absolute advantages against imported goods. Thus, it specialized in newsprint, whose high bulk, coupled with its low price, made it expensive to ship from abroad. In higher-value goods the transport-cost advantage was lost, and in such product lines as book paper and fine writing paper, the firm was forced to compete with imported German and U.S. paper. Lacking product-specific data on paper imports and annual sales data for San Rafael, market shares in these other product lines are difficult to determine, but the data that exist indicate that imported paper captured just under two-thirds of the market.[8]

As with newsprint and steel production, the domestic manufacture of glass was also controlled by a monopoly: the Vidriera Monterrey glass works in the state of Nuevo León. Founded in 1909, Vidriera Monterrey got its start producing bottles for Mexico's growing beer industry. Eventually it moved into a much wider product line, encompassing the entire range of glass products. The creation of this new enterprise totally revolutionized the glass industry in Mexico. Until the creation of Vidriera Monterrey, bottles were either imported or produced by hand in small, inefficient glass works that employed German émigré glass blowers. An 1857 census of the glass industry listed but five firms, four of which employed fewer than 100 workers. Median firm size was but 70 workers.[9] Two problems plagued the industry. First, given the extant technology, the nation's factories could not keep up with the demand for bottles for Mexico's rapidly growing beer industry. Second, there were not enough trained glass blowers in Mexico to work in the nation's factories. As a result, it was often necessary to contract foreign workers from abroad.

Mexico's smaller firms continued to hold out for a while against the Monterrey giant, but over time Vidriera Monterrey's more efficient, automated glass-blowing machinery gave it a decided edge in the market, gradually forcing the smaller producers out. Shops that blew glass bottles by hand simply could not compete with Vidriera Monterrey's U.S.-produced machinery, which was capable of producing 40,000 bottles per day. The total paid-in capital of the firm was 1.2 million pesos.[10]

A similar structure of production was found in soap manufacturing, where one huge firm, the Compañía Industrial Jabonera de la Laguna, faced numerous, small, artisanal shops. Founded in 1896 in Gómez Palacio, Durango, the Jabonera was one of the four largest soap factories in the world, employing approximately 800 men in its two soap- and glycerine-producing plants. Its productive capacity was 90 million pounds of soap, mostly of the laundry variety, and 2,000 tons of glycerine per year. The original capitalization of the firm was 2 million pesos, but this quickly grew to 5 million pesos by the end of the Porfiriato.[11] Of course, numerous cottage-industry soap factories existed as well, but none were large, and they contributed only a small proportion of total output. A 1902 industrial directory listed 56 producers, of which almost all were sole proprietorships too small even to have names.[12] Only one non–cottage industry firm, the Jabonera la Unión, competed against the Jabonera de la Laguna, but it took at most 20 percent of the market. The remainder went to the La Laguna soap works.[13]

The Compañía Nacional Mexicana de Dinamita y Explosivos, an offshoot of the Compañía Industrial Jabonera de la Laguna, monopolized the production and distribution of dynamite and other explosives. Founded in 1901 with an initial capitalization of 1.4 million pesos—later increased to 3 million pesos in 1903 and to 4 million pesos in 1904—the company controlled 100 percent of the market for explosives, including nitroglycerine, dynamite, and cartridges for firearms. Through a special concession from the federal government (see Chapter 6), the firm did not have to face any competition from foreign imports. Though the enterprise got off to a slow start, not producing any dynamite until 1907, by 1912 it was capable of producing 15 million pounds of explosives a year. When running at peak production levels, its factory in Durango employed approximately 900 workers.

As was the case in steel and paper, Dinamita y Explosivos was a vertically integrated operation. Not only did the firm produce final goods like dynamite and cartridges, but it also produced all the chemicals necessary for the manufacture of those products, including sulfuric acid, nitric acid, and aziotic cotton. Glycerine was purchased from the Jabonera de la Laguna, which held one-third of Dinamita y Explosivo's stock.[14]

In the production of cigarettes three huge firms, the Compañía Manufacturera El Buen Tono, La Cigarrera Mexicana, and La Tabacalera Mexicana, totally dominated the market. Fifty percent of La Cigarrera Mexicana's stock was in fact owned by El Buen Tono, making it a virtual subsidiary of the larger company, so in reality there were only two industry leaders, the El Buen Tono–La Cigarrera Mexicana combination, that controlled 50

TABLE 4.1
Mexican Cigarette Production, 1898–1911

Fiscal years[a]	Number of factories	Production	
		Kilos	Packages[b]
1898–1899	766	4,915,730	328,605,915
1899–1900	766	5,906,520	375,542,765
1900–1901	740	5,974,334	364,699,301
1901–1902	701	6,203,078	371,791,006
1902–1903	670	7,305,080	405,816,926
1903–1904	605	7,723,557	467,950,007
1904–1905	469	8,174,320	483,068,231
1905–1906	491	8,455,529	505,202,138
1906–1907	479	8,855,804	524,364,650
1907–1908	469	8,903,960	515,324,969
1908–1909	437	8,660,854	505,437,551
1909–1910	451	8,451,309	511,573,779
1910–1911	341	8,380,192	493,348,501

SOURCE: *Mexico* [47].

[a]July 1 to June 30.

[b]I assume that packages represent boxes of 20 cigarettes each, though the number is not stated in the source. Each package represents roughly 1.5 percent of a kilo.

percent of the market, and La Tabacalera Mexicana, which took 12 percent. Employing automated cigarette machinery imported from France, these two giants were capable of producing over 6 billion cigarettes per year. The rest of Mexico's cigarettes were produced in hundreds of small shops spread throughout the country.[15]

Though precise calculations are difficult, the data indicate that over time the two giants forced the smaller producers out of business. As Table 4.1 demonstrates, in 1898 the nation's entire output of almost 5 million kilos of cigarettes was divided up among 766 factories. Ten years later, in 1908, though production had increased by 76 percent to close to 8.7 million kilos, the number of factories had fallen by over 40 percent to 437. In other words, output per factory trebled over the ten-year period, from 6,410 kilos in 1898–99 to 19,819 kilos in 1908–9. By June 1911, the last date for which data exist, there were only 341 factories in operation, less than half the number in existence just 12 years earlier. Output per factory had now increased an additional 24 percent to 24,575 kilos. These figures probably underestimate the degree of concentration of the industry because the data on the number of factories in operation include cigar as well as cigarette factories. Since there are not the kinds of economies of scale in the production of cigars as there are in cigarettes, the cigar industry was not subject to the same degree of concentration as the cigarette industry was. Thus, if anything, these figures understate the degree to which the major producers were forcing out the nation's smaller manufacturers.

Data on the labor force also indicate that the big, mechanized firms were forcing the artisanal shops out of business. In 1895 there were 10,397 workers employed in cigarette production. By 1910 there were but 6,893,[16] approximately half of whom were employed by the nation's two major firms. If we assume that cigarette output was the same in 1895 as in 1898, the first year for which output data are available, the data indicate that output per worker increased from 31,606 packages per worker in 1895 to 74,216 packages per worker in 1910—an increase in labor productivity of 135 percent over the 15-year period—the apparent result of the substitution of automated rolling machinery in the big firms for thousands of workers rolling cigarettes by hand in hundreds of small shops. These figures, like those on output per factory, also tend to underestimate the degree of change in the industry. It is unlikely that output in 1895 was equal to the level of 1898—it was almost certainly significantly lower. Thus, if anything, the degree to which the automated machinery employed by the large firms raised labor productivity was probably greater than the 135 percent increase estimated.

The two firms that came to dominate the market were incredibly large operations. The larger of the two, El Buen Tono, had an initial capitalization of 1 million pesos in 1894. Through a series of additional stock issues and the reinvestment of profits, the value of this paid-in capital grew to 6.5 million pesos by 1907, by which time the firm employed some 2,000 workers and was producing 3.5 billion cigarettes per year. Annual sales increased with the growth of capital, so that total receipts, in real 1900 pesos, grew from just over 1 million pesos in 1894 to 5 million pesos by 1907 (see Table 4.2).[17]

In addition to these operations, El Buen Tono held 50 percent of the stock in Mexico's second largest cigarette manufacturer, La Cigarrera Mexicana, giving it effective control over that com-

TABLE 4.2
El Buen Tono Sales, 1894–1909

	Annual sales	
Year	Current pesos	Real pesos
1894	1,059,337	1,136,628
1895	1,374,427	1,476,291
1896	1,445,241	1,414,130
1897	1,472,652	1,432,541
1898	1,650,830	1,865,345
1899	1,714,029	2,004,712
1900	1,661,274	1,661,274
1901	1,526,976	1,243,466
1902	1,851,168	1,532,424
1903	2,769,942	2,203,613
1904	3,780,763	3,540,040
1905	4,408,249	3,634,171
1906	5,425,919	3,992,582
1907	6,800,318	5,078,654
1908	5,275,053	3,999,282
1909	5,316,491	3,702,292

SOURCES: Derived from *MI*, 1 Mar. 1905, p. 8; *EM*, 18 Aug. 1906, pp. 421–22, 5 Mar. 1910, p. 473, 21 Mar. 1908, p. 488; *MYB 1911*: 281; deflated, using consumer price index in Rosenzweig 1965c: 172.

pany. This essentially increased El Buen Tono's productive capacity by an additional 1.5 billion cigarettes per year, giving it roughly a 50 percent market share. The total paid-in capital of this company was 2 million pesos, and it employed 400–500 workers.[18]

The only real competition for El Buen Tono was La Tabacalera Mexicana, which though smaller than El Buen Tono was still an impressive operation. Like the larger firm, it utilized automated cigarette-rolling machinery that could turn out millions of cigarettes per day. It employed approximately 800 workers and produced roughly 1.2 billion cigarettes annually, which gave it control of approximately 12 percent of the market.[19]

The cement industry was also characterized by large, capital-intensive firms operating in noncompetitive markets. Three companies manufactured all of Mexico's domestically produced cement: Cementos Hidalgos, founded in 1906; Cementos Cruz Azul, founded in 1907; and Cementos Tolteca, founded in 1909.[20] The high-bulk, low-price ratio of cement prevented any one of them from totally controlling domestic production or from pushing foreign cement out of the market. Indeed, though these three producers had the installed capacity to satisfy the nation's entire demand, the Mexican cement industry never took more than 47 percent of the market during the Porfiriato, the majority of the market going to imports (see Table 3.2, above).

Similarly, three major companies dominated the beer industry, though there were smaller, regional producers as well. The two largest of the three giants, the Cervecería Cuauhtemoc and the Cervecería Moctezuma, were founded during the early 1890's. The third, the Compañía Cervecera de Toluca y México, is an exception in that it was established in 1865, well before the Porfiriato.

The degree of concentration that developed in the steel, soap, and paper industries did not occur in the beer industry. Beer's perishability, coupled with the lack of refrigerated transport, kept any one firm from centralizing all of national production in a single brewery. When nationally based oligopolies did develop in the 1920's and 1930's, they came about as the result of the acquisition of the smaller regional producers by the big three: Moctezuma, Cuauhtemoc, and Modelo. The Cervecería Modelo, founded in the 1920's, drove Toluca y México out of business and purchased its plant. But even during the Porfiriato, the three firms were already beginning to move beyond their regional bases and to pressure the smaller breweries that operated on a local scale. In 1901 there were 29 such regional breweries, basically one in every major city.[21]

The oldest of the non-regional producers, the Compañía Cervecera de Toluca y México, was founded in 1865 by the Swiss émigré Agustín Marendes. It is unclear at what point Toluca y México was transformed from a family-run enterprise with Marendes as both owner and manager to a joint-stock company, but by 1898 the company was listed on the Mexico City stock exchange with a subscribed capital of 1.2 million pesos.[22] What had started out as a small producer in the 1860's grew to be a major corporation by the end of the Porfiriato. The company's subscribed capital in 1910 had grown to 2 million pesos, with annual production in the area of 1 million liters of beer and a payroll of between 650 and 800 workers. The brewery was lo-

TABLE 4.3
Cervecería Cuauhtemoc Sales, 1892–1910

Year	Sales (000 liters)	Year	Sales (000 liters)
1892	498	1902	5,581
1893	986	1903	5,925
1894	1,123	1904	6,865
1895	1,980	1905	8,884
1896	2,151	1906	13,344
1897	2,474	1907	14,005
1898	3,743	1908	11,183
1899	4,504	1909	11,582
1900	4,866	1910	13,275
1901	4,685		

SOURCE: Unpublished data from Cervecería Cuauhtemoc sales department.

cated in Toluca, and the major market for the company was in nearby Mexico City, but it distributed throughout central Mexico as well.[23]

The other two breweries, both significantly larger than Toluca y México, also competed on a semi-national scale. The Cervecería Cuauhtemoc was founded in 1890 by a group of Monterrey merchants who had been importing beer from the United States. The original capitalization was only 150,000 pesos, but this was gradually increased to 2 million pesos by the end of the Porfiriato. By this time, too, the Cervecería Cuauhtemoc had eclipsed Toluca y México as the nation's most important brewery. Sales had grown from 500,000 liters in 1892 to 13.3 million liters by 1910, which was over 13 times the annual production of Toluca y México (see Table 4.3). More important, Cuauhtemoc had moved aggressively into Toluca y México's home territory by establishing a Mexico City sales office in 1902. The total number of employees of this giant operation was 1,500 workers by the close of the Porfiriato.[24] Though data on the firm's market share are sparse for the period prior to the Revolution, I calculate that in 1901 it captured 28 percent of the market for domestically produced beer.[25]

Cuauhtemoc's other major competitor, the Cervecería Moctezuma, was located in Orizaba, Veracruz. Unfortunately no data exist on the volume of sales, production, or employment, but qualitative sources suggest that it operated at a scale equal to that of the Cervecería Cuauhtemoc. Like the Cervecería Cuauhtemoc, its paid-in capital was 2 million pesos.[26]

The expansion of the Mexican beer industry pushed foreign beer out of the market. Imports fell from approximately 3 million kilos in fiscal year 1889–90 to just over 500,000 kilos in fiscal 1910–11, while demand for beer was rising. The Cervecería Cuauhtemoc's production alone in 1910 was over 25 times that of the total volume of imports.[27] By 1906, imported beer's market share had fallen to about 4 percent of total demand.[28]

Like many other large manufacturing industries, Mexico's beer industry was not just import-substituting, producing locally what had previously been imported, but was opening up a whole new market for a product that had never before been distributed on such a wide scale. For example, the annual production in 1907 of the Cervecería Cuauhtemoc alone was approximately five times the amount imported in the most active year for beer imports between 1888 and 1911.[29] In other words, tastes were beginning to change in Mexico, favoring modern goods over traditional ones. A mug of beer was beginning to replace a draught of pulque as the favored drink of the Mexican working class. In large part this was due to extensive advertising by Mexico's major producers, who quite early on began to compete on the basis of brand names and the quality that consumers associated with those brands. The Cervecería Cuauhtemoc, for example, got a great deal of mileage out of the fact that its Carta Blanca brand won first place at the 1904 world's fair in St. Louis, Missouri. To an equal degree, however, this shift in tastes could not have taken place had incomes not been rising. Much of the conventional wisdom about tendencies in real wages in Porfirian Mexico notwithstanding, in all probability the real incomes of workers, especially skilled ones, rose throughout the period. Indeed, it is hard to reconcile falling wages with a growth-oriented economy characterized by a shortage of skilled labor.

Even in the manufacture of textiles, big business was coming to dominate production. Textile production, unlike many of the other industries of the Porfiriato, was not new to Mexico. Throughout the colonial period nonmechanized sweatshops called *obrajes* spun and wove *manta*, a coarse, grey cotton cloth suitable for work clothes, and as early as the 1830's the textile industry began to move into mechanized factories, abetted by loans and other assistance from the government-sponsored Banco de Avío. But in the 1890's cotton textile manufacturing began to be transformed from an industry characterized by small firms producing for local and regional markets to large firms producing for the national market.

One of the best indicators of this change was the tremendous growth in the size of factories. In 1853 there were only 47 cotton textile factories, 9 fewer than had existed in 1845. With few exceptions, these were not particularly large operations, the median number of spindles per factory being 2,300. Only the Cocolapam factory in Orizaba, Veracruz, employed more than 10,000 spindles.[30] In 1878–79 the number of mills had grown to 99, but they were still small. In fact, median mill size had fallen to 2,000 spindles.[31] The largest of these operations had been erected during the Banco de Avío years; the newest were actually smaller than their predecessors, and they produced no high-quality textiles: the inexpensive manta was the industry's mainstay.

By the end of the Porfiriato, however, the situation had changed dramatically. Not only had the number of factories increased by 50 percent since 1878—there were now 148—but the size of the enterprises had increased as well. Median mill size was now 4,488 spindles, roughly double that in 1878–79, and the number of mills with more than 10,000 spindles had increased to 20. The nation's largest mill, Río Blanco in Orizaba, Veracruz, contained 42,568 spindles.[32] In addition, the technology employed in the new mills was qualitatively different. The larger, newer mills were now employing high-velocity, electric-powered looms and spindles, which were a far cry from the old water-, steam-, horse-, or human-powered machinery that had been employed in the mid-nineteenth century.

Of the numerous firms in the cotton textile industry, many of them joint-stock companies, only two competed on a national level. They controlled just over 20 percent of total national production and nearly 100 percent of the domestic production of fine-weave cloth.[33] The smaller firms generally concentrated on the low end of the market, producing the heavy manta. This left the market for the finer weaves to imports, which took 25 percent of the market,[34] and the few large firms that, with the help of protective tariffs, were able to compete in this more difficult market.

Of all the large manufacturing corporations set up during this period the Compañía Industrial de Orizaba, S.A. (CIDOSA) was the largest. CIDOSA was founded in 1889 to run the recently (1882) erected Cerritos and San Lorenzo mills in Orizaba, Veracruz. The company's original capitalization was 2.55 million pesos—about $2 million at the time the company was established—but by the end of the Porfiriato this had grown to 15 million pesos. CIDOSA's productive capacity expanded along with its capitalization. In 1892 the company augmented the two existing mills by erecting the nation's largest factory, the Río Blanco mill, which employed close to 3,000 workers. The number of CIDOSA's mills increased again in 1899 when the Cocolapam mill was purchased. Not only was CIDOSA the nation's largest textile enterprise, but it was also the largest manufacturing concern of any type, in terms of both capitalization and the number of workers it employed. In fact, in 1911 CIDOSA was the eighteenth largest corporation in terms of capitalization in Mexico, ranking behind only the largest railroads, mining concerns, and banks.

Originally CIDOSA's mills were run by water turbines, which were soon augmented by hydroelectric power. Like many vertically integrated manufacturing concerns, the company owned its own hydroelectric plants. Altogether CIDOSA's four mills employed over 8,000 horsepower, using 18 turbines and 45 electric motors. This motive power drove nearly 100,000 spindles, 4,000 looms, and 10 eight-color printing machines. When all of the company's four textile mills and two power plants were running at peak, they employed close to 6,000 workers.

Though textile manufacturing is usually characterized by near-perfect competition, in 1912 CIDOSA controlled 13.5 percent of the market with annual sales in the area of 7 million pesos. Seventy-five percent of the company's production was in heavy, coarse goods for the low end of the market, but it also produced fine weaves equal in quality to the best imported fabrics, the English-made machinery at Rio Blanco being able to spin yarn counts into the eighties.[35]

Behind CIDOSA in terms of market size, work force, and subscribed capital came the Compañía Industrial Veracruzana (CIVSA). Located just upriver from CIDOSA's four factories, CIVSA's Santa Rosa works rivaled those found at the larger company. Indeed, its work force of 2,000 was almost as large as that found at the Río Blanco mill, and its machinery was also capable of producing cloth equal in quality to imported goods. Like CIDOSA, CIVSA was an integrated operation, which processed raw cotton, spun it into yarn, wove it into cloth, and stamped colored patterns into it. It also generated its own power at its own hydroelectric plant. At the close of the Porfiriato the firm was capitalized at 6.03 million pesos and commanded a 6 percent market share.[36]

Other large firms also existed, though they were not as technically advanced and as dominant in the market as CIDOSA and CIVSA. They did not compete with high-quality foreign cloth as did the two Veracruz giants, and they tended to be regional rather than national producers. By the standards of an economy as small and underdeveloped as Mexico's, however, and even by international standards in cotton textile production, they were sizable operations, with capitalizations in the millions of pesos and work forces in the thousands. The firms were the Compañía Industrial de Atlixco (with 2,000 workers, 6 million pesos in paid-in capital, and 5 percent of the market),[37] the Compañía Industrial de San Antonio Abad (with 1,700 workers, 3.5 million pesos in capital, and a 4 percent market share),[38] the Compañía Industrial Manufacturera (1,200 operatives, 4 million pesos in capital, and 3 percent of the market),[39] and the Compañía Industrial de Guadalajara, which ran three mills in the state of Jalisco with a total paid-in capital of 2 million pesos and a work force of just over 500. It took but 2 percent of the market.[40]

The existence of these six large firms did not preclude the existence of smaller producers. Throughout the period small manufacturers continued to hold on against their larger, more efficient competitors. Over time, however, the tendency was for the large firms to force out the smaller ones. In general, the smaller family-owned and family-run mills did not operate in the more lucrative and competitive Mexico City market. Rather, they predominated in provincial areas, where transport costs gave them an advantage over the Veracruz giants, as in areas like Querétaro or Oaxaca or in areas where a textile industry had existed for some time. In these areas the age of the mills meant that the fixed capital costs of the enterprises were very low because the machinery had long since been paid for and depreciated. This was the case, for example, in areas like Tlaxcala or Michoacán, where much of the machinery dated from the mid-nineteenth century. Firms operating in these areas had only to cover their variable costs.

Over time, of course, the smaller firms had to choose between modernizing their equipment in order to remain competitive or going out of business. For this reason, by the first decade of the twentieth century many of the mills in Mexico City and Puebla, which competed directly with the big Veracruz firms, began to install the new, high-velocity machinery that the industry leaders used. In 1898 what the taxation authorities classified as old spindles (non–high velocity) outnumbered new spindles (high velocity) by a ratio of nearly two to one in the nation's textile industry. By 1907 new spindles outnumbered old by a six-to-one ratio, and new weaving machinery had almost entirely replaced the nation's older, slower looms.[41]

Mexico's artisan weavers did not have this option; they were quickly being driven out of existence by the technological revolution in the cloth industry. Of the 41,000 artisan cloth producers in 1895, only 12,000 remained by 1910. The fortunes of the weavers of the state of Guanajuato provide a graphic illustration of the rapid disappearance of craft-producers once the new mills began to flood the market with machine-made cloth. In 1876 the state had supported 853 cotton textile shops, but by 1910 nearly all of them were gone. The only artisans who survived in any number were the weavers of *rebozos* (shawls), who were saved by the preference of rural women for this traditional garment.[42]

All of the industrial giants that grew up during this period had several structural characteristics in common, the most obvious of which was their immense size. Not only did they employ thousands of workers, but they also commanded capital in the millions of pesos. Even more outstanding was the fact that these giants were not small enterprises that, through decades of careful management and reinvestment, had grown into large corporations. On the contrary, they were large at their founding, with initial capitalizations well into the millions of pesos. From the start this was big business.

Along with the immense size of firms went a new structure of ownership and control. Manufacturing enterprises had previously been family-owned affairs. At most, several merchant families would pool their resources in a limited partnership. Given the size of these new enterprises, however, this structure gave way to joint-stock corporations owned by unrelated stockholders. In fact, most of the large industrial corporations of the period went public quite early in their development; their shares were traded not only on the Mexico City exchange, but on those of Paris and Geneva as well.

Family-owned enterprises remained in Mexico. In some lines of manufacturing, like leather goods, cigars, and food processing, small firms continued to dominate. Even in the increasingly concentrated cotton and wool textile industries, small firms that produced for geographically isolated areas continued to hold out. Wherever there were sizable economies of scale or speed, or where the lack of a skilled labor force created incentives to mechanize production, however, big firms were pushing the small producers out. Thus, along with the increase in the size of firms came a growing concentration of the market. Because no comprehensive industrial census was ever carried out during the Porfiriato, it is not possible to calculate the percentage of national industrial production attributable to large-scale manufacturing. Data from the census of 1929, when Mexican manufacturing was much the same as it was in 1910 (see Chapter 9), can shed some light on the subject. As a percentage of the total national production of manufactures, the subsectors discussed in this study, that is, those that were becoming increasingly concentrated—steel, textiles, cement, beer, dynamite, soap, paper, glass, and cigarettes—accounted for just over half of all manufactures produced in 1929. I estimate that these industries comprised 56.5 percent of the total capital invested in manufacturing and contributed 56 percent of total value added.[43]

Along with horizontal integration came vertical integration. It was not uncommon for manufacturing concerns to own and operate their own power plants, control the sources of their raw materials, and manufacture their intermediate inputs. For example, the San Rafael y Anexas paper company generated its own electrical power, operated its own railroad, and produced its own mechanical wood pulp. It even owned its own forests and ran its own logging operation. Similarly, Fundidora Monterrey controlled every phase of production from the mining of the iron ore and coal to the rolling of finished steel products. In both industries the desire to take advantage of economies of speed, even if they were unrealized, had a lot to do with the firm's decision to integrate vertically. In paper production, for example, whenever pulp and paper mills were located in the same vicinity, wood pulp could be pumped directly from the grinders into the paper mills while still in a liquid state. This meant that the pulp did not have to be dried into "laps" (sheets of folded pulp) and then reliquefied before being processed into paper.[44]

Similarly, in the steel rail industry economical operation requires that the entire process, from the reduction of iron ore to the rolling of finished products, be carried out in the same location. In other industries vertical integration was dictated by the type of technology employed. In cotton and wool textile production, for example, the introduction of electrically powered machinery required firms to construct their own generating plants since it was not generally possible to purchase commercially produced power from a utility company. In fact, the sale of electric power often went the other way, with municipalities buying the excess electricity produced by factories.

There were two areas in which manufacturing corporations did not vertically integrate: forward integration into sales and marketing, and backward linkages into capital goods. Unlike large manufacturers in the United States, which were now establishing marketing departments to control the distribution of finished products, Mexico's major manufacturers did not try to exercise tight control over distribution. Rather, they retained the more informal, nonintegrated structure that had existed since the early nineteenth century in which jobbers and commissioned mill agents handled the distribution of goods. The segmentation of the market was probably the crucial factor here. There was probably little to be gained in the way of efficiency by streamlining distribution arrangements.

With regard to forward linkages, the fact that the major stock-holders of these firms were usually themselves merchants (see Chapter 5) meant that a relatively sophisticated, if somewhat decentralized, marketing system already existed. Jobbers purchased goods from companies in which they owned stock, at a pre-arranged discount, and then sold them to their own retailing operations. In product lines where this traditional owner-jobber-retailer network was not set up to handle the type of transactions involved—for example, the sale of cement to the government for public works projects—distribution and marketing were carried out by commissioned sales agents. Only in the case of the steel industry were corporate-run regional sales offices established.

There was also little in the way of backward linkages into the production of capital goods. Though some firms were moving into intermediate products like glass bottles, steel, and cement, the manufacture of capital goods was totally ignored. That is, unlike the United States where the cotton-textile industry gave rise to a textile machinery industry, which in turn gave rise to advanced metal working, machine tool, and engineering industries, Mexican manufacturers did not move beyond the production of final goods. This was largely the result of the high degree of risk involved in the production of specialized, non-consumer goods whose market was neither deep nor secure. In addition, the production of sophisticated capital goods required a level of scientific and technical knowledge that was largely absent in Mexico. By the time Mexico began to industrialize, the development of manufacturing technology had moved out of the shops of tinkerers and technically minded workmen and into the design and engineering departments of big corporations. Mexico was simply too far behind to try to develop its own capital goods industry. From the point of view of individual firms it was far less costly to purchase the necessary machinery from foreign manufacturers than to undertake its production in Mexico.

Thus, during the twenty years between 1890 and 1910 Mexican manufacturing was transformed. Large, vertically integrated firms replaced the small shops and artisanal producers that had historically produced most of Mexico's manufactures. The technologies these firms employed were of recent vintage and the machinery brand new. Thus the Siemens-Martin furnaces at Fundidora Monterrey were as up-to-date as any found in Pittsburgh, the looms in CIDOSA's cotton textile mills the equal of anything found in New England.[45]

This model of rapid industrialization, however, had its costs in terms of long-run industrial development. It meant that a few firms carved up the entire national market in any one product line. Oligopoly and monopoly production came to characterize modern Mexican manufacturing from its very inception. This in turn meant that start-up costs were extremely high. Investors would have to come forward who had access to capital in the millions of pesos required to operate the new giant firms and to supply the requisite foreign-produced capital goods. Given the need for such credentials, ownership was in danger of becoming ever more restricted.

FIVE

Finance and Entrepreneurship

THE SCALE OF the industrial technology Mexico imported was not only too large relative to the size of the market, it was also extremely expensive relative to the ability of the economy to accumulate and transfer capital. The contradictions inherent in the importation of foreign technology again presented themselves, and they again encouraged the development of a noncompetitive, inward-looking industrial structure.

By the time that Mexico began to industrialize during the last decades of the nineteenth century, the cost of entry to the market in manufacturing was much higher than it had been in the late eighteenth century when Great Britain began what came to be known as the First Industrial Revolution. During the early phase of world industrialization, a small group of moderately prosperous men could purchase the capital goods needed to undertake almost any kind of industrial venture. By the late nineteenth century, however, the state of manufacturing technology was such that entry into the mass production of most industrial goods required capitalizations running into the millions of dollars. What had evolved in Europe over a long period of time, financed through an extended process of reinvestment, now had to be purchased all at once.

Entry costs were further raised by the fact that the technology and capital goods that had to be imported were expensive to buy, ship, and insure in transit. Foreign technicians often had to be employed to build and operate the mill and train the work force. These expenses could increase the final cost of the mill by a substantial margin. In the cotton textile industry, for example, they added almost 60 percent to the start-up cost.

Manufacturers therefore had to raise initial capitalizations running into the millions of pesos. The original paid-in capital of the Fundidora Monterrey steel mill, for example, was 10 million pesos (roughly $5 million). The founders of the San Rafael y Anexas paper company had to come up with 5 million pesos. Even this mammoth sum was not enough to properly equip the mill, and they were forced to release yet another stock issue, increasing the paid-in capital to 7 million pesos. In the cigarette, cement, glass, and beer industries, initial capitalizations ran as high as 2 million pesos. Even in wool and cotton textile manufacturing, which do not have large economies of scale, start-up costs were very high. A medium-sized mill could cost upward of a million pesos, with some firms requiring as much as 3.35 million pesos to set up.

How, then, did Mexican manufacturers raise amounts of this magnitude in an economy as capital-scarce as Mexico's?

Government-affiliated industrial finance banks were one way that capital could have been channeled into manufacturing. This strategy was pursued with success in some nations of continental Europe. In 1830 the Mexican government also established such a bank, the Banco de Avío. A percentage of the tariff revenues on imported cotton textiles was to be used to capitalize the bank, which would then make long-term loans to new industrial ventures. Unfortunately, the bank was plagued with problems and was finally dissolved in 1842.[1] It was never revived, even after the conditions for industrialization became more propitious during the last decades of the century.

The private banking system could likewise not be counted on to serve as a source of finance capital for Mexico's new industries. Mexico's banking system, still in its infancy, was designed to do nothing more than facilitate commerce. In 1897 Mexico had only seven functioning banks, none of which was legally able to provide loans for periods exceeding one year. Even with the expansion of the banking sector during the first decade of the twentieth century, the result of federal legislation designed to augment the development of financial institutions, Mexico's entire banking system still numbered fewer than 20 firms in 1910— most of them extremely small enterprises with capitalizations in the area of only 500,000 pesos. Most important, almost all of

TABLE 5.1
Debt-Equity Ratios, Selected Manufacturing Companies,
1901–1913

Company	Years	Ratio
Fund Mont	1901–03	0.03:1
	1904–06	0.18:1
	1908–13	0.43:1
CIDOSA	1907–12	0.33:1
CIVSA	1908–13	0.12:1
Atlixco	1908–13	0.17:1
San Ildef	1907–13	0.07:1
Buen Tono	1903–09	0.07:1
Toluca-México	1905	0.12:1

SOURCES: Fundidora Monterrey data calculated from *FMIA*, 1901–13. CIDOSA data calculated from *EM*, 11 Apr. 1908, p. 30, 17 Apr. 1909, p. 52, 21 May 1910, p. 162, 27 Apr. 1912, p. 67, 19 Apr. 1913, p. 37. CIVSA data calculated from *EM*, 1 May 1909, p. 98, 26 Apr. 1913, p. 51, 23 May 1914, p. 72. Atlixco data calculated from *EM*, 24 Apr. 1909, p. 75, 12 Apr. 1913, p. 22, 21 May 1914, p. 51. San Ildefonso data calculated from *BCM*: 298; *EM*, 21 May 1914, p. 51. El Buen Tono data calculated from *EM*, 12 Mar. 1904, p. 593, 14 Mar. 1905, p. 477, 21 Mar. 1908, p. 488, 5 Mar. 1910, p. 473. Toluca-México data calculated from *EM*, 10 Mar. 1906, p. 449. For raw data and a complete year-by-year breakdown of debt-equity ratios, see Haber 1985: 88–97.

these banks were legally constituted only to serve as sources of short-term credit. In 1910 only nine banks were set up to provide loans for periods of more than one year, and these existed predominantly in order to finance urban and rural real estate transactions.

A few banks, called Bancos Refaccionarios, were set up to provide capital for manufacturing, but they could make loans for periods of no more than two years. This was far too short a term to be used in the initial financing of a factory, though in theory they could have provided working capital. As it turned out, the Bancos Refaccionarios had trouble generating their own capital, and what they did amass they put into real estate, agriculture, and mining. They provided almost no working capital for Mexico's manufacturers.[2]

Bank financing therefore played only a minor role in the development of Mexican manufacturing. As Table 5.1 shows, Mexico's major manufacturers borrowed very little money, either for their initial financing or for operating capital. Though only a fragmentary record exists, the available evidence, constructed from the balance sheets of seven of Mexico's largest manufacturing firms, indicates that these companies had incredibly low debt-equity ratios.* These companies include the Fundidora Monterrey steel monopoly; the two industry leaders in cotton textiles, CIDOSA and CIVSA, plus a third major cotton manufacturer, the Compañía Industrial de Atlixco; the industry leader in wool textiles, the Compañía Industrial de San Ildefonso; the nation's most important cigarette producer, El Buen Tono; and the third most important beer brewery, the Compañía Cervecera de Toluca y México. It should be kept in mind that these firms were among the largest and most productive of Mexico's manufacturing enterprises, and their owners among the best-connected financiers in the country. They therefore represent the upper end of the spectrum in the amount of capital they were able to borrow.

Low debt-equity ratios could indicate that these were extremely successful firms, which had high rates of profit and could therefore finance their operations out of retained earnings. This, however, was not the case: many of these enterprises were in fact money-losers (see Chapter 7). They had low debt-equity ratios not because they were successful, but because they could not obtain finance or working capital from the banking system.

Of the seven firms for which I have calculated debt-equity ratios, the Fundidora Monterrey steel company was the most highly leveraged. Even here the extent of borrowing was negligible, however. From 1900 to 1913 the firm's average ratio of debt to equity was only 0.27:1. That is, the value of the paid-in capital plus reserves was four times the value of all outstanding debt, which included accounts payable—short-term debts to suppliers for machinery or raw materials—as well as bank borrowing. Taking into account the size of the venture, this was a re-

*The debt-equity ratio of a company is a coefficient expressing the size of a company's outstanding debts (bank loans, bonds, and accounts payable) against the shareholders' equity (paid-in capital, reserves, and undistributed profits). Both items appear on the liabilities side of a company's balance sheet.

markably small amount of debt (a typical U.S. corporation in the 1980's, for example, might display a debt-equity ratio ranging from 1:1 to 5:1). Fundidora Monterrey's level of debt during the Porfiriato never exceeded 45 percent of owners' equity. More important, most of its debt was accrued because of operating losses. Very little of the company's debt was contracted in order to finance the erection of the mill. In fact, during the first three years of Fundidora Monterrey's existence, when the mill was being constructed, the level of debt was negligible; from 1901 to 1903 the debt-equity ratio averaged only 0.03:1.

Though the data for the other six manufacturing firms are less complete than for Fundidora Monterrey, they indicate an even lower debt picture (see Table 5.1). Clearly these companies borrowed very little money. The negligible amount of debt they did carry on their balance sheets was accounts payable, not bank borrowing.

Bank borrowing being of negligible importance, most of the investment capital for Mexican manufacturing came from the nation's most prominent merchant-financiers. They were the only group in Mexico with sufficient liquid wealth to finance the very expensive plant and equipment that had to be imported. Given the large capital requirements of the enterprises and the perceived risk involved in manufacturing ventures, no one financier would commit all of his resources to any single project. Instead, several financiers would combine to form a joint-stock company. The perceived inherent risk in manufacturing also encouraged financiers to require equity participation, rather than purchasing bonds or other debt instruments in the firm. Since the number of major financiers was relatively small—no more than 25—the overall effect was that a tight clique controlled Mexico's most important manufacturing companies. The same group of people combined again and again to form new enterprises, with the result that the level of interlock among corporate boards of directors was quite high.

The predominance of financiers in Mexican manufacturing was by no means an anomaly. In fact, such control may well have been a fairly consistent pattern throughout the late-industrializing world during this time period. This certainly held true in Brazil, where, as both Stanley Stein and Warren Dean have shown, a similar group of merchant-financiers controlled the major manufacturing companies.[3]

What could not be raised among the merchant-financiers was raised in foreign capital markets by means of stock issues in Geneva and Paris. Thus, while there were no subsidiaries of European manufacturing companies in Mexico, there was a good deal of portfolio investment by French and Swiss bankers and financiers. This took the form of either the direct purchase of a company's stock or, in an attempt to spread risk, the purchase of stock in a European-based, industrial holding company, like the Société Financière pour l'industrie au Mexique, which was incorporated in Geneva.

The total amount of equity capital provided by the European holding companies to Mexican manufacturers was small. The total paid-in capital of the Société Financière pour l'industrie au Mexique, for example, was only 10 million pesos (5 million francs), which was divided up between more than half a dozen companies. The paid-in capital of just one of the these companies, the Compañía Industrial de Orizaba, was 15 million pesos, one-and-one-half times the total capital of the entire investment company. Thus, European capital merely supplemented—it did not supplant—domestic sources of capital.[4]

How, then, was this capital generated? Who were the men who controlled it? The two most salient characteristics of Mexico's industrial financiers were that almost none of them were Mexican and most of them knew nothing at all about manufacturing. The majority of the principal stockholders in Mexico's major manufacturing enterprises were foreign-born merchants and financiers whose capital had been accumulated in Mexico through commerce and money-lending. These men were not the tinkerers of the English Industrial Revolution or the production-oriented engineers and scientific managers of U.S. industry. They were merchant-financiers whose principal talents lay in making deals to maintain their monopoly positions and in manipulating the economic apparatus of the state to provide them with protection from foreign competition. They knew little about production. For example, of the nine men who made up the first board of directors of Fundidora Monterrey, only one knew anything about steel making.[5] They tended not to compete with one another by means of innovations in manufacturing technology. They were skilled manipulators of the market and the state. Their backgrounds as merchants had taught them how to structure the market and avoid competition through collusion and price rigging, and their experience as financiers taught them how to enlist the support of the government in this strategy. Their presence on the boards of Mexico's major manufacturing enterprises therefore reinforced the tendency of Mexican industry to collude rather than compete.

Mexico's financier-industrialists were well positioned to shape government policies to their liking. Indeed, they were the economic backbone of the Porfirian state. They subscribed to the government's treasury bonds; they sat on the boards of the nation's most important financial institutions; and they represented the government in international financial markets when it borrowed money abroad. In fact, it was not so much a case of the state representing the interests of these financiers as it was that these financiers *were* the state. They controlled the emission of paper money through their ownership of the Banco Nacional de México—there was no government-run central bank—they shaped national monetary and exchange rate policy through the seats they occupied on the Comisión de Cambios y Monedas, and they held the strings on the flow of international loans to the Mexican government through their connections to the major banks in Madrid, Geneva, Paris, and New York.[6]

Exactly who were these financiers? Basically there were two groups: one consisting of European-born merchants whose commercial activities in Mexico led them into banking and, later, into manufacturing; the other was composed mostly of American-born capitalists who had accumulated wealth in noncommercial activities, for example, railroading, but who quickly made alliances with the merchant-financier elite and set themselves up as financiers in their own right. In practice these two groups functioned as one. In fact, they often intermarried to solidify socially what they had already accomplished financially.

Typical in many respects of the first group was Adolfo Prieto y Alvarez. Born in 1867 in Sama de Grado, Asturias, Prieto came to Mexico in 1890 to work in the banking house of Antonio Basagoiti y Arteta, one of Mexico's most important financiers, tobacco merchants, and industrialists. Basagoiti, a Basque, had built a financial empire in the tobacco trade and had then branched out into money-lending. Apparently his banking operations had enabled him to come into possession of several textile mills and cigarette factories. This was a common sequence and, in fact, seems to have been the means by which mills most often changed hands. A merchant banker would extend credit to a manufacturer—oftentimes also a merchant, though a somewhat less solvent one—in order to provide the materials necessary to run the mill. Payment was generally so set up that the entire annual production of the factory would be sold to the creditor at a price set at the time of the loan. It frequently happened that over time the factory owner would become so indebted to the *aviador* (money-lender) that he would be forced to sign over the factory.[7] Thus, by the time Prieto arrived in Mexico City in 1890 Basagoiti was already an extremely important merchant-banker and had started, through the acquisition of several textile and cigarette factories, to branch out into manufacturing.[8]

Prieto undoubtedly had some connection to Basagoiti prior to his arrival in Mexico. People did not just walk off the boat from Spain and obtain an important job in one of the country's largest merchant houses. Usually, a family or personal connection existed. These relations were often fortified through marriage, with junior partners in merchant firms marrying the daughters or nieces of the company's senior partners. Prieto was most probably the nephew of Eugenio Alvarez, who was a partner of Basagoiti's in a tobacco brokerage. He may also have been a relative of Luis Barroso Arias, an Asturiano financier who also had ties to Basagoiti.

From this base in Basagoiti's banking house Prieto built a financial empire of his own. In 1897, along with Indalecio Ibáñez, the son of Manuel Ibáñez, an Asturiano merchant whose firm was absorbed by Basagoiti, and Manuel Basagoiti, probably Antonio's son or nephew, Prieto was appointed *apoderado* (agent) of the banking house. This was a position of considerable responsibility, carrying with it the power of attorney of the firm.[9] Prieto continued to rise within the ranks of Basagoiti's operation and began to establish himself as a financier in his own right. In 1903 he and Indalecio Ibáñez founded the brokerage and banking house Ibáñez y Prieto. Ibáñez had already begun to branch out on his own and by this time had considerable investments in the San Cristóbal sugar hacienda in Veracruz, the El Progreso Industrial paper mill in the state of Mexico, and the La Tabacalera Mexicana cigarette-manufacturing company, which Basagoiti had established in 1899 with the Veracruz tobacco brokers Zaldo y Compañía.[10]

Within a few years Prieto had used the capital generated in the joint banking operation to buy stock in the Compañía Industrial de San Antonio Abad, a Mexico City–based cotton textile conglomerate, and in La Tabacalera Mexicana.[11] At the same time, along with Ibáñez, he purchased the La Victoria wool textile mill from Basagoiti, who had come into possession of it when his bank foreclosed on a bad debt. Capitalized at 1 million pesos, La Victoria was the second largest wool textile mill in the country.[12]

In addition to developing his own investments, Prieto was all the while moving up in the Basagoiti operation, eventually achieving the position of *apoderado general*. When Basagoiti returned to Spain—he sat on the board of at least one Spanish bank, the Banco Hispano de Madríd—Prieto was left in charge of the firm's operations.[13] By 1907 he was Basagoiti's representative on the board of directors of Fundidora Monterrey, a position he eventually used to gain total control of the firm. Basagoiti was Fundidora Monterrey's second largest shareholder, controlling 21.5 percent of the stock, a sizable investment that amounted to 2.15 million pesos, or just over $1 million in 1900 when the shares were purchased.[14] During the crisis of 1907–8 Prieto was appointed *consejero delegado* of Fundidora Monterrey at Basagoiti's urging.[15] His job was to serve as the representative of the stockholders and closely oversee and monitor the company's operations in order to make the mill profitable. Until this point Fundidora Monterrey had made money in only three out of its six years of operation, and it had run a net loss since 1902 of close to 700,000 pesos.[16]

From this point on Prieto gradually increased his control over Fundidora Monterrey. In 1917 he became chairman of the board and, by the mid-1920's, held a controlling interest in the company. He was to stay on as chairman until his death in 1945. True to his financier roots, Prieto never moved to Monterrey where the firm was located. Instead, he ran the company from Mexico City, where the majority of his investments, which spanned wool and cotton textiles, soap, cigarettes, and banking, were located. More important, prior to his ascension to power Prieto had no formal training or any practical experience in running a smelting or foundry operation. The actual running of the mill and all of the day-to-day technical decisions were left to American engineers.

Along with Prieto and his Basque and Asturiano counterparts were French and Swiss-born financiers. Some, like Sebastián Robert, were Parisian merchants who maintained outlets in both Paris and Mexico. Robert, who sat on the boards of two textile companies, CIVSA and La Hormiga, S.A., and the Banco Nacional de México, had accumulated his wealth in merchant activities as S. Robert y Compañía, which owned two stores in Mexico City—La Valenciana and El Centro Mercantil—and one in Paris, Maison d'Achats.[17]

Other European-born financier-industrialists were bankers who had accumulated their initial capital by importing luxury goods from Europe and reselling them to the Porfirian elite. These goods ranged from fine English woolens for the suitings of Porfirian gentlemen to French lingerie for their wives. On their wrists and necks they wore precision-made watches and expensive jewelry imported from Switzerland. Given the extravagant tastes of the Mexican upper class and their desire to imitate most everything European, sizable fortunes were built catering to their whims.

One such fortune, which was later directed into industrial investments, was that of the German-born Hugo Scherer. Scherer and his son, Hugo, Jr., accumulated their original wealth in the jewelry trade and went on to set themselves up as financiers of manufacturing, mining, agriculture, railways, and utilities. Besides running their own banking house, Hugo Scherer y Compañía, they sat on the boards of several commercial and mortgage banks: the Banco Nacional de México, the Compañía Bancaria de Fomento y Bienes Raíces de México, the Banco Central Mexicano, and the Caja de Préstamos para Obras de Irrigación y Fomento de la Agricultura. From importing and banking they moved into manufacturing and were important shareholders in the Compañía Industrial Manufacturera cotton textile conglomerate, the Compañía Compresora de Algodón, which operated a cotton compress in Torreón, Coahuila, the El Buen Tono cigarette manufacturing company, the Compañía Nacional Mexicana de Dinamita y Explosivos—the dynamite monopoly—and Fundidora Monterrey.

In addition to these holdings in manufacturing, the Scherers had interests in mining, agriculture, utilities, and railways. The younger Scherer sat on the boards of the Compañía Maderera de la Sierra de Durango—a timber and land company—the Dos Estrellas mining company, the Agujita coal company, the Guadalajara Tramways, Light and Power Company, and the Ferrocarriles Nacionales de México, and his father sat on the boards of the Santa María de la Paz mining company and the Minas del Fierro del Pacífico.

Both Scherers were well connected to the international financial centers of Europe and the United States. The elder Scherer was a director of the Mexican Mining and Industrial Company, a London-based holding company that channeled investments into Mexican mining operations.[18] His son was a member of the board of the Banco Internacional Hipotecario, which served as a conduit for the movement of capital from New York to Mexico. He also served as a director of the Société Financière pour l'industrie au Mexique. His international financial connections made him among the most influential bankers in private and government circles. In 1908, for instance, he was asked to handle the sale of 50 million pesos ($25 million) worth of bonds in New York to finance the semi-government-owned Caja de Préstamos para Obras de Irrigación y Fomento de la Agricultura. In addition, throughout the Porfiriato both Scherers, along with Basagoiti and Prieto, served on the Comisión de Cambios y Monedas, which determined government monetary policy and exchange rates.[19]

Yet another group of European-born financiers was made up

of wealthy Mexico City dry-goods merchants from Barcelonette, France. Barcelonette, a small town in the Bas Alpes near the Italian border, had been a center for the artisan production of wool textiles. When technological advances in the mid-nineteenth century made factory production more profitable, the traditional economy of the area was undermined. The craftsmen of Barcelonette, unable to compete with factory-made goods, began to migrate to other areas in search of new avenues for economic advancement. The focus of their migration was Mexico, where several of their countrymen had already achieved some success as merchants.[20] By the 1890's, several of these Barcelonette merchant families were among the most important dry-goods merchants in Mexico City. One such family was the Signorets, which came to Mexico around midcentury and established itself as petty traders in the state of Michoacán. By 1880 the family had amassed enough wealth that one of its members, León, was able to establish a Mexico City retail operation, Al Puerto de Veracruz. This enterprise was expanded in 1888 when the Signorets formed a partnership with another Barcelonette merchant, León Honnorat.[21]

From this point on, Signoret, Honnorat y Compañía were able to amass sufficient wealth in their wholesale and retail operations to establish themselves as major financiers, with investments in banking, manufacturing, utilities, ranching, and agriculture. Though a precise breakdown of Signoret's investment portfolio is not available, it is known that he served on the boards of at least three banks, all of which had ties to major foreign financial centers: the Banco de Londres y México, the Compañía Bancaria de París y México, and the Banco Central Mexicano (New York).[22]

Movement into commercial banking was quite common among merchants. By the very nature of the enterprise in which they were engaged, they gradually became bankers. Merchant activity generated large amounts of liquid capital that could be loaned at interest until the merchant needed to settle his own accounts. Moreover, since commerce moved on credit and since formal banking in Mexico existed only in its most rudimentary forms, the responsibility of supplying credit to both producers and retailers fell to the large jobbers. These informal credit and discounting operations were later formalized by the establishment of commercial banks, most of which were founded during the latter part of the Porfiriato.

Mercantile enterprises led men like Signoret not only into banking but also into manufacturing. In 1883 a group of Mexico City merchants attempted to corner the market on cotton goods by signing contracts with the major producers, thereby forming a cotton cartel.[23] In order to get around this attempt at cartelization, other merchants, Signoret and Honnorat included, were forced to set themselves up as manufacturers so as to guarantee a source of supply at a set price. In addition, the fact that the big merchants were the principal source of working capital for the mill owners—since the large commercial banks were not set up to make loans to manufacturing enterprises—also transformed many merchants into factory owners. As we have seen, as a mill's debt mounted and it became increasingly clear that payment would not be forthcoming, the merchants frequently recouped their loans by demanding a share of the mill. Thus, Signoret figured among the principal shareholders of the nation's largest cotton and wool textile concerns, CIDOSA and the Compañía Industrial de San Ildefonso.[24]

Signoret's industrial investments did not end with textiles. He was also on the board of directors of the Cervecería Moctezuma and of Fundidora Monterrey. In fact, he had been among the four founders of Fundidora Monterrey and in 1900 held 19 percent of the stock. This represented an investment of 1.9 million pesos, making Signoret the third largest shareholder behind Eugene Kelly* and Antonio Basagoiti.[25] He was also a stockholder and board member of two public utilities companies, the Compañía de Tranvias de Torreón, which operated a streetcar line,

* Eugene Kelly, the company's largest stockholder, controlled 29,997 shares, including those held by Patricio Milmo Sucs, a merchant firm that Kelly married into and that he managed after Milmo's death. Kelly was a New York banker of Irish descent, who married the daughter of Patricio Milmo, an Irish-born merchant in Monterrey. Milmo, originally Patrick Mullins, was one of the most powerful merchants in northern Mexico. None of the three men—Signoret, Basagoiti, and Kelly—who together controlled 70 percent of the shares in Fundidora Monterrey, had any experience in steel-making, smelting, or foundry operations. They were strictly financiers whose accumulated capital derived from merchant activity.

and the Compañía Eléctrica de Lerdo a Torreón, a power company. Though the extent of his holdings is unknown, Signoret also held interests in cattle ranching and agriculture.[26]

Finally, like the other major financiers of the Porfiriato, Signoret was well connected to the Díaz government. In fact, it was he who organized the fact-finding trip of merchants and manufacturers (which was partially underwritten by the Mexican government) to South America in 1902.[27]

Allied with the European-born merchant-financiers were U.S. investors. In general, they were not wealthy men when they arrived in Mexico, but like their French, Swiss, and Spanish counterparts, these Americans rapidly built themselves sizable fortunes. In one sense, they constituted a separate group within the Porfirian financial elite. Unlike the Europeans, they accumulated capital in areas other than commerce, but like their European counterparts they followed similar strategies as investors, holding diversified portfolios that covered a wide range of economic activities. Rather than concentrate on production and technical innovation, these entrepreneurs preferred to play the market, juggling their portfolios and ruthlessly manipulating the state to their advantage in order to bring higher returns. Moreover, they did not operate independently of the Europeans. In fact, they integrated themselves—often through marriage— into the already established European-born, merchant-banker-financier elite.

Thomas Braniff was perhaps typical in many respects of this American contingent. Born in Staten Island, New York, in 1830 to Irish immigrant parents, he went to California during the gold rush of the 1850's. Although he failed as a gold prospector, in California he met Henry Meiggs, the English railway engineer. Meiggs invited Braniff to work on a railroad that his company, Smith-Knight, was building in Peru and Chile. Following the completion of this line, Braniff went to Mexico to work on the railway that was being built between Mexico City and Veracruz. In the 1860's he began to amass what would become a sizable fortune. The contractors for the railway successfully pressured the Mexican government for permission to import consumer goods of "vital necessity" for their foreign-born employees. This was a concession that was much abused, being used by the officers of the company, including Braniff, to enrich themselves. Instead of providing basic, non-luxury, consumer goods for the railroad employees, the concessionaires brought a variety of contraband, which they sold on the free market.[28]

Following the completion of the railroad in 1873 Braniff stayed on as general manager of the company that ran the rail line, the Compañía Ferrocarril Mexicana. Using his interest in the railway as a nucleus, he began to purchase factories that lay along the new railroad. The first such purchase appears to have been the San Lorenzo cotton textile mill in Orizaba, Veracruz. Braniff spent over 240,000 pesos upgrading the mill, which was acquired in 1889 by CIDOSA, the textile conglomerate. Trading the mill for shares in the company, Braniff became one of CIDOSA's major stockholders. His position on CIDOSA's board of directors brought him into contact with the important French merchant-financiers of the time, like Henri Tron, León Signoret, and Eugenio Roux. Using these connections, Braniff branched out into other areas, eventually developing a portfolio with holdings in 15 mining companies, two major commercial banks, three railroads, seven haciendas, two power companies, and six manufacturing companies, as well as investments in urban real estate, investment banking operations, and commerce. At the time of his death in 1905 his financial empire was worth close to 8 million pesos ($4 million).[29] (See Tables 5.2 and 5.3.)

An examination of the distribution of Braniff's estate reveals a great deal about the investment patterns of the Porfirian entrepreneur. The most striking feature of Braniff's portfolio is its wide diversification. Manufacturing, though the largest component, accounted for only 39 percent of the fortune he had acquired. Twenty-three percent was invested in banking operations, about three-fifths of it in stocks of commercial banking companies—he was a board member of the Banco de Londres y México and the Banco Internacional Hipotecario[30]—and the remainder in personally run investment banking operations. In this respect, Braniff operated in much the same manner as Basagoiti, Prieto, and Scherer. On the one hand, he was a major stockholder in large commercial banking corporations, which provided short-term commercial credit and mortgages on agricultural properties; on the other, he operated a banking house of

TABLE 5.2
Investment Portfolio of Thomas Braniff in 1905,
by Functional Category

Category	Value of holdings (pesos)	Percent of total holdings
Manufacturing[a]	3,139,525	39.4%
Real estate[b]	1,607,178	20.2
Commercial banking[b]	1,047,575	13.1
Investment banking[b]	767,320	9.6
Agriculture[b]	585,277	7.3
Commerce[c]	338,346	4.2
Railroads[b]	235,800	3.0
Utilities[b]	182,975	2.3
Mining[b]	70,414	0.9
TOTAL	7,974,410	100.0%

SOURCE: Derived from Collado Herrera 1983: 91.
[a]See Table 5.3 for a breakdown of Braniff's manufacturing investments.
[b]For a breakdown of Braniff's investments in this line of activity, see Haber 1985: ch. 3.
[c]Braniff's only investment in commerce was one-third share of G. y O. Braniff, which Braniff set up with his sons George and Oscar to import rolling stock and machinery. His sons each held one-third of the stock.

his own, which made long-term loans to other investment bankers, merchants, and financiers. In fact, Braniff's second largest debtor at the time of his death was the firm of Ibáñez y Prieto, which owed him 208,000 pesos. Urban real estate made up another 20 percent of his portfolio, and agricultural real estate an additional 7 percent. Including the haciendas bought by Braniff but held in his wife's name and the urban real estate that he held, his investment in land totaled 2.19 million pesos, which was almost as large as his 3.14 million investment in manufacturing. Though he started out in railroading and must have had a great deal of technical expertise in that area—as opposed to manufacturing where he had none—railroads accounted for only 3 percent of his total holdings at the time of his death.

The range of manufacturing companies in which Braniff held stock was as varied as his portfolio in general. Just as he divided his investments among a wide range of activities, he divided up his manufacturing interests among a wide range of companies. He held 22.9 percent of the stock in the San Rafael paper mill, 6.1 percent of the stock in CIDOSA, 4.3 percent of the stock in the San Ildefonso wool textile mill, and 1.2 percent of the stock in the El Buen Tono cigarette-manufacturing company. In addition, he held shares in a small tannery and in a marble-cutting company (see Table 5.3). Apparently his investments in Fundidora Monterrey and the Société Financière pour l'industrie au Mexique, on whose boards he had served, had been liquidated before his death.[31]

Like the other financiers of the Porfiriato, Braniff was closely tied to the Díaz government. He served on the 1903 Comisión de Cambios y Monedas, along with Scherer and Basagoiti, which drafted the 1905 monetary reform that put Mexico on a bimetallic standard. He was also an active supporter of Díaz. In 1900, when Díaz was running for his fifth term as president, Braniff, together with a group of other financiers, organized public rallies in support of the dictator's reelection campaign.[32]

By the turn of the century, in order to enter large-scale manufacturing in Mexico, one had first to be a financier and, prior to that, to have been a merchant. This explains, in large part, the notable absence of Mexicans among the major stockholders of manufacturing companies. In effect, the merchant-financier-

TABLE 5.3
Investments of Thomas Braniff in Manufacturing, 1905

Company	Shares (number)	Share value[a]	Total
CIDOSA	9,175	190	1,743,250
San Rafael, Fab. de Papel	14,500	70	1,015,000
San Rafael, pref. shares[b]	1,510	100	151,000
El Buen Tono	750	152.5	114,375
San Ildefonso, Fab. de Tejidos	1,300	80	104,000
Cia. de Marmoles Mexicanos	218	50	10,900
Fab. de Curtiduria la Velocitan	200	5	1,000
TOTAL	—	—	3,139,525

SOURCE: Derived from Collado Herrera 1983: 70.
[a]Market value, according to his will.
[b]Seven-percent-interest shares. Together with his common shares, Braniff's total investment in the San Rafael paper mill amounted to 22.9 percent of the firm's stock.

industrialist nexus excluded the Mexican-born from industry, because large-scale commerce had historically been dominated by foreigners. During the colonial period Mexico's major merchants were almost exclusively Spaniards—primarily Basques and Asturianos—but after independence Frenchmen, Swiss, Germans, Italians, and Englishmen joined the merchant elite. Neither the "Mexican national character" nor any legal obstructions precluded the Mexican-born from entering commerce. Rather, foreign-born merchants used their extensive network of contacts both in Europe and in the foreign community in Mexico to control mercantile activity. Since commerce moved on trust and credit, it would have been extremely difficult for an outsider to engage in large-scale commerce without being related by either blood or marriage to a European merchant family.

The upshot was that the Mexican-born did not become merchants. Even the *criollo* (Mexican-born) children of foreign merchants rarely entered commerce. Because merchants generally did not marry until they had amassed considerable wealth, they also tended not to have children until late in life. Lacking sons old enough to work for them, but needing employees to whom they could entrust their most sensitive business matters, the merchants usually sent to Europe for nephews or other relatives. When the merchant died, it was these European-born nephews, who had invested years of their lives in making the business grow, who inherited the firm.[33] The merchant's criollo sons, if there were any, usually went into one of the professions or into the clergy. We may recall, for example, that Antonio Basagoiti sent for Adolfo Prieto in Asturias because he lacked sons to whom he could entrust the running of his commercial and banking operations. It was Prieto who eventually wound up running the entire Basagoiti operation and who used it to build a financial empire of his own. Prieto in turn married late and had but one child, a daughter. When he died in 1945, it was his two Asturiano nephews, Carlos Prieto and Santiago Arias Prieto, who inherited his business interests.

If it was necessary to be a merchant prior to becoming a financier and industrialist, then it should follow that in areas where Mexicans did succeed in merchant activity they should also have been among the area's industrialists. This was indeed the case.

Whereas the Europeans had the trans-oceanic trade all locked up and controlled all the big jobbing and retail houses in Mexico City, the Mexican-born figured among the more prominent merchants in more marginal areas of the country, like the north, and were therefore found on the boards of the major manufacturing enterprises in those areas.[34]

One such area was Monterrey, where circumstances transformed what had been an economic backwater into a major commercial center. Crucial to its development were the U.S. Civil War, the westward expansion of the U.S. economy, and the growth of American mining and smelting interests in northern Mexico during the Porfiriato. During the Civil War the Union blockade of the Confederacy's ports forced the South to carry on its external trade via the Mexican port of Matamoros. The merchants of Monterrey benefited enormously from this unprecedented trade. Also, as a result of the westward growth of the United States, Monterrey by the end of the nineteenth century no longer sat in the middle of nowhere, but was now less than 200 miles from a rapidly expanding economy. The possibilities for smuggling were tremendous, and large fortunes were built in the Texas-to-Mexico contraband trade. Finally, American investors, most notably the Guggenheims, began to sink large sums of money into mining ventures in the area and built several huge smelters in the city proper. The upshot was that a rapidly growing economy was created in what historically had been an economically marginal area.[35]

A similar process took place in other northern Mexican cities, and within a generation the North's native-born, small-time, regional merchants became major financiers. They replicated the process that had occurred in Mexico City among their European-born counterparts, moving from commerce to money-lending, and eventually setting themselves up as bankers and industrialists.

Among the most successful of these Mexican-born merchant-financiers was Isaac Garza. Born in Monterrey in 1853, he began his career in commercial activities in 1870, working in a textile retailing operation in San Luis Potosí. Four years later, he returned to Monterrey to work in the dry-goods store of José Calderón. Gradually, Garza moved up in the Casa Calderón, as the

operation was called, and helped move the firm out of commerce and into manufacturing. His ascendance in the commercial house was, no doubt, abetted by his marriage to Calderón's
niece, Consuelo Sada. Garza's big coup came with the idea to
produce beer in Monterrey for the local market, instead of importing it from St. Louis. Along with Calderón and other associ-
ates of the merchant firm, he formed the first board of directors
of the Cervecería Cuauhtemoc, named for the last Aztec em-
peror who had resisted the Spaniards. Since none of these men
actually knew anything about beer brewing, they invited Joseph
M. Schnaider, the son of the owner of the St. Louis brewery
from which they had been importing beer, to serve on the board
as well. The Cervecería proved to be one of the fastest growing enterprises in northern Mexico, quickly becoming one of the
three largest beer breweries in the country.

From beer brewing Garza branched out into other lines of
manufacturing. He was one of the original stockholders in the
Fundidora Monterrey steel works, purchasing 1,200 shares (1.2
percent of all shares outstanding) at a total cost of 120,000 pesos,
when the company issued its first stock in 1900. Garza's other
main industrial interest was the Vidriera Monterrey glass works,
which initially produced glass bottles for the Cervecería Cuauhtemoc's beer and later monopolized national glass production.[36]

Like the Mexico City financiers, the merchant-financiers of the
North held diversified portfolios, formed joint-stock companies
in order to spread risk, and invested cautiously. In fact, they frequently entered into partnerships with the Mexico City financial
elite. For example, Manuel Cantú Treviño, a Monterrey-based
merchant, financier, and textile mill owner, was an important
stockholder in two companies dominated by Mexico City interests, the Compañía Industrial de Atlixco (the giant textile manufacturer) and Fundidora Monterrey.[37]

By the close of the Porfiriato a small clique of financiers, most
of them of European origin, controlled Mexico's major manufacturing companies. They were the only group in the country that
had sufficient liquid wealth to capitalize the type of large-scale
industrialization that Mexico was undertaking. In company after
company, from textiles to steel, from beer to dynamite, this

tightly knit group guided the investment decisions that determined the range of products and the organization of production.

This was an economic elite that knew how to structure the market in order to avoid competition and had the economic and political clout to do so. This group's expertise lay more in ruthlessly manipulating the state and the market than it did innovating new processes or techniques of production. It also occupied a privileged political position; it was the economic backbone of the Díaz dictatorship. It was therefore well positioned to obtain the tariff protection and subventions it sought, and it could enlist the support of the government in limiting domestic competition. In this, as the next chapter takes up in detail, it was all too successful.

SIX

The Strategy of the Firm

A NONCOMPETITIVE industrial structure evolved in Mexican manufacturing for two reasons. First, the scale of the technology employed was inappropriate for the size of the market. Second, a small group of financiers skilled at manipulating both the market and the state held an unusual degree of political and economic power. As an elite, they were also fairly cohesive, combining again and again in new enterprises. At the same time, poorly developed capital markets kept other groups from challenging their hold on industry, since the merchant-financier elite was the only group sufficiently wealthy to finance new industrial firms.

For these reasons Mexico's industrialists pursued a rent-seeking strategy, in which they exploited their financial and political advantages to discourage competition. That is, rather than make innovations in new processes or techniques of production, they sought to limit competition and earn monopoly rents. Given the fact that their entrepreneurial experience and talents were in commerce and money-lending—not in production—and given the fact that demand for many of their products was highly inelastic, this strategy made sense from the point of view of maximizing returns to the firm. Indeed, the returns were low and uncertain (see Chapter 7), and would have been lower still if firms had not pursued anti-competitive strategies.

How, exactly, did they go about this? How did Mexico's merchant-financier-industrialists manipulate the market to minimize competition? What did they do when a new entrant threatened to disrupt the market? How did they get the government to assist them in creating barriers to entry? How did the strategies adopted to solve the problems created by the scale of technology influence the structure of industry? When and why did monopoly and oligopoly come to characterize Mexican manufacturing?

In some product lines it was not necessary for entrepreneurs to structure the market. Product-specific factors in these industries made it virtually impossible for more than one or two firms to survive. The best example of this situation was the steel industry, where the scale of technology was so large relative to the size and depth of the market that only those with sufficient capital and connections could have entered the market to compete with Fundidora Monterrey. Since Fundidora Monterrey was continually losing money and seldom operated at more than one-third of capacity, there was little incentive for other firms to enter the market. The nation's only other steel-producing enterprise, La Consolidada, was a complementary operation to that of Fundidora Monterrey, buying pig iron from the Monterrey giant and producing specialty steel alloys and castings that the larger company was not equipped to handle. La Consolidada produced only 5 percent of Mexico's total domestic steel production; the rest was Fundidora Monterrey's.[1] Fundidora Monterrey's real competition was from foreign imports. Essentially, the company was able to close off the market for steel rails and structural shapes for construction purposes, while it conceded the market for tubing, sheeting, and other flat-rolled products.[2]

The cement and beer industries, unlike steel, were characterized by regional monopolies. Cement's high bulk-to-price ratio and beer's perishability meant that costs of transport beyond regional markets were prohibitive. Single firms tended, therefore, to dominate a single regional market.

This is best exemplified in the beer industry where each major city, with the exception of Mexico City and Orizaba, Veracruz, had only one brewery. Of the 29 breweries in operation throughout the country in 1901, only three marketed their product outside their immediate area.[3] These three giants—the Cervecería Cuauhtemoc, the Cervecería Moctezuma, and the Compañía Cervecera de Toluca y México—did not initially compete with one another in the same markets. Rather, each carved out a regional market for itself and expanded at the expense of the smaller producers in nearby cities. Indeed, the history of the

Mexican beer industry is the history of these larger firms as they swallowed up the smaller, local breweries. Moctezuma dominated in the area around Veracruz and the Gulf Coast, Cuauhtemoc controlled the north, and the Cervecería de Toluca y México took the lucrative Mexico City–Toluca market.[4] By the 1920's the process of consolidation was well enough advanced that these three firms began to compete on a national scale. Only then did they begin to follow strategies designed to minimize competition.

In the cement industry there were also just three large firms: Cementos Tolteca, Cementos Cruz Azul, and Cementos Hidalgo. The last, located in the state of Nuevo León, controlled the important and growing Monterrey market. The others, both located in the state of Hidalgo, divided the Mexico City market between them. Interestingly, none of these firms was able to run its plants at capacity even though there was sufficient demand (see Tables 3.1 and 3.2), since the cost of transport prohibited them from marketing their products at a distance of more than 250 kilometers from the point of production.

In other industries, however, many firms found it necessary to discourage competition if they hoped to make a profit. Economies of scale and the lack of a capital market to finance new enterprises discouraged them from entering the market, but firms also needed to find ways to maintain their privileged positions against would-be competitors. The structure of the market may have been such that only one large firm could prosper, but that *one* was not necessarily the firm that did in fact control the market at that time. It is conceivable that new firms could have come along and dislodged the reigning giant.

The manipulation of the market took various forms, but it almost always involved closing off access to some important factor of production, like technology, raw materials, or government protection. Where this was not possible, firms sometimes tried to close off access to the distribution and marketing network. If all else failed, they simply bought out the competition. Often a combination of these strategies was employed: firms tried to corner the market in some vital factor of production at the same time that they went about buying out their competitors. They employed a whole arsenal of anti-competitive weapons designed to create barriers to entry and to maintain their dominance of the market.

One strategy that firms pursued was to monopolize the raw materials necessary for the production of a particular product, by integrating vertically. To some extent backward integration could theoretically have allowed for economies of speed, thereby creating cost savings that would make the firm more competitive. But firms often integrated vertically far beyond the degree needed to take advantage of economies of speed. Vertical integration was as much the product of the drive to monopolize the market as it was to lower production costs.

This was the case, for example, in the manufacture of soap, where the Compañía Industrial Jabonera de la Laguna was able to monopolize access to the most important raw material, cottonseed oil, and thereby create a barrier to entry. It later used this advantage to establish a national monopoly in the production of dynamite. The company began in 1883 as a soap and candle factory called La Nacional, in the state of Chihuahua. Its founders were Juan Terrazas, a scion of the powerful Terrazas-Creel clan that essentially owned the entire state of Chihuahua, and John Brittingham, a 24-year-old self-promoter from St. Louis, who had the good sense to marry into the Terrazas family. The firm primarily produced candles for the mines, with soap a secondary product line.[5] The company originally used tallow acquired from local ranchers to make its products, but soon augmented it with cottonseed oil, which the firm processed in its own mill. Throughout the 1880's La Nacional operated one of only two such mills in Mexico; the other mill, in nearby Gómez Palacio, Durango, was quite antiquated. In 1891 when a group of Monterrey-based merchants and American financiers took over and reconstructed the competing mill, Brittingham and Terrazas quickly proposed a merger of the two firms the following year[6]—the first in a succession of mergers designed to forestall competition.

The newly formed joint-stock company, La Esperanza, S.A., had the capability to operate in the national market. Distribution was carried out through commissioned sales agents, the company's location at the strategic rail junction of Gómez Palacio providing ready access to the national rail grid. Sales climbed quickly, from 3.6 million pounds of soap in 1893 to 8.4 million pounds in 1896.[7] Not only was La Esperanza now operating on a national scale, it was extending its operations to the international market as well. One of the by-products of the crushing of cottonseed for its oil was cottonseed cakes, which were used for animal feed and were sold in the English market through a sales agent in Liverpool. The income from this operation was then used to purchase the caustic soda, soda ash, jute bags, and camel hair mats that La Esperanza imported from England. In 1906, the only year for which data are available, the company shipped 22,000 tons of cottonseed cakes to its Liverpool agent.[8]

The profitability of this monopoly operation attracted competitors, among whom were the local cotton planters of the Laguna district, who realized that they could crush their own cottonseed and make their own soap.[9] These newly formed firms threatened to cut off La Esperanza's access to its most important raw material, cottonseed. Moreover, they threatened to divide the market and force La Esperanza to take a smaller market share and lower prices. Reacting to the threat and seeking to maintain control over national soap production, Brittingham again proposed a merger scheme. In 1898 the Compañía Industrial Jabonera de la Laguna was formed with a capitalization of 2 million pesos. Half of the capital was subscribed by the present factory owners, with shares subdivided according to each firm's average production over the preceding three years. In addition, the factories agreed to transfer their production facilities to the new company for 50 percent of their appraised value. The other half of the newly formed company's capital was subscribed by the region's cotton planters and was subdivided according to a scheme similar to that governing the division among the factory owners.

Most important, Brittingham's scheme required the cotton planters to sign 25-year contracts obliging them to turn over their entire output of cottonseed to the company, thereby achieving vertical integration and the control of the requisite raw materials. This was a clause that many of them would later regret, for Brittingham's long-term contracts turned out to be an incredible boon to the factory owners but a disaster for the cotton planters. The prices that the company paid to the planters were exceedingly low. In 1908, for example, cottonseed sold on the free market for 20 to 22.5 pesos for a *carreta* of 1,380 kilos, but the Compañía Industrial Jabonera de la Laguna paid the planters only one-third this price.[10] This state of affairs did nothing to endear Brittingham to his new partners. When the 25 years were up, the first thing the planters did was to dissolve the company and form a new one, this time without Brittingham.

Whether Brittingham's partners liked him or not, the merger gave the Jabonera de la Laguna an almost complete monopoly of the domestic production of soap, cottonseed oil, and glycerine. No one could enter the market against the company because it controlled the region's cottonseed market. Not content with this success, Brittingham attempted to organize an even larger syndicate, which would have monopolized the entire national production of cottonseed. Apparently he was unable to raise the 15–16 million pesos necessary to finance the syndicate, but in the final analysis it did not matter because no competing group of capitalists sought to undo Brittingham's monopoly.[11] Only one other firm of any size existed, the Compañía Jabonera La Unión in Torreón, Coahuila. This firm appears to have sold much of its cottonseed oil to the Jabonera de la Laguna. Even including that sale, La Unión could have taken at most 20 percent of the market between 1906 and 1914. Of course, numerous cottage-industry soap factories existed as well, but none were of significant size, and certainly none came even close to competing with the Jabonera de la Laguna, which was among the four largest soap factories in the world.[12]

If a firm failed to achieve a monopoly of the requisite raw materials, it would often try to monopolize the requisite technology. Given the fact that almost all the technology and capital goods utilized by Mexican manufacturing were imported, it was possible, by obtaining the sole rights to the use of a patent or a machine developed elsewhere, to monopolize the manufacture of a particular product. This strategy was most effectively pursued by Vidriera Monterrey, which turned its control of the patents for automated glass-bottle blowing into a national monopoly during the final years of the Porfiriato. The firm secured the exclusive Mexican rights for glass-production processes developed elsewhere and then branched out from bottles into a wide array of glass products. Today it monopolizes a number of product lines and is the core company in the giant Grupo Vitro industrial conglomerate.

Like the Compañía Industrial Jabonera de la Laguna, this company was the brainchild of John Brittingham, who in 1905 purchased the sole rights to use the Owens patents, held by the Toledo Glass Company, for automated glass-bottle production in Mexico. Two years later he further locked up his control of automated glass-making technology by acquiring from the Toledo Glass Company the exclusive rights to other important patents and the exclusive right to use Toledo's Owens machinery in Mexico.[13]

Brittingham, as we have seen, always thought big. The glass-bottle monopoly he intended to establish was to be just the beginning. His ultimate goal was to use it to gain control of the beer industry and create a monopoly there as well. Brittingham planned to build a glass works as an adjunct to the Cervecería Chihuahua, a regional beer producer that he owned in partnership with some of the other stockholders in the Jabonera de la Laguna. The glass works would then be used to establish a national beer syndicate, under Brittingham's control.

This scheme, like his attempt to establish a national cotton syndicate, never materialized. In 1909, however, Brittingham arranged a joint enterprise with the owners of the Cervecería Cuauhtemoc, which had previously established an unsuccessful bottle plant employing émigré glass blowers. Brittingham's La Owens de México company was merged with Cuauhtemoc's defunct Vidrios y Cristales, and a joint-stock company formed, with a subscribed capital of 1.2 million pesos, one-third of which was awarded to Brittingham (unpaid) in exchange for the rights to use the valuable Owens patents. One-third was apportioned to Cuauhtemoc for the purchase of its old buildings and installations at the Vidrios y Cristales works. The remaining third was paid in cash, half by Brittingham and his partners and half by the Cervecería Cuauhtemoc interests. Construction began in 1910, with the plant coming on line in 1911. Vidriera Monterrey's productive capacity was 40,000 bottles per day, roughly 12 million bottles per year.[14]

The control of the technology for automated glass production enabled Vidriera Monterrey to monopolize the bottle market. It also gave its parent company a decided advantage over its competitors, who were forced either to blow glass by hand, as did the Compañía Cervecera de Toluca y México, to import expensive foreign glass, or to buy bottles from Vidriera Monterrey.[15] In later years, the control of Mexico's sole glass-bottle production facility was one of the major factors that gained for Cervecería Cuauhtemoc a dominant position in the market (see Chapter 9).[16]

Barring the ability to monopolize the necessary technology or raw materials, a firm might turn to manipulating the state. All of Mexico's new manufacturing enterprises with capitalization in excess of 100,000 pesos operated under some form of federal concession that gave them tax-exempt status. In some industries the concessionaires obtained exclusive rights to tax exemptions in the production of a particular line. That is, if an entrepreneurial group was politically well connected and was important enough to the state, it could get the federal government to make it the sole concessionaire. The most notorious—and abused—of these concessions was held by the Compañía Nacional Mexicana de Dinamita y Explosivos, which turned its connections with the Díaz government into a monopoly in both the production and importation of dynamite and other explosives.

The history of this particular company is highly instructive in understanding the modus operandi of establishing a federally subsidized national monopoly. In 1897 Augusto Genin, one of Mexico's most important French-born financiers, representing the Société Financière pour l'industrie au Mexique and the Société Centrale de Dynamite de Paris, obtained a concession from the Ministerio de Fomento to build an explosives factory. Three years later Saturnino Sauto and Tomás Reyes Retana, representing the Jabonera de la Laguna, obtained a similar concession. Though neither had as yet produced any dynamite, or for that matter had even begun to erect a factory, the two concessionaires merged in the following year (1901) to create the Compañía Nacional Mexicana de Dinamita y Explosivos. Each of the three founding corporations subscribed one-third of the company's capital, which was originally 1.4 million pesos, later increased to 3 million pesos in 1903 and to 4 million pesos in 1904.[17]

In order to preclude the possibility of having to buy out other would-be competitors, the newly formed company successfully petitioned the Díaz government for a new concession. The agreement, which had a duration of 14 years, was a masterpiece of the kind of paper entrepreneurialism that Mexico's emergent industrialists were so good at. First, the company got the government to establish both an import tax *and* a consumption tax on dynamite. Then it maneuvered to get its products exempted from both of these taxes, thereby putting both importers and other national producers at a considerable disadvantage. The consumption tax was fixed at 210 pesos per ton, the import tax at 30 pesos. The average price of imported dynamite between 1904 and 1909 was 301 pesos per ton, exclusive of taxes and transport costs. The combined taxes, then, of 240 pesos would have levied an 80 percent tariff on imports, clearly giving the company a high degree of protection. Assuming that a hypothetical domestic competitor could have produced dynamite at the cost of imports, the 210-peso consumption tax would have added 70 percent to the final sale price of its product. The government further agreed that if it should ever lower either of these taxes it would pay the company the equivalent amount per ton of explosives produced in order to compensate for the drop in the rate of protection. Finally, in a seeming concession by the company, Dinamita y Explosivos "agreed" that if dynamite prices rose beyond the "normal price" it would import the amount necessary in order to restore equilibrium to the market. The imported dynamite would enter the country "as if it were the product of the firm's own operations," that is, without payment of either the consumption or the import tax. What this effectively meant was that what the company could not produce it was allowed to import duty-free. The concessionaires had in fact gotten the government to award them a federally subsidized monopoly on dynamite production *and* distribution.[18]

Crucial to the creation and maintenance of this monopoly was the fact that its financier board members were extremely well connected. They were tied to the Paris banks, which were a crucial source of finance for the Díaz government; in addition, the concessionaires made an effort to include key government figures on the board of directors of the company. They even went so far as to include the son of the president, Porfirio Díaz, Jr.

Besides the president's son, other board members included Julio Limantour, brother of the secretary of the treasury, Enrique C. Creel, the secretary of foreign affairs, and Roberto Nuñez, undersecretary of the treasury.[19] If monopoly profits were going to be made through the abuse of a state concession, then the strategy of the concessionaires was to at least cut in members of the government for a piece of the action.

The fact that the company was politically well connected was important not only for maintaining its exclusive concession on dynamite importation and production, but also because one of the company's principal customers was the Mexican government itself. Approximately one-quarter of the firm's work force of 900 operatives was engaged in the production of cartridges, whose primary consumer was the Mexican army.

Political connections were also crucial because the abuse of the concession by the company aroused many complaints from the mining sector. The company did not produce a single stick of dynamite until 1907—ten years after the award of the first concession—and appears never thereafter to have met national demand. In 1907, according to my estimates, it met 20 percent of the nation's needs through its own production: roughly three million pounds of explosives. The firm's productive capacity increased rapidly thereafter, but it never met more than 60 to 80 percent of the nation's requirements, which increased throughout the Porfiriato as the mining sector continually expanded.[20] Invoking the import clause of the concession, Dinamita y Explosivos bought explosives from the U.S. dynamite trust that were then brought into the country duty free and sold at inflated prices.[21]

If a firm was unable to obtain control over the factors of production, it could still restrict entry to the market by controlling the distribution network for final goods. In large part this explains the relatively high level of concentration in the cotton textile industry, where Mexico's most important jobbers were also its most important retailers and the owners of its largest, most productive mills. Although there was no national textile monopoly, the owner-jobber-retailer nexus gave the producers of the finer weaves of cotton cloth an edge over their competitors in imported products. In fact, one of the major problems facing foreign firms seeking to export to Mexico was the fact that they had difficulty gaining entry to the distribution network once they got their cloth into the country.[22]

Thus, though there were nearly 150 cotton textile factories in Mexico by the close of the Porfiriato, two enterprises, both tied to the big Mexico City jobbing-houses, controlled the nation's entire production of high-quality, fine-weave goods. They also took a large share of the market in common cloth. As already discussed, CIDOSA and CIVSA together produced one-fifth of all the cotton cloth manufactured in Mexico during the first decade of the twentieth century (see Chapter 4).[23] It seems unlikely, however, that this level of market power in common cotton cloth could have been used to raise the price of their goods significantly over the competitive level.

Since the major stockholders in the country's largest, most productive textile mills were also Mexico's most important jobbers in the cloth trade, it was not difficult to establish a national distribution system. In fact, in addition to having an interest in the factories, the large jobbers with few exceptions also controlled one or more retail department stores. The owner-jobber-retailer sold to himself at a 25 percent discount from list price, with each stockholder in the mill agreeing to take a certain percentage of production. The remainder was sold to small jobbers at a 15 percent discount, and to large and medium retailers at an 8 percent discount. Small retailers, who generally operated in Mexico's provincial areas, bought odd lots from the large retailers or from small jobbers. For wholesale transactions the terms were usually 60 to 90 days' credit. Small retailers generally paid cash.[24] In this way, the production of the large mills was distributed throughout the country, with the large owner-jobber-retailers covering distribution in the large cities, smaller retailers handling secondary cities—buying either from the large jobbers or from mill agents—and petty traders handling the countryside.

This was not a very efficient way of controlling competition in the market for coarse-weave goods. Smaller, provincial producers employed commissioned mill agents, who directly linked retailers and the mill in order to get around the distribution cartel set up by Mexico City's owner-jobber-retailers. The Compañía Industrial de Parras, for example, which was located in

Coahuila and was controlled by the powerful Madero family, operated in this way, using commissioned mill agents to sell the factory's cloth throughout Coahuila, Zacatecas, and Durango.[25] The partial control of distribution, especially in the lucrative Mexico City market, did, however, give the big firms an edge over their competitors and was certainly important in controlling the market for fine-weave goods.

A process similar to that which allowed the concentration of cotton textile manufacturing also occurred in wool textiles. Two large corporations, both controlled by major Mexico City merchant interests and both employing large-scale production methods, dominated this subsector. The largest of these, the Compañía Industrial de San Ildefonso, was founded in 1896 by the Gascony-born merchant-industrialist Ernest Pugibet, along with many of the same stockholders who controlled the Compañía Industrial de Orizaba and the Compañía Industrial Veracruzana. Together, this group of merchants and financiers raised an initial capital of 1.5 million pesos. This was soon doubled so that the firm could construct its own hydroelectric plant.

Without census data on wool textiles, it is not possible to determine market shares. However, only a few other large firms competed against San Ildefonso. Of its major competitors only one was a joint-stock company, La Victoria, S.A., which was controlled by many of the same Basque and Asturiano merchants who controlled the Compañía Industrial de Atlixco and the Compañía Industrial de San Antonio Abad cotton textile conglomerates. La Victoria was capitalized at 1 million pesos. The other large woolen factories, of which there were very few, were family owned or were controlled by simple partnerships among Mexico City's large merchant houses.[26]

If all else failed, a firm could maintain market dominance by buying out its competitors. As we have seen, mergers and buy-outs were frequently part of a larger strategy designed to control some crucial factor of production. The Compañía Industrial Jabonera de la Laguna, for example, merged with would-be rivals to control the supply of raw materials. A corporate merger likewise gave rise to the Compañía Nacional Mexicana de Dinamita y Explosivos. The merged company then created a barrier to entry by persuading the government to declare high tariffs and consumption taxes at the same time that it awarded the company an exclusive tax exemption.

In some cases, mergers and buy-outs were not just complementary to another strategy, but served as the centerpiece of a firm's attempt to control the market. This was the case, for example, in the production of paper, where the San Rafael y Anexas paper company dominated the market, and also in the cigarette industry, where El Buen Tono alone controlled roughly 50 percent of the market.[27] The fact that Mexico's financial elite was relatively small and cohesive facilitated this process. The number of potential rivals was small, and the social and financial connections that already existed between the owners of rival firms facilitated their merging.

Since there was no independent capital market outside of the network of merchant-financier families, a merger strategy in many industries could provide market dominance over the long run. This was not the case in countries that had well-developed stock exchanges and capital markets, since the high prices imposed by a monopoly attracted competitors who could use the national capital market to finance the erection of rival production facilities. This is what happened in the United States to many of the giant firms that had gained market dominance through the great merger movement of the 1890's. Unless a firm could erect a barrier to entry, new firms arose to challenge those enterprises earning monopoly rents.[28]

By means of an aggressive strategy of buy-outs and mergers a near-monopoly was established in the paper industry. Mexico's paper industry had been dominated by small firms producing small amounts of low-quality goods. These firms appear to have changed hands with some frequency, the market not being secure enough to sustain profits and continued growth over the long run.[29] With the founding of the Compañía de las Fábricas de San Rafael y Anexas in 1890, all this changed. The San Rafael mill, located in the Chalco district of the state of México, was originally an iron foundry owned by N. M. Rothschild and Sons, the London banking house. Rothschild, through its Mexican representative, Watson Phillips and Company, sold the foundry to the firm of J. H. Robertson and Company, who in turn sold it to the Spanish merchant firm of Ahedo y Compañía in 1879.* It was this latter firm that in 1890 converted the San Rafael foundry into a paper mill.[30]

By national standards Ahedo y Compañía's mill was large. Until it began operations in 1892 the combined value of production of Mexico's twelve existing paper factories had been barely over 1 million pesos per year. San Rafael's Swiss-made machinery, driven by 15 water-powered turbines, had a capacity of 12 tons of paper per day, which was about three times that of all its competitors combined. In 1893 the merchant partnership that founded the mill dissolved when Andrés Ahedo left the firm. The sole remaining partner, José Sánchez Ramos, then accepted Thomas Braniff's offer to form a new partnership. Together they organized the joint-stock company, San Rafael y Anexas, S.A., in 1894, with an initial issue of 5 million pesos of stock.

San Rafael undertook an aggressive strategy of mergers that gave the firm a monopoly in the production of newsprint, the most lucrative product line in the paper market. By 1905 the company had acquired the Santa Teresa, La Planta de Zavaleta, La Agencia de Tlalmanaco, Belém, and El Progreso Industrial mills. The result was that it faced only two small competitors, the Loreto and Peña Pobre mills, each of which was owned, ironically, by German technicians imported by San Rafael to supervise its own operations.

The only serious threat to San Rafael's control of the market came in 1902 when a group of rival capitalists erected the El Progreso Industrial mill, located in the Tlalnepantla district of the state of México. Within two years of its operation, however, El Progreso Industrial was bought out by San Rafael. After a long process of negotiation, its Scottish and Asturiano stockholders, many of whom were from the same merchant-financier clique that controlled the Atlixco and San Antonio Abad textile

---

*J. H. Robertson was a Scottish mill-superintendent who came to Mexico to work in the Miraflores cotton textile mill in the state of México. He soon bought the mill from its owners and set himself up as an industrialist in his own right. He and his son Felipe became major stockholders in both the Compañía Industrial de San Antonio Abad, to which pertained the Miraflores mill, and the Compañía Industrial de Atlixco. Felipe was to play a key role in the founding of the El Progreso Industrial paper mill. (Beato 1981: 81, Walker 1986: 134.)

companies, agreed to trade their shares for those in the San Rafael operation, thereby uniting the two companies. Historically, San Rafael dismantled newly acquired mills and transferred their machinery to its centralized operations in the state of México. In the El Progreso Industrial case, however, it maintained the mill as it was, using its modern machinery for the production of high-quality book, envelope, waxed, coated, and linen paper.

Besides acquiring its competitors, San Rafael also pursued a strategy of vertical integration in order to erect a barrier to entry through the control of raw materials. The company owned, in addition to the two paper mills, two haciendas, Santa Catarina and Zavaleta, which had extensive forests covering parts of the states of Puebla, México, and Morelos. At Zavaleta it operated a plant for the preparation of mechanical wood pulp. Power, for both wood pulp preparation and paper production, was generated by the company's own hydroelectric plants and supplemented by sales from independent power companies. Finally, San Rafael acquired a considerable interest in the San Rafael y Atlixco railway, thereby gaining control over all stages of production, from tree harvesting to power generation, pulp preparation, transport, and the rolling of the final product.

Not only did this vertically integrated structure allow the company to exercise greater control over the flow of primary and intermediate goods—and take advantage of the sizable economies of speed in paper manufacturing—but it also served to discourage the development of rival firms by limiting access to many of the most important inputs. Indeed, the firm integrated far beyond the degree necessary to capture economies of speed, the purchase of woodlands being a case in point. Such a strategy of vertical integration alone could not have hoped to succeed in blocking entry, however: Mexico was full of woodlands, and the company could never have purchased all of them.

A comparison of the history of the International Paper Company (IPC) in the United States and San Rafael in Mexico is useful to understanding the differences in the process of industrial concentration in the two countries. Like San Rafael, IPC followed a strategy of mergers and consolidations with rival firms at the same time that it integrated vertically. And like San Rafael, it concentrated on controlling the lucrative market for newsprint. But contrary to the pattern in Mexico, the monopoly rents that IPC earned after its formation in 1898 brought into the market rival firms that were financed through the stock and bond markets. Within the next seven years, 20 new producers entered the market. As a result of this new competition, IPC's share of eastern newspaper capacity slipped from 64 percent in 1900 to 48 percent in 1905.[31] In Mexico, the absence of well-developed capital markets and the cohesiveness of the merchant-financier families who dominated the economy enabled a merger strategy like San Rafael's to be quite successful over the long run. Indeed, San Rafael's newsprint monopoly was broken only in 1936, when the Mexican government decreed that the distribution of newsprint was a strategic industry that should be controlled by the state, not by private industry. It therefore created PIPSA, a state-run distribution monopoly.

At the same time that San Rafael monopolized newsprint, U.S. and German producers dominated the market in other, higher-value product lines. San Rafael could maintain its control of the newsprint market in large part because the cost of transporting a high-bulk, low-price item like newsprint from overseas to Mexico City would have been prohibitive. In higher-value goods, however, this cost advantage would have been diminished. Without more specific data on paper imports or annual sales data for San Rafael, it is difficult to determine market shares, but available data suggest that the company captured about 35 percent of the 2.5 million pesos in total Mexican paper sales per year.[32]

The largest cigarette firms pursued similar merger strategies. The Compañía Manufacturera El Buen Tono, founded by Ernest Pugibet in 1875 as a family enterprise, was the largest of Mexico's cigarette manufacturers. In 1894 Pugibet, seeking to raise additional capital to expand production and control the market, reorganized the firm as a joint-stock company, with a capitalization of 1 million pesos. As in the textile industry, the firm's other major stockholders were Mexico City's most important merchant-financiers, including Thomas Braniff, Hugo Scherer, and Henri

Tron. They were joined on the board of directors by influential members of the government including Roberto Núñez (undersecretary of the treasury), Pablo Macedo (president of congress), Manuel González Cosío (secretary of war), and Porfirio Díaz, Jr. Through a process of additional stock issues and the reinvestment of profits, the subscribed capital of the company quickly grew to 6.5 million pesos by 1907.

The strength of this capital allowed El Buen Tono to establish itself as the undisputed giant of the cigarette industry. Not only did the firm control roughly 35 percent of the nation's output—the company's French-made machinery was capable of producing roughly 3.5 billion cigarettes per year[33]—but it was able to purchase a controlling interest in Mexico's second largest cigarette company, La Cigarrera Mexicana. El Buen Tono held half of La Cigarrera Mexicana's paid-in capital of 2 million pesos. This not only reduced the number of competitors in the cigarette market from three to two, but it also gave El Buen Tono effective control of additional productive capacity. La Cigarrera Mexicana's machinery could produce from 4 to 5 million cigarettes per day (1.5 billion cigarettes per year). Altogether, then, El Buen Tono controlled roughly 50 percent of national production.[34]

Slightly smaller than La Cigarrera Mexicana was El Buen Tono's only real competitor, La Tabacalera Mexicana. Originally a merchant partnership between the tobacco magnates Antonio Basagoiti and Zaldo Hermanos y Compañía, it had been formed by the merging of the disparate operations that each partner controlled. In order to raise additional capital the firm went public in 1907. La Tabacalera Mexicana produced about 4 million cigarettes per day (approximately 1.2 billion cigarettes annually).[35] Since imports were negligible,[36] this gave the company roughly 12 percent of the national market, the remainder going either directly or indirectly to El Buen Tono or to the hundreds of small shops spread throughout the country, which were rapidly disappearing in the face of this competition.

In the final analysis, then, Mexico's industrialists employed a wide array of anti-competitive strategies designed to maintain their control of the market. Like U.S. manufacturers during the same period, Mexican entrepreneurs merged their firms with rivals and erected barriers to prevent new competitors from entering the market.* They had several advantages over their U.S. counterparts that made their attempts at market control more common and effective. First, the lack of a national capital market meant that a small group of merchant-financier families were the only entrepreneurs who had the ability to capitalize rival firms. They could use social and family connections to build empires and to restrict entry to the market through their control of capital. In the United States, as we have already pointed out, rival firms attracted by monopoly rents could be financed by the stock and bond markets. Indeed, many of the consolidations formed in the United States during the great merger movement of the 1890's soon found themselves challenged by new competitors and were forced to take smaller market shares and to lower their prices.[37]

Second, the process of consolidation in the United States was largely the result of the merger of a number of evenly matched firms that had been in existence—and in competition with one another—for a number of years. Indeed, as Naomi Lamoreaux has argued, their merger was largely the result of the fact that the intense competition had forced prices so low that strong measures were necessary to restore price stability.[38] In only one out of five mergers did one firm have a definite advantage over the rest.[39] This was not the pattern in Mexico, where generally one recently established, large firm, which was powerful at its founding, possessed sizable advantages over its competitors in terms of technology, access to capital, and influence with the government. That is, prior to consolidation, firms did not have the opportunity to move down the learning curve and were not

---

*The anti-competitive tactics of Mexico's major firms were similar to those employed in the industrial consolidations of the 1890's in the United States. Just as Mexican firms tried to control particular processes or technologies, so U.S. firms used the control of patents to restrict entry to the market. In the competition between General Electric and Westinghouse, for example, they were the primary weapons for control of the market. The two electrical giants later pooled their patents and used their control of technology to enforce stable oligopolistic behavior in the industry. Similarly, U.S. firms also tried to lock up access to raw materials. This, for example, was the strategy of the U.S. Steel Corporation, which set out to buy or lease the best iron-ore lands in the Lake Superior region. By 1907 U.S. Steel controlled between 70 and 75 percent of the ore lands in the area, which effectively prevented the emergence of new rivals and limited the production of its existing competitors. For a discussion of these strategies, see Lamoreaux 1985: ch. 5.

forced to compete with one another. Indeed, Mexico's monopolies and oligopolies never competed with other domestic firms. They dominated the market at their inception.

A third advantage for Mexican entrepreneurs was the influence they had with the government, which ensured that their attempts to monopolize the market would be facilitated by the state. In the United States, on the other hand, there were efforts to break up consolidations perceived as inimical to long-run economic growth. In fact, the Mexican government itself saw anticompetitive strategies as necessary to overcome the obstacles that the nation's incipient industries faced. For this reason there were no laws against mergers and consolidations.

Finally, the nature of the market in the two countries made the situation of Mexican entrepreneurs qualitatively different. In the United States the scale of technology was better suited to the size of the market since it had evolved in the U.S. setting. In Mexico, this was not the case, notably where the market was not strong enough to permit the existence of more than a single firm. Given the costs and the potential returns, once this firm was established there was little incentive for other firms to enter the market against it. Thus, Mexico's entrepreneurs reacted to market opportunities, but these opportunities were limited by the scarcity of capital, the scale of technology, the uneven distribution of income, and the politicized nature of doing business in Mexico.

SEVEN

Profits

UNDERLYING MEXICO'S concentrated industrial structure was a surprisingly low level of profitability. Firms pursued the strategies that they did, and the market was organized the way it was, because the problems associated with the industrialization of an economy like Mexico's made profits relatively low and uncertain in many lines of manufacturing. The anti-competitive practices of Mexico's big manufacturing firms were therefore partially a defensive response to low rates of return.

The purpose of this chapter is to develop some estimates of the profitability of the major manufacturing enterprises of the Porfiriato. The profitability of these firms is then followed into the Revolution in Chapter 8 and into the Great Depression in Chapter 9. Chapter 10 then charts the recovery of profitability during the period 1933–38. In Chapter 11, I develop estimates of the overall rate of return to investors during the entire period for which it has been possible to gather data, roughly 1896 to 1938.

Because profits are not things, but rather abstract concepts, they may be measured in any number of ways. I have therefore developed three different measures of the rate of profit based on three different conceptions of what profits are and who receives them, namely, the rate of return on capital stock, the yield on common stock, and the financial returns to investors. All of these conceptions of profits refer to the profitability of individual companies and rely implicitly upon the methods of cost accounting.[1]

The body of evidence employed in this analysis of profits is the corporate accounts and stock market data for 12 of Mexico's largest industrial enterprises, gathered primarily from the Mexican financial press. For the period 1896–1914 the two most notable publications were *El Economista Mexicano* and *La Semana Mercantíl*, both of which disappeared with the Revolution and were replaced by the *Boletín Financiero y Minero*. For the Fundidora Monterrey steel company a complete set of annual reports, containing detailed balance sheets and profit and loss statements, is available in the Library of the Banco de México.

The firms in my sample represent a broad range of industries, spanning paper, steel, beer, soap and glycerine, cigarettes, and cotton and wool textiles. Of the major large-scale industries operating in Mexico during this period the only ones not represented here are explosives, cement, and glass. Although the firms in question represent a diverse array of product lines, they had several characteristics in common. First, all were publicly held joint-stock companies whose shares were traded on the Mexico City stock exchange. No family-owned firms, simple partnerships, or privately held joint-stock companies are included. This is an unfortunate limitation, but unavoidable since only publicly held corporations had to publish their balance sheets or declare their earnings.

In addition, all the firms in my sample were extremely large enterprises, many of which had the ability to influence the market. Some of them, like Fundidora Monterrey (steel), San Rafael y Anexas (paper), and the Compañía Industrial Jabonera de la Laguna (soap and glycerine), held monopolies or near-monopolies in their respective product lines. Others functioned in oligopolistic markets: for example, the two firms that represent beer manufacturing (the Compañía Cervecera de Toluca y México and the Cervecería Moctezuma) and the two that represent cigarette manufacturing (El Buen Tono and La Cigarrera Mexicana). Data on La Tabacalera Mexicana, the third of Mexico's major cigarette producers, are available since 1910 and are included in the sections on profits after that date, thereby enlarging the total number of firms in the sample to 13. In the textile industry the ability of the leaders to influence the market was probably more limited. In cotton textiles the sample includes four of the nation's major producers (CIDOSA, CIVSA, the Compañía Industrial de Atlixco, and the Compañía Industrial de San Antonio Abad). In wool textiles the sample includes only the Compañía Industrial de San Ildefonso, the nation's largest producer.

Finally, all the sample firms were enterprises that were able to stay in business over the medium term. No data exist on the rate of company failures, though it is clear from reading the *Memorias* of the Ministerio de Fomento that a number of firms that received government concessions never made it off the ground. Thus, if my sample has a bias, it is toward the profitable end of the spectrum. The sample is therefore representative not of manufacturing as a whole, but only of those large firms that, early in their development, were able to carve out a relatively secure position in an uncertain environment. Even with this inherent bias in the data, the rates of return observed are hardly spectacular; they are, in fact, surprisingly low.

The rate of return on capital stock, which is one measure of the rate of profit, compares a firm's net profits to the value of its physical and cash assets—cash and other negotiable instruments, inventories, land, machinery and other equipment, and buildings—generally valued at cost minus depreciation. Capital stock differs from total assets in two respects. First, debts owed to a company are not included. Carried forward from year to year in the calculation of assets, the debt figures may produce a highly overinflated, and therefore unreliable, valuation of the firm. Second, the value of stocks held in other companies is not included in capital stock. In order for a company's profit figures to be comparable to those on capital stock, the dividends earned from these stockholdings must be deducted from profits. If subsidiary investments are included in capital stock and dividend earnings are included in profits, serious distortions in the rate of return on capital stock figures could result. Suppose, for example, that a firm lost money on its own operations but made money on its subsidiary investments. Estimates of the rate of return on capital stock that fail to make the appropriate adjustment would not reflect the firm's actual profitability.

For the period 1901–10 I developed estimates of profits, capital stock, and the rate of return on capital stock for four of Mexico's most important manufacturing concerns: Fundidora Monterrey, which held a monopoly on steel production, El Buen Tono, which controlled just over half of national cigarette production, and the nation's two largest cotton-textile enterprises, CIDOSA and CIVSA, which together controlled roughly 20 percent of national production.*

I attempted to construct similar series for the other eight firms sampled, but the incomplete nature of their accounts and the low number of observations in the sources precluded putting together reliable series. Similarly, by means of a regression analysis of the rate of return series against stock market data (dividends, share prices, and yields), I attempted to estimate missing values for the four-firm sample for the years in which the sources provided no data. The correlation coefficients, however, were too low for the stock market data to serve as a reliable indicator of the rate of return on capital.[2]

It should be made clear at the outset that it is not our purpose to calculate the exact profit of any given firm in any given year but only to estimate profitability over the medium term. Even with the best of data and the most sophisticated of accounting techniques this would be impossible. In any given year changes in the method of valuation of inventories, the acceleration of physical plant depreciation, or the decision to write off a bad debt can significantly alter the profit that a company reports. The skillful manipulation of accounts can produce profits in bad years and losses in good years. Given the fragmented and incomplete nature of the existing data and the peculiar accounting procedures of Mexican companies during the period in question, the theoretical and methodological problems associated with the calculation of profits are rendered even more severe. Over time, however, these manipulations tend to balance out. Firms that are consistently losing money cannot conceal that fact over the medium term; the losses, or the profits, must eventually show up. Moreover, when a company's accounts are examined carefully, the grossest accounting manipulations become apparent, making it possible to rework the accounts to correct for them.

---

*El Buen Tono's market share was 35 percent, but it held a controlling interest in the nation's number-two firm, effectively giving it another 15 percent of the market.

Corporate annual reports are often designed to conceal from the stockholders the true financial state of the firm. The firms in this sample were no exception. Since the Secretaría de Hacienda established no regulations covering the depreciation of physical plant, the manipulation of accounts most often took the form of decelerating the rate of depreciation. During bad years firms simply stopped depreciating their physical plant altogether, thereby artificially puffing up profits. Eventually, of course, the firm would have to make up for this lack of depreciation. The usual occurrence was that in a particularly good year, when profits were high, the firm wrote off all of the lapsed depreciation. Generally speaking, series constructed from such unadjusted data tend to demonstate smoother trajectories, the concealment of losses in bad years and the accelerated depreciation in good years producing a more even profit picture over time.

I have therefore adjusted the reported data. First, the rate of depreciation actually carried out was estimated by examining the company's balance sheets from year to year. I then added this depreciation back to capital stock and profits so as derive their values before depreciation was factored out. I then worked out more consistent and reasonable depreciation schedules and deducted the resulting figures from capital stock and profits. In dealing with bad debts, instead of writing off the entire debt in a single year, as firms tended to do, I spread their writing-off over a period of years on the assumption that a firm's uncollectible debts were probably accrued over a period of time and that their writing-off should reflect that fact.* Since debts are not in-

---

*An analysis of the depreciation of physical plant for El Buen Tono and CIDOSA indicates that both firms depreciated their plant at the rate of approximately 5 percent per year, though they did so on an extremely irregular basis. I therefore spread the rate of depreciation out more evenly from year to year. That is, the firm's overall rate of depreciation was accepted as accurate, but I worked out a new depreciation schedule in order to compensate for wide annual variations in the amount depreciated. In the case of Fundidora Monterrey an analysis of the depreciation of the physical plant indicated that the firm consistently underdepreciated, in addition to depreciating on an extremely irregular basis. I therefore worked out an entirely new depreciation schedule, depreciating the plant at the flat rate of 5 percent per annum. For a complete discussion of the method employed in carrying out these adjustments, as well as for the adjustments to profits to compensate for the writing off of bad debts, see Haber 1985: appendix A.

cluded in capital stock, the adjustments were made only to the profit data.

These adjustments produced more reasonable capital stock and profits series that better reflect the actual financial state of the firms. In the case of CIVSA, however, the incomplete nature of the firm's accounts did not permit any adjustments to the data. For this reason I am less confident in the estimates on its rate of return than in those constructed for Fundidora Monterrey, El Buen Tono, and CIDOSA. It is important to note, however, that even for the three cases where adjustments were feasible, they were carried out only to compensate for the grossest of accounting manipulations. The series presented here are estimates and should not be taken as exact figures.

Since companies generally valued their physical plant at cost minus depreciation, not replacement value, the capital stock figures probably underestimate the true value of the firm's assets. This tends to produce higher rates of return and bias the results upward. On the other hand, it could be argued that the results presented here are biased downward because transfer-pricing by firms could have made corporate profits appear lower than they actually were. This was certainly the case in the cotton textile industry, where the major stockholders sold to their own wholesaling operations at discount, thereby taking profits in distribution, not in production. How much this would have biased the results is hard to judge, since other major purchasers also enjoyed discounts, and since it is a common business practice for firms to sell at discount to their largest customers. In addition, there would have been little incentive to hide profits in this way, since there was no corporate income tax. Finally, if a firm's major shareholders were in fact raking off profits through transfer-pricing, they would not have cared if the firm failed to pay dividends. This was not the case, however, since stock prices were highly sensitive to dividend earnings. Thus, it is doubtful that firms practiced transfer-pricing as a means to mislead stockholders into thinking that profits were lower than they really were. Firms did indeed tend to mislead their shareholders, but in the opposite direction: by not depreciating physical plant they indicated higher profits than they actually made, not lower profits.

Table 7.1 presents the adjusted series on profits, capital stock, and the rate of return on capital stock for the four companies.* The most striking aspect of the data is the vast difference in the profitability of Fundidora Monterrey in relation to that of El Buen Tono, CIDOSA, and CIVSA, each of which achieved rates of return in most years of 10 percent or more. The median rate of return for both CIDOSA and CIVSA was 10 percent. For El Buen Tono the returns were even higher, with a median rate of return of 14 percent between 1902 and 1910. Conversely, Fundidora Monterrey more or less broke even during this same period, and in no single year did its rate of return on capital exceed 2 percent.

The difference in profitability was largely a function of the type of product manufactured. CIDOSA, CIVSA, and El Buen Tono had several advantages over Fundidora Monterrey. They produced low-cost, consumer nondurables (cotton textiles and cigarettes) that had relatively large markets; Fundidora Monterrey, on the other hand, manufactured relatively high-cost intermediate goods, the market for which was confined almost exclusively to the railways and to government public works projects. Furthermore, because the optimal firm-size in cotton textile and cigarette production is smaller than in an integrated steel operation, these firms did not have the kind of capacity utilization problems that Fundidora Monterrey did. Finally, the high ratio of fixed-to-variable costs in steel production meant that Fundidora Monterrey could not easily control its costs by cutting wages or hours or by running fewer shifts as El Buen Tono, CIDOSA, or CIVSA could.

Although the rates of return for these three firms were indeed healthy, it is perhaps curious that they made less money than might have been expected. Given the fact that they controlled huge market shares, were technologically the most advanced producers within their respective product lines, and had directors who were closely tied to the Díaz government, it might be considered surprising that their rates of return were not higher. And if we take inflation into account, rates of return become even less impressive. On average, between 1902 and 1910 the rate of inflation in Mexico was 4 percent annually.[3] The average

---

*The rate of return is simply the net profit divided by capital stock.

TABLE 7.1
Estimated Rates of Return on Capital Stock, 1902–1910

(Current pesos)

Year	Capital stock	Profit	Rate of return
Fundidora Monterrey			
1903	11,004,871	185,754	2%
1904	11,940,647	2,970	0
1905	12,172,824	−85,313	−1
1906	12,445,387	109,555	1
1907	12,500,000	−418,974	−3
1908	12,641,801	−480,912	−4
1909	12,611,891	−112,856	−1
1910	12,022,884	162,255	1
El Buen Tono			
1902	4,788,500[a]	277,533	6
1903	4,698,904	508,208	11
1904	5,766,552	711,515	12
1905	7,015,000[a]	961,500[b]	14
1906	8,258,000[a]	1,212,200[b]	15
1907	8,846,493	1,386,985	16
1908	8,770,000[c]	1,410,180	16
1909	8,704,561	1,188,428	14
1910	8,200,000[c]	1,173,604	14
CIDOSA			
1907	16,245,619	2,055,550	13
1908	20,140,874	1,443,620	7
1909	20,473,445	1,544,321	8
1910	20,200,000[d]	2,218,958	11
CIVSA			
1903	5,723,000[e]	820,212	14
1904	5,815,000[e]	576,951	10
1905	—	—	—
1906	—	—	—
1907	6,826,000[f]	826,322	12
1908	7,162,986	612,895	9
1909	—	—	—
1910	7,500,000[f]	761,441	10

SOURCES: Fundidora Monterrey calculated from *FMIA*, 1902–11. El Buen Tono calculated from *MYB 1912*, p. 125; *EM*, 21 Mar. 1903, p. 540, 8 Aug. 1903, p. 428, 12 Mar. 1904, pp. 593–94, 4 Mar. 1905, p. 477, 21 Oct. 1905, p. 42, 21 Mar. 1908, p. 448, 5 March 1910, p. 473. CIDOSA calculated from *MYB 1908*, p. 524; *MYB 1909–10*, pp. 423–24; *MYB 1912*, p. 123; *EM*, 6 Aug. 1904, p. 401, 30 Sept. 1905, p. 580, 11 Apr. 1908, p. 30, 17 Apr. 1908, p. 52, 21 May 1910, p. 162, 27 Apr. 1912, p. 67. CIVSA calculated from *MYB 1908*, pp. 524–25; *MYB 1912*, p. 123; *EM*, 23 Apr. 1904, p. 76, 6 May 1905, p. 118, 1 May 1909, p. 48, 26 April 1912, p. 51.

NOTE: For a complete discussion of how profits, capital stock, and the rate of return on capital were calculated and a discussion of the method employed in the adjustment of the raw data, see Haber 1985: appendix A.

[a]Estimated using regression analysis comparing capital stock to annual sales. This produced an extremely good fit, with a correlation of .93. It should be noted that much the

real rate of return for CIDOSA and CIVSA therefore falls to approximately 6 percent per year, and for El Buen Tono to 10 percent. In real terms, Fundidora Monterrey lost money in every single year of operation within the same period.

Even more startling is the observation that data on stock yields and dividends for a larger sample of 12 firms indicate that the moderate rates of return observed for CIDOSA, El Buen Tono, and CIVSA were in fact above the norm. The surprisingly low returns of these three companies, in other words, represent the high end of the spectrum for Porfirian manufacturing.

The yield on common stock is calculated by dividing a share's dividend earnings by its market price. It is the inverse of a share's price-earnings ratio. Yields tell us two things. First, they are a measure of how much of a return an investor had if he purchased a particular stock in a particular year. For example, if he bought a stock at a price of 100 pesos per share, and the stock earned 10 pesos in dividends that year, the yield would have been 10 percent. He might also have made money through a capital gain. We will return to this possibility shortly.

Second, and more important, the yield on common stock is a measure of the general rate of return to investors across the entire economy. It is an indicator of the return on investments expected by the financial community. That is, the yield on the stock of a company reflects not only the profitability of that particular company, but also the profit opportunities available in other firms or in other sectors of the economy. The stock of firms whose earnings per share tend to be below average are generally traded at below their par values, and the stock of firms that pay higher than average dividends per share are usually traded at prices above their par values. Yields from company to company

---

(*Notes to Table 7.1, continued*)

same results would have been attained for the 1905 and 1906 estimates if capital stock had been estimated by calculating the proportional change necessary in 1905 and 1906 to account for the difference in the values between 1904 and 1907.

[b]Estimated using regression analysis comparing profits to annual sales. This produced an extremely good fit, with a positive correlation of .96.

[c]Estimated from plant depreciation figures in 1909 annual report.

[d]Estimated from partial data on the value of physical plant.

[e]Estimated from partial data on the value of machinery.

[f]Estimated on the reasonable assumption that capital stock increased proportionally from 1904 to 1908, and likewise from 1908 to 1912.

therefore tend to equilibrate over time, as arbitrage drives the market price of low-dividend stocks down and the market price of high-dividend stocks up. Naturally, there will still be some differences in expected returns to compensate for differences in risk. Series on yields therefore tell us a great deal about the rate of return that investors expected from different types of investments during different periods.

In order to estimate the average yields of Mexico's major manufacturers I developed series on earnings per share, market prices, and yields for a 12-firm sample. The price per share series were calculated by averaging the end-of-the-month quotes for each company as reported in *El Economista Mexicano* and the *Boletín Financiero y Minero*. If no shares actually changed hands, the average of the buy and the sell prices was used. These series were then adjusted to account for stock splits and stock dividends. Earnings data were compiled by noting all payments actually distributed to shareholders during the course of the calendar year, not those declared. This is significant, since firms usually did not pay dividends until the year following their declaration. In cases where this method of reporting produced gaps in the series, it was necessary to impute the dividends paid by using series on declared dividends. The declared dividends series were constructed from data contained in the *Mexican Yearbook* and similar publications. From these series on the price of common stock and earnings per share, series on yields were derived.

An examination of Tables 7.2 and 7.3 reveals that the results obtained from the four-firm sample on the rate of return on capital stock tend to overestimate the profitability of Porfirian manufacturing. From 1896 to 1910 the median yield on common stock was only 4.6 percent per annum. Behind these low yields were very erratic dividend payments. Quite a few firms failed to pay dividends in many years, indicating that there were no profits to be distributed (Table 7.4). The most notorious was Fundidora Monterrey, which paid no dividends at all during the Porfiriato. Other firms with records almost equally dismal include three of the nation's most important textile producers, the Compañía Industrial de Atlixco, the Compañía Industrial de San Ildefonso, and the Compañía Industrial de San Antonio Abad. Between

TABLE 7.2

Yields on Common Stock, Selected Manufacturing Companies, 1896–1910

(Percent)

Year	Buen Tono	San Ildef	CIDOSA	S.A. Abad	Atlixco	CIVSA
1896	6.6%	0%	—	—	—	—
1897	7.6	0	7.6%	9.8%	—	—
1898	7.6	3.2	—	13.2	—	—
1899	6.1	3.8	—	0	—	—
1900	7.0	3.9	—	0	—	—
1901	7.6	0	3.8	0	0%	10.0%
1902	3.7	0	3.5	0	0	8.1
1903	3.6	0	7.7	0	0	8.1
1904	6.7	0	6.8	0	0	8.4
1905	4.4	0	5.6	0	0	6.0
1906	4.8	29.4	4.6	4.2	6.9	4.9
1907	5.3	6.1	5.5	6.2	6.6	5.0
1908	6.1	7.6	4.5	9.1	9.4	5.9
1909	6.3	0	5.6	0	0	5.9
1910	3.5	3.9	5.2	7.9	0	5.8

Year	Jabon	San Raf	Fund Mont	Toluca-México	Cig Mex	Cerv Moct
1901	5.0%	0%	0%	—	—	—
1902	8.5	6.4	0	7.4%	11.2%	—
1903	4.1	13.8	0	8.1	11.2	—
1904	7.8	6.8	0	9.7	15.0	—
1905	7.8	0	0	7.5	0	—
1906	7.4	6.0	0	4.7	0	—
1907	7.7	3.9	0	2.8	6.2	—
1908	11.7	9.8	0	7.6	0	4.0%
1909	11.1	0	0	5.6	6.6	2.9
1910	10.6	6.5	0	2.2	5.9	6.5

SOURCES: Calculated from *EM*, 1896–1911.

NOTE: The full names of companies are Compañía Manufacturera El Buen Tono, Compañía Industrial de San Ildefonso, Compañía Industrial de Orizaba, Compañía Industrial de San Antonio Abad, Compañía Industrial de Atlixco, Compañía Industrial Veracruzana, Compañía Industrial Jabonera de la Laguna, Compañía Industrial de San Rafael y Anexas, Compañía Fundidora de Fierro y Acero de Monterrey, Compañía Cervecera de Toluca y México, La Cigarrera Mexicana, Cervecería Moctezuma.

1901 and 1910 Atlixco paid dividends only in 1906, 1907, and 1908, and San Ildefonso in only 7 of the 15 years between 1896 and 1910. San Antonio Abad was equally erratic, paying out profits to its shareholders in only 8 years between 1895 and 1910. The San Rafael paper company and the La Cigarerra Mexicana

TABLE 7.3
Yields on Common Stock, Composite Values, 1896–1910
(Percent)

Year	High	Low	Median	Average
1896	6.6%	0%	—[a]	3.3%
1897	9.8	7.7	7.6%[b]	8.3
1898	13.2	3.2	7.6[c]	8.0
1899	6.1	0	3.8[c]	3.3
1900	7.0	0	3.9[c]	5.5
1901	10.0	0	0 [d]	2.9
1902	11.2	0	3.7[e]	4.4
1903	13.8	0	4.1[e]	5.1
1904	15.0	0	6.8[e]	5.6
1905	7.8	0	0 [e]	2.8
1906	29.4	0	4.9[e]	6.6
1907	7.7	0	5.3[e]	5.0
1908	11.7	0	6.9[f]	6.3
1909	11.1	0	4.3[f]	3.7
1910	10.6	0	5.5[f]	4.8
Avg. 1896–1910	10.9%	0.7%	4.6%	5.0%
Avg. 1901–1910	10.6%	0%	4.2%	4.7%

SOURCE: Derived from Table 7.2.
[a]Two firms. [b]Four firms. [c]Three firms.
[d]Nine firms. [e]Eleven firms. [f]Twelve firms.

cigarette company also paid dividends erratically. During the period between 1901 and 1910 San Rafael failed to pay dividends in 1901, 1905, and 1909. Similarly in the 9 years between 1902 and 1910 La Cigarerra Mexicana did not distribute profits to its shareholders in 1905, 1906, and 1908. Thus, of the 12 firms for which it was possible to gather stock market data, half paid out dividends erratically, implying an equally erratic income flow within the firms.

It might be argued that this erratic payment of earnings to shareholders does not indicate that the firms in question were not profitable. This would be the case if firms were reinvesting all of their profits in new plant and equipment. This, however, seems a highly unlikely scenario for three reasons. First, the market price of the stock of the companies in question was highly sensitive to the lack of dividends; share prices fell significantly in years in which there were no earnings distributed. This would not have been the case if there were retained earnings, since new expenditures on plant and equipment would have increased the value of the firms' assets and therefore kept share prices from falling. Share prices may actually have increased in a situation such as this, depending on the amount of earnings retained. Second, had these firms indeed been engaged in significant programs of capital spending, the payment of dividends

TABLE 7.4

Real Dividends, Selected Manufacturing Companies, 1895–1910

(Earnings per share, 1940 pesos)

Year	Buen Tono	San Ildef	CIDOSA	S.A. Abad	Atlixco	CIVSA
1895	60	—	85	72	—	—
1896	64	0	106	85	—	—
1897	58	0	100	51	—	—
1898	65	18	120	49	—	—
1899	68	20	125	0	—	—
1900	77	18	114	0	—	—
1901	62	0	32	0	0	37
1902	24	0	23	0	0	29
1903	24	0	54	0	0	29
1904	50	0	56	0	0	33
1905	45	0	50	0	0	27
1906	57	57	50	9	20	27
1907	68	8	59	11	20	30
1908	66	8	47	11	20	29
1909	62	0	42	0	0	27
1910	31	4	36	9	0	23

Year	Jabon	San Raf	Fund Mont	Toluca-México	Cig Mex	Cerv Moct
1901	50	0	0	—	—	—
1902	85	12	0	27	62	15
1903	49	27	0	29	29	5
1904	88	13	0	11	30	45
1905	78	0	0	36	0	22
1906	80	18	0	27	0	27
1907	80	11	0	18	16	32
1908	111	24	0	44	0	22
1909	104	0	0	29	12	17
1910	89	14	0	11	38	32

SOURCE: Derived from *EM*, 1895–1911. Deflated using implicit price index in Haber 1985: appendix B.

NOTE: Adjusted for splits and stock dividends. For full company names, see note, Table 7.2. For dividend payments in current nondeflated values, see Haber 1985: ch. 5.

would have simply ceased altogether for a period of years, instead of being erratic. Companies undertaking capital modernization programs do not pay out dividends in the irregular and erratic manner that these firms did. Third, the four companies for which we have estimated rates of return on capital stock indicate that those firms with moderately healthy rates of return paid out dividends in every single year, while those with low rates of return did not do so. Fundidora Monterrey, which had very low or negative rates of return, never paid any dividends. The three firms that were profitable, El Buen Tono, CIDOSA, and CIVSA, distributed earnings on a consistent basis. Clearly, they had more reliable and consistent income flows than was the norm for Porfirian manufacturing. Indeed, a comparison of the dividends paid per share, adjusted for differences in par values, indicates that between 1901 and 1910 these three companies paid out approximately twice as much as did the other firms in the sample: an average of 41 pesos annually per share. The other nine companies paid only 20.4 pesos.

How did these yields compare with secure, relatively risk-free investments? Exactly how risky did investors think manufacturing investments were? In order to answer this question we can compare the yields in manufacturing to those in two investments that were perceived as being relatively risk free: Mexican government bonds and common stock in the Banco Nacional de México.[4] I have divided the 12-firm sample of manufacturing companies into two groups: those that were relatively low risk, defined as companies that paid dividends in every year observed, and those that were high risk, that is, those that failed to pay dividends in one or more years. Included in the low-risk category were El Buen Tono, CIDOSA, CIVSA, the Compañía Industrial Jabonera de la Laguna, the Cervecería Moctezuma, and the Compañía Cervecera de Toluca y México. In the high-risk group were the remaining six companies: the Compañía Industrial de San Ildefonso, the Compañía Industrial de San Antonio Abad, the Compañía de las Fábricas de Papel de San Rafael y Anexas, La Cigarrera Mexicana, and Fundidora Monterrey. In order to keep the numerous instances in which firms failed to pay dividends from artificially biasing the results down-

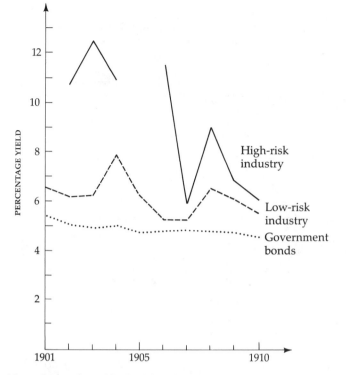

Yields on low-risk and high-risk industrial stocks compared to government bonds, 1901–1910. Source: Table 7.5.

ward, I included in the series only positive observations, since we are interested in seeing how high a yield investors expected in years in which there were profits. The results are presented in Table 7.5 and are graphed in the figure above.

The data indicate that the investment community considered manufacturing to be a fairly risky enterprise. On average the low-risk stocks paid 0.9 percentage points above Banco Nacional de México stock and 1.3 points above government bonds, a not insignificant risk premium, considering that this equaled a 17-percent and 27-percent difference respectively between low-risk manufacturing and the yields on these two securities. The high-risk stocks carried an even higher risk premium, paying on

TABLE 7.5
*Average Yields on Industrial Stocks Compared to Government Bonds
and Banco Nacional de México Stock, 1901–1910*

(Percent)

Year	Low-risk industry	High-risk industry	Government bonds[a]	Bank stock
1901	6.6%	—[b]	5.4%	5.9%
1902	6.2	10.7%	5.1	5.3
1903	6.3	12.5	4.9	—
1904	7.9	10.9	5.0	5.3
1905	6.3	—[b]	4.7	5.0
1906	5.3	11.6	4.7	5.2
1907	5.3	5.8	4.8	5.2
1908	6.6	9.0	4.8	—
1909	6.2	6.6	4.7	—
1910	5.6	6.0	4.6	—
Avg. 1901–1910	6.2%	9.1%	4.9%	5.3%[c]

SOURCES: Series on manufacturing stocks derived from Table 7.2, above; series on government bonds calculated from *EM*, 1901–10; series on Banco Nacional de México stock from Renaud 1987.

[a] Average of three government bonds (see n. 4, this chapter).

[b] All stocks observed in this category had yields of zero in this year because all failed to pay dividends.

[c] 1901–7.

average 4.2 percentage points above the yield on government bonds and 3.8 percent above the yield on Banco Nacional de México stock. That is, they carried a risk premium of 72 percent against bank stock and 86 percent against government bonds.

What did this mean for the individual investor? How much money could one have made, or lost, speculating in manufacturing stocks in the Mexico City stock exchange? In short, for the typical investor, what was the bottom line?

Money is made in the stock market in two ways. One of these, earnings in the form of dividends, has already been discussed. Stockholders may also receive a return in the form of capital gains derived from a stock's appreciation over time. Any attempt to estimate the real return to investors must take into account both of these variables. In addition, in order for a longitudinal study of this type to be meaningful, all values must be expressed in constant (or real) terms. An analysis that does not simultaneously factor in both dividend earnings and capital gains, or which uses values that have not been adjusted for inflation, can produce misleading results. In fact, it is possible for an investor to lose money on a stock that is paying dividends and whose nominal market price is increasing over time. This could be the case, for example, if the rate of inflation is higher than the combined rate of return from dividend income and nominal capital gains. Even though the investor is receiving dividends and the value of his stock is increasing on the stock market, the depreciation of his investment through inflation is occurring at a faster rate. The end result is a net real loss.

The method employed here takes all of these factors into account. The return to investors was calculated as follows. First, all dividend and share-price data from the 12-firm sample on stock yields were converted to constant 1940 pesos. Next, series on capital gains were constructed from the series on real stock prices. Annual capital gains or losses were then added to annual real dividends to obtain the total real return to investors. Finally, this value was divided by the real market price of the stock in the first year in the series to calculate the real rate of return.

Table 7.6 presents the returns possible to an investor who purchased a portfolio of stocks in 1901 and sold it in 1910. An equal distribution of stocks within the portfolio in terms of the value of the stock purchased is assumed. That is, at the beginning of the period our hypothetical investor would have divided his resources evenly among all the available stocks. The results are presented both as the overall return over the course of the cycle and as the implicit annual compound rate of growth.

From the point of view of the real returns to investors, the results are surprisingly low. An investor who divided his resources evenly in 1901 among the 12 stocks listed in Table 7.6, after all dividends for 1901 had been paid, and sold the portfolio in 1910, after collecting all dividends paid during 1910, would on average have made just 3.0 percent per annum in real terms. Of the 12 stocks in the portfolio, our hypothetical investor would have lost money on three; none would have provided a real return of more than 10 percent, and only three would have paid more than 7 percent. Even if we were to exclude the Cervecería Moctezuma, since its coverage extends only from 1908 to 1910,

TABLE 7.6
Real Return to Investors, 1902–1910
(1940 pesos)

Company name	1901 stock price	Capital gain[a]	Total dividends, 1902–10	Total return[b]	Real annual rate of return[c]
San Ildef	295	−204	77	−127	−6.1%
Buen Tono	812	70	427	497	5.5
San Raf	151	70	119	189	9.4
CIDOSA	847	−154	417	263	2.0
Jabon	1,000	−157	764	607	5.4
Cig Mex	228	−37	127	90	3.8
Toluca-México	322	162	259	421	9.7
Atlixco	153	18	60	78	4.6
CIVSA	371	27	254	281	6.5
Fund Mont	261	−81[d]	0	−81	−4.1
S.A. Abad	79	34	40	74	7.6
Cerv Moct	560	−84[e]	71[f]	−13	−0.8[g]
Average real rate of return to portfolio[h]					3.0%

SOURCES: Calculated from *EM*, 1901–10.
[a] Real difference in average stock price, 1901–10.
[b] Total real dividends plus real capital gains. Calculations assume that stock purchases were made at end of 1901 after payment of all dividends.
[c] Implicit compound rate of return, 1901–10.
[d] 1902 versus 1910 stock price.
[e] 1908 versus 1910 stock price.
[f] Dividends paid for 1908, 1909, 1910.
[g] Total return 1908–10 spread over three years.
[h] Assumes equal distribution of investor's resources among all stocks within the portfolio.

the results still would have been a very unimpressive 4.0 percent per year. In short, given the fact that all of the firms sampled were highly capital-intensive, oligopoly or monopoly producers, which had influential connections in the Díaz government and utilized the most advanced production methods then available within their respective product lines, the return to investors was low.

Overall, what all three measures of profits indicate is that manufacturing during the Porfiriato was not a good way to get rich quick. Contrary to much of the popular mythology about business in Porfirian Mexico, investing in manufacturing was as good a way to lose money as it was to make it. This is not to say that no one got rich. In a stock market as risky and volatile as existed in Mexico, a smart trader who sold short at exactly the right times could conceivably have made a good deal of money, but on average, firms did not make particularly high profits, nor did their investors reap large returns.

Why, then, did entrepreneurs bother to make sizable investments in manufacturing? Why invest in enterprises that provided low rates of return? The answer is that their investments in manufacturing were part of an overall strategy of profitability: losses in some areas would be compensated by higher than normal profits in others. This allowed investors to control both the new, promising areas of economic activity, like manufacturing, and the older, more established areas like commerce and real estate speculation. This was the reason that investors held such diversified portfolios.

Implicit in this strategy was the belief that the Mexican economy would continue to grow as it had during the 1880's and 1890's. To the nation's elite, it appeared that Mexico was on the way to becoming a modern nation, and they intended to be on top of the process. Mexico's financiers undoubtedly realized that over the short term their enterprises would not be particularly lucrative, that Mexico was not really ready for steel mills, cement factories, and other incredibly huge operations that required large and well-integrated consumer markets. Over the short run these investments would make lower-than-average profits, or might even lose money, but over the medium term their owners would find themselves in the enviable position of controlling the largest, most important firms in a rapidly expanding and highly profitable manufacturing sector. In this belief they could not have been more mistaken.

EIGHT

The Revolution and Its Aftermath, 1910-1925

IT WAS THE BELIEF of the *Científicos* and the investment community that the building of a vibrant economy, replete with railroads, steel mills, and large-scale commercial agriculture, would carry Mexico into the modern world. Though some sectors of society would undoubtedly suffer along the way, the end result would be the development of an enlightened polity and society. Mexico, after the process was complete, would be a developed country.

In this analysis the group surrounding Díaz completely misread the situation. On the one hand, the process of economic growth created dislocated and marginalized groups who, in order to defend their declining standard of living, eventually mobilized to defend their class interests. These groups included the peasants of the center-south who had been forced off their lands in the Porfirian land grab, as well as urban and rural proletarians seeking better working conditions, an end to the company store, higher wages, and the right to organize unions. On the other hand, the process of economic growth also created groups of capitalists who opposed Díaz's rule. The commercial elite from the north, typified by the wealthy Madero family from Coahuila and Nuevo León, felt that even though they had grown wealthy under the Pax Porfiriana, they had been excluded from exercising political power. Since economic growth and the distribution of its rewards were a highly politicized process, this northern elite was resentful that the Mexico City interests monopolized the political system. Allying itself with intermediate groups like petty capitalists and medium-sized commercial agriculturalists, and giving lip service to the need for social reforms, this group sought to harness the rage from below in order to propel itself into power.

In this task the commercial and financial class from the north failed. Díaz fell easily: the dictator was old, the system corrupt, the classes that had supported it lacked faith in the continued ability of the Pax Porfiriana to produce peace and profits. The problem was that once Madero and his wealthy cohorts forced Díaz out, they were not able to control the peasants, ranch hands, artisans, and industrial workers who had helped put them into the presidential palace. The history of the Mexican Revolution, then, is essentially one of class war, in which the ruling class from the north had to fight a long and bloody war in order to keep the workers and peasants from gaining control of the state. They finally achieved their goal with the assassination of key leaders of the lower classes, including Emiliano Zapata and Francisco Villa, as well as by a series of compromises written into the constitution of 1917, which provided, at least on paper, some of the reforms that the workers and peasants had been fighting for.

The story of exactly how this occurred is a long one and has been told many times over. It is therefore not my purpose to retell that story. Rather, my concern is with what happened to the old Porfirian industrialist class and the manufacturing plant they had built.

One of the clichés of Mexican history is that the Revolution of 1910–17 completely destroyed the Porfirian order and created a new, more efficient productive base, guided by an "authentic," nationalist bourgeoisie. As John Womack has pointed out, the Revolution is generally seen as a period of unrelenting destruction and mayhem in which the productive apparatus of the Porfiriato was destroyed and the old Porfirian monopolists forced to flee the country.[1] Most scholars, when looking at this period in Mexican history, have described it in terms of "a wrecking process," "revolutionary ruin," "lost years for Mexico," or "utter chaos."[2] This belief, springing more from ideological assumptions than from empirical evidence, has blinded many scholars to the possibility that the Revolution could have produced anything other than widespread destruction. That is, they have assumed that "without 'order' there can be no progress, without peace there could be no production."[3]

In many respects the Revolution accomplished exactly the opposite of what most scholars have supposed. Most of Mexico's manufacturing plant emerged intact from the fighting; it was not destroyed. Mexico's industrial barons did not permanently abandon the nation, creating a vacuum to be filled by a national bourgeoisie; they stayed put. Moreover, the Revolution did not bring about a new surge in entrepreneurial behavior, giving rise to a new, more efficient industrial base. If anything, firms disinvested in the years following the Revolution. Similarly, the Revolution did not break the hold of the monopolies and oligopolies that controlled Mexican manufacturing; the basic organization of industry did not change. In short, if Mexican industry during the Porfiriato was characterized by large, vertically integrated monopolies and oligopolies that relied on government protection to make up for structural inefficiencies, these characteristics were even more evident in the years following the Revolution. That is, to a certain extent the Revolution, rather than tearing down the industrial structure of the Porfiriato, reinforced it.

Until the end of 1913, three years after Francisco I. Madero's call to arms, the Revolution had little effect on the economy. As late as March 1913 the Mexican financial press was reporting that business was up, one article noting that "the statistics that mark commercial traffic, railroad revenues, etc., have not been reduced by the conflicts occurring in various regions of the country but, contrary to what one would expect, they have incurred slight increases."[4]

Data on manufacturing production corroborate these reports. In the cotton textile industry, for example, annual production in the years 1910–13 was only slightly lower than it had been from 1905 to 1910. In fact, series on the total amount of raw cotton consumed, the number of spindles and looms in operation, and the number of workers employed in those years all indicate that the industry was doing at least as well as during the earlier period. The only noticeable decline was in the number of mills in operation, from 132 mills in 1908 to 118 in 1913 (see Table 8.1). Partial data for the beer industry indicate a similar response to

TABLE 8.1
Cotton Textile Industry, Main Economic Indicators, 1895–1925

Fiscal year	Operating mills	Active spindles	Active looms	Workers [a]	Cotton (metric tons) [b]	Capital [c] (000 pesos)
1895	110	411,496	12,335	19,975	21,540	—
1896	—	430,868	12,874	—	21,988	—
1897	—	458,795	13,874	—	24,199	—
1898	112	469,547	14,581	—	25,067	—
1899	120	491,443	14,759	23,731	26,518	—
1900	134	588,474	18,069	27,767	28,985	—
1901	133	591,506	18,733	26,709	30,262	—
1902	124	595,728	18,222	24,964	27,628	—
1903	115	632,601	20,271	26,149	27,512	—
1904	119	635,940	20,506	27,456	28,841	—
1905	127	678,058	22,021	30,162	31,230	—
1906	130	688,217	22,774	31,673	35,626	—
1907	129	693,842	23,507	33,132	36,654	—
1908	132	732,876	24,997	35,816	36,040	—
1909	129	726,278	25,327	32,229	35,435	—
1910	123	702,874	25,017	31,963	34,736	—
1911	119	725,297	24,436	32,147	34,568	—
1912	126	762,149	27,019	32,209	33,154	—
1913	118	752,804	26,791	32,641	32,821	—
1914	90	—	—	—	—	—
1915	84	—	—	—	—	—
1916	93	—	—	—	—	—
1917	92	573,072	20,489	22,187	—	—
1918	104	689,173	25,017	27,680	20,334	—
1919	110	735,308	26,995	32,815	31,095	—
1920	120	753,837	27,301	37,936	31,694	—
1921	121	770,945	28,409	38,227	35,924	—
1922	119	803,230	29,521	39,677	34,654	81,765
1923	108	802,363	29,668	38,232	32,343	71,968
1924	116	812,165	29,888	37,732	30,517	74,229
1925	130	838,987	31,094	43,728	40,997	77,568

SOURCES: Derived from Rosenzweig 1965c: 106; Sterrett and Davis 1928: 105; Yamada 1965: 26, 29; Mexico [6]: II, 124–25; Mexico [54]; Mexico [49]: 170; Mexico [50]: 166; de la Peña 1938: 7; Mexico [46]: table 2; EM, 4 July 1914, p. 138; Mexico [48]: II.327, III.685, IV.439, V.563; Mexico [30]: 14.

[a]Number of workers employed; does not include managerial personnel. Prior to the Revolution workers generally worked a 12-hour day; after the Revolution this was shortened to 8 hours.

[b]Total cotton consumed during the year. This is taken as a proxy for production on the reasonable assumption that the ratio of cotton consumption to output of finished products did not change substantially over time.

[c]Accumulated capital investment in physical plant, valued at cost minus depreciation at year end.

the early years of the Revolution. Though global data are lacking, the sales figures for one of the big three firms, the Cervecería Cuauhtemoc, indicate that until 1914 it was business as usual, with record sales of over 16.5 million liters in 1912. Sales dipped appreciably the following year to 11.7 million liters, but this was still well above the company's pre-revolutionary average (see Table 8.2).

Although the early years of the Revolution appear not to have interfered significantly with the production and distribution of consumer nondurables like beer and textiles, the political instability created by the overthrow of Díaz did have negative effects on the manufacturers of producer goods. In the steel industry, for example, the production of pig iron—the first step in the production of steel—fell from an all-time high of 71,000 tons in 1911 to just under 33,000 tons in 1912, and further to a little under 12,000 tons by 1913. The cement industry was similarly affected, with annual production falling by 10,000 tons per year between 1910 and 1913 (see Table 8.3). In 1913, total production was half of what it had been just three years earlier. Perhaps the most surprising feature of these output data from the steel and cement industries, however, is that the plants did not shut down entirely after 1910. Apparently there was still enough construction taking place to keep both industries running during the early years of the Revolution.

The data on profits mirror this finding. Estimates on the rate of return on capital stock for CIDOSA, Fundidora Monterrey,

TABLE 8.2
Cervecería Cuauhtemoc Sales, 1911–1925

Year	Sales (000 liters)	Year	Sales (000 liters)
1911	14,172	1919	7,735
1912	16,519	1920	14,929
1913	11,732	1921	16,689
1914–15[a]	3,359	1922	13,156
1916	2,758	1923	12,335
1917	4,640	1924	11,564
1918	4,977	1925	15,736

SOURCE: Unpublished data from Cervecería Cuauhtemoc sales department.
NOTE: For 1892–1910 data, see Table 4.3 above.
[a] Combined year.

TABLE 8.3

Utilization of Installed Capacity in the Cement and Steel Industries,
1911–1925

(000 metric tons)

Year	Cement industry			Steel industry[a]		
	Capacity	Output	Utili-zation[b]	Capacity	Output	Utili-zation[b]
1911	152	50	33	110	71	65
1912	177	40	23	110	33	30
1913	177	30	17	110	12	11
1914	177	25	14	110	0	0
1915	177	10	6	110	0	0
1916	177	20	11	110	0	0
1917	177	30	17	110	12	11
1918	177	40	23	110	21	19
1919	177	40	23	110	21	19
1920	222	45	20	110	15	14
1921	222	50	23	110	42	38
1922	222	70	32	110	24	22
1923	222	90	41	110	44	40
1924	222	107	48	110	19	17
1925	222	110	50	110	49	45

SOURCES: Cement industry, unpublished data from the Cámara Nacional de Cemento. Steel industry, figures calculated from *FMIA*, 1911–26.

[a]See note *a* to Table 3.1.

[b]Production divided by installed capacity, expressed as a percent.

and CIVSA (no data are available on El Buen Tono for the early years of the Revolution) indicate that these companies did only slightly worse from 1911 to 1913 than they did prior to the Revolution. CIDOSA had a rate of return on capital stock in 1911 of 6 percent and in 1912 of 8 percent, which was just slightly under its 10 percent average for the Porfiriato (see Table 8.4). Similarly, CIVSA managed a rate of return of 12 percent in 1912 and 10 percent in 1913,[5] which was more or less what it had made prior to the Revolution. Even Fundidora Monterrey, which barely broke even during the Porfiriato, managed to turn a profit in 1911 and in 1912. In fact, 1911 was a record year for the company, the first one in which its profits reached 3 percent of capital stock, with an unusually high (for Fundidora Monterrey) rate of capacity utilization of 65 percent. The rate of return fell to 1 percent in 1912 and to negative 6 percent in 1913.

Data on yields tell a similar story. As Table 8.5 demonstrates,

TABLE 8.4
Estimated Rates of Return on Capital Stock, 1911–1925
(Current pesos)

Year	Capital stock	Profit	Rate of return
Fundidora Monterrey			
1911	12,150,506	331,785	3
1912	11,627,366	75,033	1
1913	11,379,415	−670,124	−6
1914	11,262,387	−829,849	−7
1915	10,183,267	−1,002,244	−10
1916	10,320,282	−613,450	−6
1917	9,855,241	2,064,243	21[a]
1918	10,160,729	333,128	3
1919	10,099,372	537,713	5
1920	12,527,242	1,132,825	9
1921	13,364,126	899,535	7
1922	13,689,525	497,746	4
1923	14,148,271	1,526,247	11
1924	14,041,756	−78,673	−1
1925	14,155,461	708,500	5
El Buen Tono			
1918	10,650,733	1,264,375	12
1919	9,706,661	2,036,842	21
1920	—	—	—
1921	—	—	—
1922	—	—	—
1923	13,186,402	2,115,842	16
1924	12,837,403	1,570,457	12
CIDOSA			
1911	20,128,326	1,259,368	6
1912	19,176,892	1,465,242	8
1913	—	—	—
1914	—	—	—
1915	—	—	—
1916	—	—	—
1917	—	—	—
1918	—	—	—
1919	—	—	—
1920	18,411,047	2,596,762	14
1921	—	—	—
1922	17,300,000	2,197,799	13
1923	—	—	—
1924	16,363,224	595,799	4

SOURCES: Fundidora Monterrey data calculated from *FMIA*, 1910–26. El Buen Tono data calculated from *BFM*, 28 May 1919, p. 8, 27 Aug. 1920, p. 1, 28 Aug. 1920, pp. 1, 8, 21 Apr. 1924, p. 1, 10 Sept. 1925, p. 1, 28 Oct. 1925, p. 1. CIDOSA data calculated from *MYB 1912*, p. 123; *EM*, 19 Apr. 1912, p. 37, 27 Apr. 1912, p. 67; *BFM*, 30 Jan. 1920, p. 8, 3 Feb. 1920, p. 8, 2 July 1921, p. 8, 5 Apr. 1923, p. 4, 28 Mar. 1925, p. 1, 29 Mar. 1927, p. 1, 1 Apr. 1927, p. 1.

NOTE: For a complete discussion of how profits, capital stock, and the rate of return on capital were calculated and a discussion of the method employed in the adjustment of the raw data, see Haber 1985: appendix A.

[a]Fundidora Monterrey's rate of return of 21 percent was not the result of productive activities, but a financial gain from the refinancing of the company's bonds.

TABLE 8.5
Yields on Common Stock, Selected Manufacturing Companies, 1911–1925

(Percent)

Year	Buen Tono	San Ildef	CIDOSA	S.A. Abad	Atlixco	CIVSA
1911	5.9%	4.0%	5.7%	9.4%	5.3%	6.4%
1912	5.3	4.7	6.4	0	3.9	5.9
1913	0	6.8	3.6	0	5.0	5.8
1914	3.2	—	6.0	0	0	2.4
1915	0	—	—	0	0	0
1916	0	0.4	0	0.4	0	0
1917	—	0	—	—	0	0
1918	8.3	10.1	6.8	31.0	0	4.7
1919	7.6	8.1	13.0	14.3	0	7.0
1920	12.1	10.9	14.2	12.2	0	10.7
1921	13.5	18.8	20.4	33.3	15.0	12.7
1922	12.6	13.2	12.2	0	7.7	16.3
1923	12.1	9.4	11.0	0	8.3	6.9
1924	11.1	10.1	5.0	0	14.3	12.3
1925	9.7	5.0	5.5	0	11.3	4.8

Year	Jabon	San Raf	Fund Mont	Toluca-México	Cig Mex	Cerv Moct	Tab Mex
1911	8.7%	6.5%	0%	9.0%	5.5%	5.2%	0%
1912	10.7	7.9	11.3	0	6.6	6.6	—
1913	4.2	4.2	0	4.2	0	4.3	—
1914	0	0	0	3.1	0	4.4	0
1915	0	0	0	0	0	0	—
1916	0	0	0	0	0	0	—
1917	—	0	0	0	—	0	—
1918	9.9	0	0	0	0	8.5	2.5
1919	19.9	10.3	0	0	14.5	14.5	11.7
1920	22.9	16.1	6.4	0	12.5	—	0
1921	5.2	6.7	5.3	10.0	17.1	—	10.1
1922	0	8.6	0	0	16.3	11.0	25.5
1923	13.4	14.2	0	0	14.8	5.9	12.1
1924	19.8	6.8	0	0	22.6	6.6	6.3
1925	—	8.3	0	0	13.4	7.2	11.8

SOURCES: Calculated from *EM*, 1910–14; *BFM*, 1916–26.
NOTE: For full names of companies and for yield data for the period 1896–1910, see Table 7.2, except for La Tabacalera Mexicana (Tab Mex) for which there are no data for that period.

almost all of the firms sampled had good yields in 1911, 1912, and 1913. In fact, as Table 8.6 shows, median yields in 1911 and 1912 were actually higher than before the Revolution. In 1913, there was a marked drop in stock yields, but even a median yield of 4.2 percent was still healthy compared to the pre-revolutionary period. Behind these relatively strong stock yields was a surprisingly steady stream of dividend payments to shareholders. In 1911, 11 of the 13 firms sampled paid dividends to their shareholders. Only Fundidora Monterrey, which never paid dividends even during the Porfiriato, and La Tabacalera Mexicana, for which no data exist prior to 1910, paid none. The performance for 1912 and 1913 is much the same, though the data indicate a drop in dividend payments in 1913 (see Table 8.7). In short, whether we look at series on production or on profits, the data

TABLE 8.6

Yields on Common Stock, Composite Values, 1911–1925

(Percent)

Year	High	Low	Median	Average
1911	9.4%	0%	5.7%	5.5% [a]
1912	11.3	0	6.3	5.8 [b]
1913	6.8	0	4.2	3.2 [b]
1914	6.0	0	0	1.6 [b]
1915	0	0	0	0 [c]
1916	0.4	0	0	0.1 [b]
1917	0	0	0	0 [d]
1918	31.0	0	4.7	6.3 [a]
1919	19.9	0	10.3	9.3 [b]
1920	22.9	0	11.5	9.8 [b]
1921	33.3	5.2	13.1	14.0 [b]
1922	25.5	0	11.0	9.5 [a]
1923	14.8	0	9.4	8.4 [a]
1924	22.6	0	8.5	7.3 [a]
1925	13.4	0	6.4	6.4 [b]
Avg. 1911–1925	14.5%	0.3%	6.1%	5.8%
Avg. 1911–1917	4.8%	0%	2.3%	2.3%
Avg. 1918–1925	22.9%	0.7%	9.4%	8.9%

SOURCE: Derived from Table 8.5.
[a] Thirteen firms.   [b] Twelve firms.   [c] Ten firms.   [d] Seven firms.

TABLE 8.7

Dividend Earnings, Selected Manufacturing Companies, 1911–1925

(Earnings per share, current pesos)

Year	Buen Tono	San Ildef	CIDOSA	S.A. Abad	Atlixco	CIVSA
1911	30.00	2.00	20.02	5.00	4.00	13.00
1912	30.00	2.00	20.02	0	3.00	12.00
1913	0	3.00	11.26	0	3.00	12.60
1914	14.06	—	20.02	0	0	5.40
1915	0	3.00	20.02	0	0	0
1916	0	0.60	0	2.00	0	0
1917	23.44	0	14.34	6.00	0	0
1918	23.44	2.72	13.59	11.46	0	5.30
1919	23.44	2.99	34.87	8.00	0	14.33
1920	39.84	4.02	40.25	6.00	6.00	21.79
1921	46.88	7.14	53.62	12.00	3.00	22.03
1922	46.88	5.13	34.48	0	3.00	30.31
1923	46.88	4.12	38.67	0	6.00	13.91
1924	46.88	4.14	15.54	0	6.00	21.92
1925	46.88	2.03	15.24	0	0	8.22

Year	Jabon	San Raf	Fund Mont	Toluca-México	Cig Mex	Cerv Moct	Tab Mex
1911	40.00	8.00	0	20.00	6.00	14.00	0
1912	50.00	10.00	7.00	0	6.00	12.00	—
1913	20.00	5.00	0	6.00	0	8.00	10.00
1914	0	0	0	4.00	0	8.00	0
1915	0	0	0	0	0	0	6.00
1916	0	0	0	0	0	0	6.00
1917	41.02	0	0	0	3.82	0	2.82
1918	21.72	0	0	0	0	10.16	2.00
1919	55.72	0	0	0	4.50	37.24	12.00
1920	76.38	6.00	3.00	0	4.50	23.94	0
1921	16.32	10.00	2.00	5.00	6.00	37.24	12.00
1922	0	5.00	0	0	7.50	33.25	35.00
1923	40.00	6.00	0	0	9.00	19.95	20.00
1924	51.75	8.24	0	0	14.00	19.95	10.00
1925	—	5.00	0	0	11.00	19.95	20.00

SOURCES: Calculated from *EM*, 1910–14; *BFM*, 1916–26.

NOTE: For full names of companies see Table 7.2 above; "Tab Mex," La Tabacalera Mexicana. Data adjusted to account for stock splits and stock dividends. For real earnings per share, see Table 8.10, below.

indicate that at least until mid-1913 it was more or less business as usual.

With the overthrow of Francisco Madero in 1913, however, the situation changed qualitatively: by the end of the year Mexican manufacturers found themselves in the middle of a civil war, and production, sales, and profits dropped accordingly. Mexico's industrialists were now confronted by two major problems: occupation by revolutionary armies and the disruption of the national system of transport and communication.

One of the most pressing needs of any army is a source of finance. Mobilizing tens of thousands of men to fight prolonged campaigns is a costly undertaking. For this reason there was little incentive for revolutionary armies to destroy the factories they occupied. Rather than being a target for demolition, Mexico's manufacturing plants were viewed as strategic assets that could be used to generate income for the armies that controlled them. What typically occurred in occupied areas was that either the army would seize the local factories and run them for its own benefit, or it would threaten to do so unless a forced loan was paid. To cite one example, in April 1914 the forces of Pablo González took control of Monterrey. For most of the year González occupied and ran the Cervecería Cuauhtemoc, where he continued to employ the brewery's work force. By November the company's stocks of raw materials had been used up. At this point, having extracted what he could from the operation, González returned the factory, apparently undamaged, to its owners.[6]

There were similar occurrences in other manufacturing enterprises, including the Miraflores cotton textile mill in the state of México and the La Estrella cotton textile mill in Coahuila. In August 1914 Miraflores, which was part of the Compañía Industrial de San Antonio Abad textile conglomerate, was occupied by the forces of Emiliano Zapata, who continued to operate the factory. It was not until 1919, when the Zapatistas finally laid down their arms, that the mill was returned to its owners. Though part of the factory was damaged by fire during its occupation, it was returned essentially intact.[7] The La Estrella mill, which was owned by the Compañía Industrial de Parras, was seized by the government of the state of Coahuila in October 1915. In August 1917 it was returned to its owners, again apparently undamaged.[8]

On occasion these property seizures created profit opportunities for Mexico's financier-industrialists. One such opportunity occurred in 1914 when the forces of Francisco Villa took over the La Laguna region, where most of the nation's cotton is grown. Villa continued to employ the workers on the cotton plantations in order to generate income for his army. This created a major problem for the Compañía Industrial Jabonera de la Laguna, which relied upon the cottonseed from these plantations as its primary raw material for the manufacture of soap and glycerine. At the same time, Villa had no way to market his cotton crop. The company, through its president and general manager John Brittingham, therefore arranged to purchase Villa's cotton, which was to be paid for C.O.D. at the U.S. border. In return Villa agreed to ensure the delivery of the seed to the soap factory. The price paid to Villa for the cotton was actually well under its market value, and Brittingham turned a large profit on the transaction by selling the cotton in Liverpool at inflated, World War I prices. Brittingham, however, had not heard the last of Villa. Whether Villa realized that he had been paid too little for the cotton is unknown, but by 1915 he was threatening to seize Brittingham's soap works and run it himself unless the company provided him with several forced loans. In total Villa obtained $350,000 from the soap and glycerine company.[9]

Because of these financial considerations, the bulk of Mexico's industrial plant came through the Revolution relatively unscathed. Revolutionary armies often removed the belting from machinery when they retired from a factory—apparently the belting had military uses—but in general they caused little serious damage. Here and there, a few factories were destroyed, but by and large these were small operations. Reading through the correspondence of the Departamento de Trabajo for these years, one finds few cases in which entire factories were seriously damaged.[10] Of those that were totally destroyed by the Revolution, none were large firms. Generally speaking, Mexico's larger manufacturers—Brittingham's Compañía Industrial Jabonera de la Laguna is a good example—had the political and financial resources with which to defend themselves. They therefore came through the Revolution in rather good condition.

More serious than the threat of takeover by revolutionary armies was the breakdown of communications and transport. Mexico's manufacturing boom of the Porfiriato was based upon the unification of the market by the railroads. The national railway network allowed manufacturers to take advantage of economies of scale by producing for a wider market than had previously been available, permitting the development of new industries and the integration and expansion of old ones. The major economic effect of the Revolution was to undermine this transport system, thereby restricting the market and making many manufacturing plants unprofitable. In addition, the breakdown of long-distance transport prevented manufacturers from obtaining the raw materials and spare parts they needed to continue functioning.

With the eruption of Civil War in late 1913 the nation's system of commerce and communications fell apart. As in the U.S. Civil War, the control of the railroads was of strategic importance. Thus, the railways, and the accompanying telegraph lines, were unavailable for commercial purposes. Instead of carrying manufactures, raw materials, and foodstuffs, the railways were full of troops and military equipment. Moreover, the intense fighting around the rail junctions destroyed many of the rail lines. Throughout most of 1914 rail transport between the north and Mexico City was interrupted. Between Mexico City and the port city of Veracruz the situation was much the same, both rail lines being cut. The situation in Veracruz was complicated even further by the fact that the city was occupied by U.S. troops for part of the year. It was for this reason that the use of donkeys and mules doubled during the period 1910–20, though as transportation they were considerably less efficient than the railways.[11]

The problems of distribution arising from the breakdown in communications and transport were further complicated by the breakdown of the national system of currency and exchange. During the Revolution silver and gold coin disappeared from circulation and were replaced by paper currencies issued by each of the warring factions. Since each army printed bills as it saw fit, and since bills were not backed by anything except the belief that the army in question was going to continue to control a particular area, this money was constantly being discounted and devalued. Inflation was rampant, and the different currencies of different areas were not easily interchangeable. In short, the functioning of the national market was further hampered by the lack of a national monetary system.

The inability to obtain the necessary inputs and to deliver finished goods to market forced factories to close across the country. By August 1913, 86 cotton textile factories had written to the Departamento de Trabajo saying that the transport situation was forcing them to cease operations. Throughout 1914 and 1915 the owners and workers of Mexico's major manufacturing enterprises requested some type of intervention to allow the factories to obtain the raw materials and spare parts that they needed in order to continue producing.[12] Those that remained in operation did so on a limited basis. In the cotton textile industry, for example, the number of mills in operation dropped from 118 in 1913 to 90 in 1914. By 1915 only 84 of the nation's more than 148 mills were in operation (see Table 8.1, above). Other consumer goods industries were also hard hit, among them beer brewing. The nation's leading producer of beer, the Cervecería Cuauhtemoc, cut back production by more than 80 percent. As Table 8.2 demonstrates, from a high of 16.5 million liters shipped from the brewery in 1912, combined sales for 1914 and 1915—the brewery was occupied for half of 1914 by the army of Pablo González—were only 3.4 million liters. In 1916, total sales were only 2.8 million liters, less than 20 percent of what they had been in 1912.

Though production data for other consumer goods industries are not available, we can infer from the payment of dividends to their stockholders that the situation was akin to that in the Cervercería Cuauhtemoc and the cotton textile industry. As Table 8.7 indicates, by 1915 the majority of firms were no longer paying any dividends at all, implying that at best they were covering only their variable costs. In that year only 3 of the 13 firms sampled paid out any profits to their shareholders. A similar situation obtained in 1916 and 1917. Although some firms continued to make money and pay dividends, the data indicate that they did so at a much reduced level during this period. Because of the lack of a price index for the revolutionary years, it is not possible to convert these nominal values to real values, but it is certain that the Revolution produced extremely high rates of inflation. Thus, in the face of rising prices, earnings per share were falling. The poor dividend payments are reflected in the series on yields. The average yield for the 13 sample firms hovered around zero for the years 1915 to 1917 (see Table 8.6, above).

In the producer goods industries the situation was even worse than in consumer goods. The lack of articulation between the producer and consumer goods sectors meant that the market for intermediate goods was chiefly confined to the construction industry. Given the disruption of the market, the inability to move goods on the railways, the complete cessation of government infrastructure projects, and the lack of private construction because of the Revolution, the intermediate goods sector was essentially shut down from 1914 to 1916. For example, during those three years not a single ingot of pig iron came out of Fundidora Monterrey's blast furnace (see Table 8.3, above). The company posted sizable losses in each of these years, losing a total of 2.4 million pesos (see Table 8.4, above). In the cement industry, output fell from 60,000 tons in 1910 to 10,000 tons in 1915, implying a capacity utilization rate of only 6 percent (see Table 8.3, above). Of Mexico's three big cement manufacturers only the smallest, Cementos Tolteca, continued to operate, and this was on a limited production schedule. The largest and most efficient cement producer, Cementos Hidalgos, closed its gates in 1911 for lack of sufficient demand. The second largest, Cementos Cruz Azul, tried to continue producing, but, given the unfavorable market conditions, it incurred sizable losses and eventually passed into the hands of the Banco Nacional de México.[13]

In the producer goods industries that were articulated with the consumer goods sector, newsprint and glass bottles, the situation was almost as serious. In the paper and newsprint industry the industry's largest single plant, San Rafael, in the state of Mexico, was taken over by Zapatistas from 1914 to 1919.[14] This left only San Rafael's other mill—El Progreso Industrial—and the relatively small Loreto and Peña Pobre mills in operation. The extent to which these smaller operations were able to meet demand is unknown, though the lack of raw materials and spare parts must have forced them to curtail operations.[15] This was further complicated by the fact that the owner of the Peña Pobre mill was a German national blacklisted by the U.S. government from receiving exports of American-made machinery and spare parts during the First World War. On the demand side there were also developments encouraging contraction. The largest single market was the newspaper industry, which was severely curtailed by the Revolution. Both of the nation's major financial publications of the Porfiriato, *La Semana Mercantil* and *El Economista Mexicano*, ceased publication with the outbreak of civil war in 1914. In the glass bottle industry data on market demand also suggest a major contraction. The largest consumer of the Vidriera Monterrey's bottles was the Cervecería Cuauhtemoc, whose output fell by better than 80 percent between 1912 and 1916, implying a similar contraction for the bottle producer.

Thus, the commercial crisis of 1914–16, as well as the problems of armed seizure and forced loans, produced a major downturn in industrial production. Though the effect on intermediate goods producers was stronger than it was for consumer goods producers, the Revolution created extremely unfavorable conditions throughout the manufacturing sector. The steel and cement industries were both essentially inoperative throughout the period; 40 percent of the cotton textile mills were closed; paper, beer, and glass producers were forced to operate on a limited scale; and few manufacturers were realizing profits high enough to permit them to pay any dividends.

Even with these adverse conditions, however, many enterprises continued to operate. Thus, as significant as the drop in manufacturing output from 1914 to 1916 was the fact that many firms, especially in the consumer goods sector, continued to function even during the worst phases of the fighting. Indeed, several firms consistently turned profits and paid dividends. CIDOSA paid hefty dividends throughout the Revolution, missing but one year (1916); La Tabacalera Mexicana paid dividends in all years except 1914, and San Ildefonso in every year except 1917; and the stockholders in El Buen Tono earned dividends in three of the six years of fighting (1912, 1914, and 1917).

Common to all of these profitable firms was the production of low-cost, consumer nondurables. Although the nation managed to get along without newsprint and steel, it still needed items of everyday necessity like cloth and cigarettes. Intermediate goods producers essentially shut down for the duration of the Revolution, but firms that produced mass-market consumer goods continued in operation, turned small profits, and paid dividends to their shareholders.

More important, the industrial sector as a whole recovered from the downturn quite rapidly. Because few of the nation's major manufacturing enterprises sustained severe physical damage during the course of the fighting, by 1917 the output of both producer and consumer goods began to climb at a brisk pace. Within a few years industrial output was once again at the level it had been prior to the Revolution. In the cotton textile industry, for example, all of the indices of economic activity indicate a fairly swift recovery. If we take the quantity of cotton consumed as a proxy for production, the data indicate that the volume of production in 1919 was the same as it had been in 1905. Similarly, series on the number of mills in operation, the number of spindles and looms in service, and the number of workers employed, also point to a rapid upturn after the crisis of 1914–16. By 1919, the nation's 110 active cotton factories were employing 735,308 spindles, 26,995 looms, and 32,815 workers, which was only slightly lower than the record levels for the Porfiriato (see Table 8.1, above). Sales data for the Cervecería Cuauhtemoc indicate a similar recovery in the beer industry, beginning in 1917. In 1920 the company had its second-best year ever, shipping close to 15 million liters of beer (see Table 8.2, above).

Even without production and sales figures for other consumer goods producers, the data on profits, dividends, and stock prices suggest that the experiences of the cotton textile industry and the Cervecería Cuauhtemoc were the norm. As Tables 8.4, 8.5, and 8.7, demonstrate, by 1920 the profits of consumer goods producers were fast approaching their Porfirian levels, and companies were once again paying substantial dividends to their shareholders. Both El Buen Tono and CIDOSA posted impressive profits within a few years of the end of the fighting. CIDOSA's rate of return on capital stock in 1920 and 1922 was 14 and 13 percent, respectively, which was about 4 percent higher than the firm's average for the Porfiriato. El Buen Tono's returns were even more impressive, achieving a rate of 12 percent in 1918, 21 percent in 1919, 16 percent in 1923, and 12 percent in 1924 (see Table 8.4, above).

Data on stock yields and dividend earnings indicate that the experience of these two companies was fairly typical. By 1920 almost all of the firms sampled were paying dividends again. The only exceptions among the consumer goods manufacturers were the Compañía Industrial de San Antonio Abad, which paid dividends in 1920 and 1921 but then failed to pay anything from 1922 to 1925, and the Compañía Cervecera de Toluca y México, which paid one dividend in 1921 but then never paid again.

In producer goods the recovery from the disaster of 1914–16 was almost equally rapid. In the cement industry, for example, annual output in 1918, 1919, and 1920 was in line with what it had been prior to the outbreak of hostilities. Though the recovery of steel production took a bit longer, Fundidora Monterrey's blast furnace was again at work by 1917. In 1918 output of pig iron was 21,000 tons, which was higher than in 1905, 1907, and 1908, though still lower than the average for the Porfiriato (see Table 8.3, above). With this revival of production Fundidora Monterrey finally started to make money, achieving rates of return that rose from 3 percent in 1918, to 9 percent in 1920 (see Table 8.4, above).

The revival of the physical apparatus of Mexican manufacturing was accompanied by the renewed political activity of the nation's industrialists. In November 1917, just after the promulgation of Mexico's new constitution, the nation's manufacturers called a national conference of industrialists in Mexico City. Realizing that the rules of the game were being rewritten by the new state taking shape, they joined together to defend their interests. There were basically three issues on their agenda. The first was to bring pressure on the post-revolutionary government to continue previous levels of tariff protection.[16] The second issue was to make it known to the government that the industrialists opposed articles 27 and 123 of the new constitution.[17] Article 27 reserved for the state the right to allocate land resources and subsoil rights, stating that "the nation shall at all times have the right to impose on private property such limitations as the public interest may demand."[18] Article 123 established the eight-hour workday, the six-day week, a minimum wage, and equal pay for equal work. It also gave labor the legal right to organize and to strike. Finally, the convention proposed to form regional industrial chambers, which could be used to bring pressure on the government to protect the interests of Mexico's industrialists, specifically monopolies and protective tariffs.[19]

It was therefore not the case, as many have assumed, that the industrial barons of the Porfiriato were run out of the country in 1910. In fact, leading the charge against the government at the 1917 conference was none other than Adolfo Prieto, the Asturiano financier, who had risen through the ranks at the Antonio Basagoiti operation to become one of the nation's leading industrialists of the Porfiriato. The other leaders of the conference were, like Prieto, large manufacturers whose origins were distinctly Porfirian. This was not, in any sense of the word, a new "authentic, national bourgeoisie" made up of small, Mexican-born industrialists. In fact, one of the first things that the leadership of the conference did was to diminish the power of small industrialists by not giving them their own group within the larger organization, putting them instead in with the catchall grouping "Miscellaneous Industries."[20] In short, not only did the nation's industrialists stay put during the Revolution, but they were already trying to influence government policy even before the fighting had stopped.

In an immediate physical sense, then, the Mexican Revolution had little effect on the manufacturing sector. Mexico's major manufacturing companies came through the fighting largely intact, and the entrepreneurs who had controlled these companies before the Revolution continued to do so. In fact, Mexican manufacturers made more money after the Revolution than ever before. Rates of return on capital stock, stock yields, and real returns to investors all jumped markedly during the period 1918–25. All the indices of profitability indicate that returns during this period were roughly twice what they had been during the Porfiriato. At the same time, output and capacity utilization were also climbing. As Tables 8.1, 8.2, and 8.3 indicate, the volume of production in the steel, cement, beer, and cotton textile industries were all increasing rapidly, with concomitant jumps in capacity-utilization rates.

The Revolution did, however, have a significant psychological effect on Mexico's industrialists, and this was harmful to the manufacturing sector over the medium term. Though the Revolution caused little real physical damage to Mexico's manufacturing plant, it did create a crisis of confidence among investors. It may have brought the northern bourgeoisie to power, but it forced them to compromise with other groups, notably organized labor. In fact, the alliance between the northern bourgeoisie and the urban working class helped defeat the peasantry. Even this victory was not a total one, however. The peasants of the center-south were still a factor that the new state had to take into account, despite their defeat on the battlefield. The new state had therefore to address the interests not only of the ascending capitalists of the north, but of the working class and peasantry as well. This complex series of alliances explains why the Mexican Constitution of 1917 both protects private property and takes it away from the old landed elite, why it both supports the rights of capital and strengthens the rights of the working class. Thus, though the old financier-industrialists of the Porfiriato and their enterprises were still very much in existence, they no longer controlled the reins of political power to the degree they had prior to the Revolution. Labor now played a larger role in the state, and this had a profound impact on the outlook of investors.

One of the characteristics of this crisis was a deceleration of investment in new plant and equipment. As Table 8.8 indicates, the adjusted book values of the physical plant category of capital stock for two of the three sample firms indicate that a process of disinvestment was under way during the early 1920's. In fact, the data on CIDOSA and El Buen Tono, the nation's largest cotton textile and cigarette producers, respectively, suggest that they were following a policy of running their already established plants into the ground. Disaggregated capital-stock figures for the two companies show that the book values of their physical plants were decreasing over time.[21] CIDOSA's physical plant value, for example, fell 16 percent from 11,544,394 pesos in 1920 to 9,653,661 pesos by 1924. A similar devaluation occurred in El

TABLE 8.8

Estimated Value of Physical Plant, Fundidora Monterrey,
CIDOSA, El Buen Tono, 1903–1925

(Current pesos)

Year	Fund Monterrey	CIDOSA	Buen Tono
1903	8,388,005	—	3,020,282
1904	9,235,571	—	3,588,333
1905	9,832,630	—	—
1906	10,032,228	—	—
1907	9,525,527	12,343,085	5,616,185
1908	9,081,831	16,003,944	6,063,705
1909	9,316,921	16,493,259	5,630,373
1910	9,364,689	16,145,026	5,200,000
1911	9,087,041	15,919,062	—
1912	9,336,536	15,562,002	—
1913	9,226,429	15,059,801	—
1914	8,989,250	14,557,600	—
1915	8,509,309	14,055,399	—
1916	8,160,556	13,553,198	—
1917	7,819,332	13,050,997	—
1918	7,829,935	12,548,796	7,138,226
1919	7,374,466	12,046,595	6,748,277
1920	9,133,171	11,544,394	—
1921	10,420,513	11,042,193	—
1922	10,217,106	10,539,992	—
1923	10,237,919	10,037,791	5,526,097
1924	10,340,039	9,653,661	5,624,739
1925	9,871,560	9,151,460	—

SOURCE: See Tables 7.1 and 8.4, above.
NOTE: All values in current pesos, calculated at cost minus depreciation. It is not possible to calculate real values without knowing the vintage of the equipment. For a discussion of the estimation procedure used, see Haber 1985: appendix A.

Buen Tono, where the physical plant, valued at 7,138,226 pesos in 1918 fell 21 percent to 5,624,739 by 1924. Thus, much of the increase in the rate of return on capital stock for CIDOSA and El Buen Tono can be attributed to a fall in the value of capital, not to an increase in net profits. Only in the case of Fundidora Monterrey does it appear that any new investment took place. The physical plant category of capital stock for this firm rose 41 percent between 1919 and 1921, from 7,374,466 pesos to 10,420,513 pesos. After 1921, however, the company put the brakes on new capital spending; the value of physical plant declined by 5 percent to 9,871,560 pesos by 1925.

Data from the federal tax register on the cotton textile industry indicate that the deceleration in new investment in plant and equipment was not confined to a few companies. The value of capital per active mill—measured at cost minus depreciation—decreased from 687,000 pesos in 1922 to 597,000 pesos by 1925, a drop of 13 percent in just four years. Even though the number of active mills had increased from 119 to 130, the total value of their physical plant had actually decreased from just under 81.8 million pesos in 1922 to 77.6 million pesos in 1925. As we will see in the following chapter, this decline in the value of capital stock continued into the early 1930's (see Table 8.1).

At the same time that many of the nation's older industries were being decapitalized, some new industries were being established. This new investment was not of the same magnitude as that of the closing years of the Porfiriato, but neither was it insignificant and it helped offset, to some degree, the decline in capital spending of the industries founded during the Porfiriato. Part of this new investment is attributable to U.S. manufacturing companies that were setting up plants in Mexico. Examples include Ford Motors, Du Pont de Nemours, and Palmolive. Some of these ventures were in new lines of activity, Ford Motors being a case in point, but were not as yet large in scale. Ford's plant, for example, was little more than a warehouse where a few mechanics bolted together knocked-down assembly kits. Other American investments in manufacturing simply took the place of already existing companies, Du Pont's acquisition of the old Compañía Nacional Mexicana de Dinamita y Explosivos works being an example. In any case, the big influx of foreign direct investment in manufacturing would not occur for another 30 years.

New domestically capitalized firms were also coming into existence at this time. Unlike the foreign corporations, however, they almost always competed in the same lines of activity as did the older, Porfirian companies. In fact, it was often the case that they merged with the older companies, thereby retaining the highly concentrated nature of the market. In the cement industry, for example, Cementos Monterrey was founded, but it soon merged with the old Cementos Hidalgo to create Cementos

Mexicanos. In the beer industry the Cervecería Modelo was established. Located in Mexico City, it drove the Compañía Cervecera de Toluca y México to the wall, eventually buying out the older, less efficient firm. In one case, that of cigarettes, the market did indeed become more competitive. In 1924 El Aguila, S.A., was founded, setting up a plant in Mexico City. The following year, it established a second plant in Irapuato, Guanajuato. Capitalized at 12.8 million pesos and utilizing newer, more efficient machinery than its Porfirian competitors, it soon came to dominate the market and threatened to drive El Buen Tono, La Cigarrera Mexicana, and La Tabacalera Mexicana out of business, a subject we will return to in the next chapter.

Another manifestation of the crisis of confidence in the investment community can be found in the behavior of the stock exchange. Both stock yields and the real financial returns to investors jumped markedly after the Revolution. During the period 1918–25 yields were more than double what they had been from 1896 to 1910, median stock yields increasing from 4.6 percent per annum to 9.4 percent (see Tables 7.3 and 8.6). Real financial returns to investors increased sixfold, jumping from an average of 3.0 percent annually during the period 1901–10 to 18.7 percent per annum from 1918 to 1925 (see Tables 7.6, above, and 8.9). This jump in returns was not a function of an increase in real dividend earnings. In fact, real dividends during the period 1919–25 were lower than during the 1902–10 period. The average annual real dividend paid per share, which was 26.45 pesos from 1902 to 1910, fell during the period 1919–25 to 18.44 pesos (see Tables 7.4, above, and 8.10).

The increase in both yields and financial returns was the product of the undervaluation of stocks because of the uncertainty created by the Revolution. The same psychological uncertainty that discouraged firms from reinvesting in new plant and equipment—thereby producing a slowdown in the rate of growth of capital stock—caused the real values of stocks to decrease. Between 1912 and 1918 the real values of shares held in the sample firms declined on average by 75 percent. The stock in some firms had even larger drops in real value. For example, the real value of shares in the San Rafael paper company in 1918 was only 15 percent of their 1912 value. The smallest decrease registered

TABLE 8.9

Real Return to Investors, 1918–1925

(1940 pesos)

Company name[a]	1918 stock price	Capital gain[b]	Total dividends 1919–25	Total return[c]	Annual rate of return[d]
San Ildef	23	29	36	65	21.1%
Buen Tono	235	370	359	729	22.3
San Raf	34	58	49	107	22.5
CIDOSA	167	183	275	458	20.7
Jabon	184	165[e]	271[f]	436	22.4[g]
Cig Mex	32	71[h]	70	141	27.3
Toluca-México	47	−28	5	−23	−9.1
Atlixco	23	44	31	75	23.0
CIVSA	96	118	158	276	21.4
Fund Mont	28	11	5	16	6.7
S.A. Abad	31	11	27	38	12.1
Cerv Moct	100	248	225	473	28.3
Tab Mex	67	147	105	252	25.0
Average real rate of return to portfolio[i]					18.7

SOURCES: Derived from *BFM*, 1916–26.

[a]For full names of companies, see note to Table 7.2.

[b]Real difference in average stock price, 1918–25.

[c]Total real dividends plus real capital gains.

[d]Implicit compound rate of return from 1918–25.

[e]Real difference in average stock price 1918–24.

[f]Real dividends, 1919–24.

[g]Compound rate of return over six-year period 1919–24.

[h]1919 stock price.

[i]Assumes equal distribution of investors' resources among all stocks within the portfolio in 1918.

was that of the San Antonio Abad textile company; the real market price of a share of its stock fell from 83 pesos in 1912 to 31 pesos in 1918 (both in 1940 pesos), a decline of 63 percent. At no time during the period 1918–25 did the real market price of the stock in any of the sample firms come close to regaining its pre-revolutionary value. Even with the rally in stock prices that occurred after 1918, these stocks still traded in 1925 for roughly half their 1912 values.[22]

Indeed, an analysis of the ratio of capital-stock market values to book values for the three companies for which it was possible to put together reliable capital-stock series indicates that investors were extremely wary of investing in manufacturing after the

TABLE 8.10

Real Dividend Earnings, Selected Manufacturing Companies, 1911–1925

(Earnings per share, 1940 pesos)

Year	Buen Tono	San Ildef	CIDOSA	S.A. Abad	Atlixco	CIVSA
1911	918	91	639	96	138	370
1912	1,021	78	567	83	138	368
1913	—	—	—	—	—	—
1914	—	—	—	—	—	—
1915	—	—	—	—	—	—
1916	—	—	—	—	—	—
1917	—	—	—	—	—	—
1918	235	23	167	31	23	96
1919	323	39	280	59	51	214
1920	329	37	282	49	43	202
1921	380	41	287	39	44	189
1922	495	52	418	39	52	247
1923	488	55	444	40	45	255
1924	568	55	412	44	56	238
1925	605	52	350	42	67	214

Year	Jabon	San Raf	Fund Mont	Toluca México	Cig Mex	Cerv Moct	Tab Mex
1911	837	225	141	402	199	484	—
1912	884	226	112	301	165	332	—
1913	—	—	—	—	—	—	—
1914	—	—	—	—	—	—	—
1915	—	—	—	—	—	—	—
1916	—	—	—	—	—	—	—
1917	—	—	—	—	—	—	—
1918	184	34	28	47	—	100	67
1919	293	58	35	83	32	268	108
1920	333	58	47	52	36	—	116
1921	342	68	41	55	38	—	130
1922	364	100	44	41	61	400	182
1923	362	88	34	29	77	423	208
1924	349[a]	78	36	25	83	403	212
1925	—	92	39	19	103	348	214

SOURCES: Calculated from *EM*, 1910–14; *BFM*, 1916–26.

NOTE: For full names of companies, see Table 7.2 above; "Tab Mex," La Tabacalera Mexicana. Data adjusted to account for stock splits and stock dividends and deflated using index of implicit prices developed in Haber 1985: appendix B. No data available for 1913–17 because of lack of price deflator.

[a] Company put into liquidation by stockholders.

Revolution. This ratio measures the degree to which the investors under- or overvalue the capital stock of a company. This ratio is based on and is similar to Tobin's q. It differs from Tobin's q in that it measures book value at cost minus depreciation, not at replacement cost, which for historical data is not generally possible since firms almost never valued their assets at replacement cost in their financial statements. Indeed, most uses of Tobin's q by historians have measured book value in the way that I have here. Theoretically, when the ratio is higher than 1, firms will issue new stock and make new expenditures on capital stock, since they will receive greater income from the issue of new shares than the actual price of the additions to capital stock. When the ratio is less than 1, firms will not invest, since the income from new stock issues would be less than the cost of additions to capital stock. Since there are obvious problems with measuring book values and market values of capital stock, and since the capital market in Mexico was extremely thin, our concern here is not what the ratio was in any particular year, but how this ratio changed over time. For this reason, in Table 8.11 I have reduced the ratios to an index with 1907 equal to 100 in order to chart how investors changed their perceptions of the value of their assets from the Porfiriato to the post-revolutionary period.

The data for all three companies indicate that after the Revolution investors perceived that manufacturing was not a desirable investment. As Table 8.11 shows, the market value / book value ratio for all three companies dropped by roughly one-half between the end of the Porfiriato and the early 1920's. In other words, after the Revolution investors radically reassessed how much they valued their investments in manufacturing companies, seriously undervaluing their assets compared to the prerevolutionary period. This explains why stock yields were so high. Investors perceived that the market was extremely risky, which partially explains why they undervalued their investments. They therefore demanded a risk premium in order to keep their money in Mexico. Similarly, the real returns to investors were high because the uncertainty created by the Revolution had bid stock prices down so low by 1918 that any increase

TABLE 8.11

Capital Stock, Ratio of Market to Book Values,
Fundidora Monterrey, CIDOSA, El Buen Tono, 1902–1925

(1907 = 100)

Year	Fund Mont	CIDOSA	Buen Tono
1902	—	—	68
1903	115	—	72
1904	106	—	62
1905	131	—	102
1906	134	—	98
1907	100	100	100
1908	101	80	87
1909	97	80	85
1910	127	66	94
1911	96	60	—
1912	79	56	—
1913	76	—	—
1914	72	—	—
1915	—	—	—
1916	—	—	—
1917	—	—	—
1918	49	—	41
1919	49	—	50
1920	57	53	—
1921	42	—	—
1922	36	62	—
1923	28	—	46
1924	28	64	52
1925	33	56	—

SOURCES: Market values calculated from *EM*, 1902–14; *BFM*, 1918–25; book values from same sources as Tables 7.1 and 8.4.

NOTE: Book value equals capital stock (physical plant, land, inventories, cash assets) minus depreciation. Market value equals market price of stock, adjusted for splits and stock dividends, multiplied by number of shares. Ratio calculated by dividing market value by book value. This ratio then reduced to an index with the 1907 value equal to 100. The data presented here indicate the relative degree of change over time for each company, not the differences in the absolute ratio between individual companies in any particular year.

in real stock prices or real dividends afterward resulted in extremely high rates of return.

If profits were increasing after the Revolution and if these profits were not being pumped back into the system in the form of new investment, where did they go? Without an analysis of the investment portfolios of Mexico's major financiers of this period, it is not possible to provide a conclusive answer to this question. However, it may have been that these profits, after being paid out as dividends, left the country. Some evidence for this supposition exists. In 1927 Joseph Sterrett and Joseph Davis hinted at problems of capital flight in their report to the International Committee of Bankers, which was established to oversee the repayment of Mexico's foreign debt. In a tone of understatement reserved only for bankers, they noted that the low level of deposits in Mexican banks was due in large part "to a tendency, on the part of many concerns, to keep deposit accounts abroad rather than in Mexico because of the fluctuations in currency and exchange and fear of untoward developments of various kinds."[23] It may well have been that the 1920's marked a period of capital flight. This would certainly have been consistent with the low level of confidence among Mexican investors and would have made a great deal of sense, given the possibilities that existed in the New York Stock Exchange during this period. Conclusive proof, however, must await further research.

What is clear, however, is that the untoward events that Sterrett and Davis hinted at were just around the corner. From 1926 to 1932 the Mexican economy went into a tailspin. Why that occurred, and how it affected the manufacturing sector, is the subject of our next chapter.

NINE

The Crash, 1926-1932

FOR ENTREPRENEURS who were wary about undertaking new investments in the early 1920's, the developments of the latter part of the decade bore out their pessimism. From 1926 to 1932, demand fell, output declined, profits disappeared, and new investment slowed dramatically. This general economic contraction had adverse consequences for the industrial sector. Consumer demand, as noted previously, was already perilously low and served as a bottleneck to the development of a strong market for manufactured goods. Now, with the economic downturn, demand fell further. Firms had to cut back production, lay off workers, and suffer considerable losses. Of the large firms under consideration in this study, almost all were hit hard by the downturn of 1926-32. Some were forced into financial restructuring. Smaller enterprises were doubtless forced to the wall as well.

Several forces were driving the contraction of the economy—some of them internal to Mexico, some international and beyond Mexico's control. Internally, political conflict and the organization of the Mexican working class further decreased the confidence of investors, thereby discouraging new investment. Externally, the export sector, long the motor of Mexican economic growth, began to contract under the combined weight of a fall in export prices and the movement out of Mexico of the foreign companies that controlled the oil industry.

Within Mexico, the changes brought by the Revolution began to play themselves out: foreign investors became wary of changes in the laws regarding the ownership of the nation's subsoil rights; the peasantry, not victorious in the Revolution but not totally defeated either, stepped up its demands for agrarian reform; and the liberal-bourgeois interests that controlled the Mexican state escalated their long-standing feud with the Catholic church, which boiled over into a full-scale war between church and state, the Cristero War of 1926–29. At the same time, the Mexican working class continued to organize, with union membership growing to over one million by 1928. This in turn drove up wages, further pressuring already shaky enterprises. In the cotton textile industry, to cite but one example, the nominal wages of male workers rose by 34 percent between 1925 and 1929. Because of falling prices, real wages increased even faster, rising by 43 percent over the four-year period.[1]

None of these conflicts, with the possible exception of the debate over subsoil rights, seriously slowed the pace of economic growth. Labor, though increasingly organized, was controlled by the government through the corrupt Confederación Regional de Obreros Mexicanos. It could obtain wage increases, force employers to comply with the eight-hour day, and engage in militant rhetoric; but it was not a threat to Mexican capitalism. The wage increases threatened profits, but they did not threaten the owners of capital as a class. In addition, the wage increases were confined to a small group of organized workers; most workers remained non-unionized, and therefore their incomes probably did not grow. In addition, the rise in workers' incomes would not necessarily have had negative effects on the growth of the economy as a whole, since rising wages would have pushed up aggregate demand. In rural Mexico a similar situation prevailed; the peasantry was clamoring for land redistribution, but had not succeeded in accomplishing its goal. The large-scale restructuring of land tenure would not occur until the mid-1930's. The Cristero Rebellion, though a drain on government resources, never spread beyond the area centered around the states of Jalisco, Colima, and Michoacán; it was never a serious threat to the government in Mexico City, nor did it disrupt the functioning of the national economy in any significant way.

The major effect, then, of internal developments during the 1920's was to increase the sense of uneasiness and lack of confidence that had been prevalent among the industrialist class since 1917. A stable government, accepted as legitimate, that could effectively mediate the demands of industrialists and workers, landowners and peasants, had yet to be established. It was not entirely clear in which direction the country was heading, nor was it certain that the country would not be plunged into yet another round of revolution.

In only one area of the economy did political events contribute in a major way to slowing the rate of economic growth. The debate over ownership of the nation's mineral and petroleum wealth—whether that resource was part of the national patrimony, as the Constitution of 1917 claimed, or belonged to the largely foreign companies that held title to the land that lay over it, which was the interpretation of the mining and mineral code enacted during the Porfiriato—had a good deal to do with the petroleum companies' shifting their operations out of Mexico. It should be kept in mind, however, that market-oriented factors were at work as well in that decision, including the discovery of easily tapped oil deposits in Venezuela and rising production costs in Mexico. The end result was that Mexican oil output dropped sharply during the 1920's: from a high point of 182 million barrels in 1922, to 140 million in 1925. The drop accelerated thereafter, since no new exploration took place and the existing wells became played out, with output falling to 90 million barrels in 1926, 64 million barrels in 1927, and 50 million barrels in 1928. In 1932 Mexico produced only 33 million barrels of oil—a mere 18 percent of the amount produced in 1922.[2]

The contraction in the export sector was not confined to the oil industry. At the same time that oil output was declining, revenues from silver and other metals also dropped. During the latter half of the 1920's primary-product producers all over the world saw the terms of the trade swing against them: they now faced a buyer's market for the commodities they produced. Prices of agricultural products and minerals began to slip after 1925, when renewed European production after the First World War was added to expanded wartime production outside of Europe.[3] Beginning in 1926, the prices of Mexico's major mineral exports began to decline sharply. The price of silver, for example, fell from 80 cents (U.S.) per ounce in 1926 to 62 cents in 1927. The prices of copper, lead, and zinc, Mexico's other major mineral exports, fell in roughly equal proportions to the drop in the price of silver.[4]

The drop in prices and output in petroleum and mining caused a major contraction in export revenues, since these two goods accounted for 70 percent of the nation's exports.[5] In 1926 Mexico exported some $334 million worth of goods. By 1928, this had shrunk to $299 million, a decline of 10 percent in just two years. The contraction continued, with export earnings falling to $275 million in 1929. Between 1929 and 1932 export earnings plunged by a whopping 29 percent per year. At the depth of the crisis in 1932, total export revenues amounted to only $97 million, less than a third of their level just six years earlier.[6] The drop was not compensated for by decreases in import prices. Indeed, not only did the volume of exports decline by 37 percent between 1929 and 1932, but the terms of trade deteriorated by 21 percent as well. Thus, the purchasing power of Mexico's exports fell by over 50 percent in just three years.[7]

Exactly how much this contraction of the export sector harmed employment is difficult to judge, since the data are unreliable and cover only urban areas. If we use the available figures to measure the magnitude of change rather than absolute amounts, they indicate that the number of unemployed workers tripled between 1930 and 1932.[8] In the cotton textile industry, to cite a specific example, employment fell by 24 percent between 1926 and 1932, the greater part of this decline occurring after 1929.[9] The increase in unemployment caused by the external shock was aggravated by another shock from abroad: the deportation of Mexican workers living in the United States. One reaction in the United States to the Depression was to blame foreign workers for the high levels of unemployment—a refrain still heard today. The response of the Hoover administration, never noted for its compassion or sense of equity, was to expel over 310,000 Mexicans between 1930 and 1933. These deported workers swelled the ranks of an already underemployed work force by an additional 6 percent.[10]

Assessing the effect of this increase in unemployment on consumer demand is difficult, since reliable, nationwide statistics on incomes and employment are lacking. However, data from the cotton textile industry indicate that, at least for some workers, real wages did not decline during the Depression. In the cotton goods industry, male workers who had been able to hang on to their jobs actually saw their real incomes increase by 28 percent between 1926 and 1929, and by 15 percent between 1929 and 1932.[11] As was the case in the United States during the Great Depression, decreases in the price level outstripped the decline in nominal wages, thereby raising the purchasing power of workers fortunate enough still to have a job. This rise in real wages would have offset to some extent the decline in consumer demand brought about by declining employment levels.

The decline of the export sector also had significant fiscal effects that served to push down aggregate demand still further. During the early 1920's, fully one-third of all government revenues came from production and export taxes on oil, bringing in 86 million pesos in 1922. By 1927, with the contraction of oil output, petroleum revenues were down to 19 million pesos and accounted for only 12 percent of total revenues.[12] Disaggregated figures on petroleum's share of federal revenues are not available after 1927, but aggregate data on tax revenues from natural-resource production and exportation, most of which was oil and silver, indicate that they continued declining. In 1925, total taxes on raw-materials production totaled 57 million pesos, or 17.7 percent of government revenues. By 1929 they had fallen to 30 million pesos (9.3 percent of fiscal revenues), and by 1932 stood at only 15 million pesos, which accounted for only 7 percent of government income. Overall, total federal revenues fell throughout the period, from a high of 322 million pesos in 1925 to 307 million pesos in 1927, 289 million pesos in 1930, and 212 million pesos in 1932.[13]

The government's reaction to this decline in revenues made the crisis even more severe. Its pro-cyclical policies during the crisis further decreased aggregate demand and exacerbated an already grave situation.[14] In terms of fiscal policy, the economic planners in the Mexican Ministry of the Treasury were convinced, as were governments everywhere at the time, that it had to run a balanced budget. Thus, government expenditures fell along with government revenues. In fact, even though revenues were declining, the government ran large surpluses each year from 1928 to 1931, with a whopping 14 percent surplus in 1929.[15]

Because the government was committed to maintaining a balanced budget, it was forced to cut expenditures and raise taxes. The country was in no condition to attract new foreign loans— in fact, Mexico's international creditors were already pressuring the government to make good on previous loans on which it had defaulted—and it was not possible simply to run the printing presses and issue additional currency because the Mexican public was unwilling to accept Banco de México notes.[16] Thus, the government responded to the falling revenues by raising taxes, reducing the wages of government workers, and laying off public employees. These measures only exacerbated the contraction of the economy by further decreasing aggregate demand.

In terms of monetary policy the story was much the same: the government's goal was to maintain a fixed exchange rate, and this served to heighten booms and busts in the economy. Whenever the nation's balance of payments was in an unfavorable position, gold flowed out of the country, thereby causing a decrease in the money supply. As a result, a depreciation of the peso occurred, creating in effect a de facto exchange rate system, and the national monetary authorities then propped up the old fixed exchange system by minting less currency and decreasing the money supply even further. The result, therefore, of a pressured balance of payments situation was that the government reduced the money supply in order to shore up the international price of the peso, which in turn only served to depress the means of payment and reduce the level of aggregate demand.[17] This only added fuel to the fire. In 1926, for example, the treasury minted 29.4 million pesos of silver coin and 30 million pesos of gold. The following year, in response to the threat on the peso, it minted only 5.6 million pesos in silver, holding gold coinage relatively stable at 30.3 million. This contractionary monetary policy continued into 1928, when the government minted only 1.3 million pesos worth of silver and 26.9 million pesos in gold. After 1929 these policies became even more draconian. Indeed between 1929 and 1931, when the Mexican government demonetized gold, the combined effect of the outflow of gold coin to cover trade deficits and the deliberate attempt by the treasury to decrease the money supply produced a real drop of 54 percent in the monetary base.[18]

The overall effect of this contraction in export earnings, government spending, and the monetary base was a fairly strong depression. Though the estimates are rough, the available data indicate that real per capita Gross Domestic Product fell by 5.9 percent in 1927, 0.9 percent in 1928, 5.4 percent in 1929, and 7.7 percent in 1930. In 1931 real GDP per capita grew by 1.5 percent, but the recovery was not long lasting. The following year GDP fell by an incredible 16 percent, so that over the six-year period 1926–32, real GDP per capita fell 30.9 percent.[19]

The effect of this general economic contraction on the manufacturing sector was mixed. In general, it was exactly the opposite of what had happened during the Revolution: the manufacturers of consumer goods were hardest hit, while the manufacturers of producer goods did relatively well. This is not the common pattern during depressions. Producer goods industries usually suffer more than consumer goods industries because spending by final goods producers on inventories and equipment almost totally ceases, yet consumer demand is still sufficient to keep the consumer goods industries operating.

In Mexico the pattern was reversed, for two reasons. First, with the exceptions of the newsprint and bottle industries, the nation's intermediate goods producers were not well articulated with the consumer goods industries (see Chapter 4, above). In addition, no capital goods industries existed. Thus, a deceleration in orders for new plant and equipment had an adverse effect on foreign machinery companies, not on other Mexican firms. Second, government spending on refurbishing the Porfirian rail system and the construction of a highway system puffed up the demand for construction materials, primarily steel and cement. Consumer goods producers, on the other hand, were hit hard by the crisis, as incomes and employment declined along with the rest of the economy.

Hardest hit was the cotton textile industry. As consumer demand fell with the crisis, so did the ability of the working class to purchase cotton cloth. Sales, output, and profits fell precipitously. As Table 9.1 shows, revenues from cotton cloth sales

dropped off dramatically between 1925 and 1932: a total of 30 percent. During the early years of the crisis, it is interesting to note,
the drop in sales revenue was not accompanied by a major decrease in output. Taking the amount of raw cotton consumed by
the industry as a proxy for production, the data in Table 9.1 do
not indicate a significant change in output between 1925 and
1930, nor is there evidence of change in the number of factories
in operation or the number of active spindles and looms. To
some extent this could have been caused by a decrease in cloth
prices, which would have resulted from a general fall in prices.
More important in explaining the divergence in output and sales
revenues was that factories could shut down only if the Secretaría de Industria, Comercio, y Trabajo permitted them to do so.
Beginning in 1926 textile manufacturers asked permission, but
the government refused to grant it, forcing them either to stay
open or to pay a required three-months' severance pay to the
dismissed workers. In the states of Puebla and Tlaxcala, where
the nation's oldest and least efficient mills were located, industrialists tried to get government permission to close down in
order to sell their stockpiled inventories. Instead of granting
their request, however, President Calles, as arbitrator, ordered
the owners to operate the mills by turn, each mill to run 24 hours
per week for four months, thereby protecting the jobs of the
workers.[20] By March 1928 Mexico's mills had a nine-months'
supply of product in their warehouses, and many factories were
selling off stock below their costs of production.[21] The end result
was that while the mills stayed open and the workers and machinery continued to be active, Mexico's textile factories were
simply worked less intensively. Raw cotton consumption—a
proxy for the volume of output—per mill fell substantially, from
315 tons in 1925 to 272 tons in 1929. At the same time, the number of workers, looms, and spindles per mill all decreased even
though the number of operating mills did not fall. As machinery
wore out or workers retired or quit, they were not replaced.
Thus, in 1925 the average mill employed 336 workers, 239 looms,
and 6,454 spindles. By 1929 this had fallen to 273 workers, 208
looms, and 5,787 spindles (see Table 9.1).

From the point of view of the textile-mill owners the situation
was made even more severe by the 10 to 25 percent increase in

TABLE 9.1
Cotton Textile Industry, Main Economic Indicators, 1925–1932

Fiscal year	Oper- ating mills	Active spindles	Active looms	Workers	Cotton (metric tons)	Sales (000 current pesos)	Capital (000 current pesos)[a]
1925	130	838,987	31,094	43,728	40,997	108,419	77,568
1926	138	842,793	31,296	43,776	41,522	95,438	77,260[b]
1927	144	821,211	30,437	41,238	41,170	91,069	77,122
1928	—	—	—	—	39,356	96,400	76,500[c]
1929	145	839,109	30,191	39,515	39,437	97,162	75,905
1930	—	845,607	30,820	38,988	40,585	91,145	76,396[c]
1931	143	840,498	30,732	36,247	34,627	74,244	66,098
1932	137	832,386	30,056	33,474	34,434	75,977	63,345

sources: Derived from Sterrett and Davis 1928: 105; *Mexico* [54]; de la Peña 1938: 7; *BFM*, 22 June 1933, p. 1; *Mexico* [30]: 14.
    note: See notes for Table 8.1, above.
    [a] Accumulated capital investment in physical plant, valued at cost minus depreciation at year-end.
    [b] At end of first semester.
    [c] Includes knitting mills.

wages granted to the textile workers in a government-arbitrated agreement in December 1926. Many of the owners, especially those from Puebla and Tlaxcala, refused to pay the increase, claiming that they were already losing money. The government responded in defense of the workers in January 1927 by decreeing that companies not complying with the new wage rates were required to pay a higher production tax than those who were paying the new rates.[22] Even an increase in import duties, which were already among the highest in the world, failed to turn the situation around for the industry.

By mid-1931, forcing the mills to stay open was no longer a tenable strategy as factory owners began to threaten to dissolve their companies and declare bankruptcy unless workers agreed to a cut in pay and a temporary shortening of the work-week. This was even the case with a firm as large and powerful as CIDOSA, which in 1931 called a special meeting of the stockholders to decide whether to dissolve the company, given the crisis faced by the firm. As it was, even with a reduced work-week of 36 hours, the firm was losing money. In the end, the workers agreed to a cut in pay and a shutdown of three months.

The pay cut was sizable, with a reduction of from 11 to 20 percent depending on the salary paid prior to the crisis. In general, workers who earned the highest wages suffered the biggest cuts. In addition, the union also agreed to a reduction in the size of the work force by approximately 5 percent, allowing 304 workers to be laid off permanently—the company had originally asked for 430 positions to be eliminated. While the factory was shut down, the workers received 25 percent of their salaries, based on the 36-hour weekly pay. In exchange the company agreed that when work started again the work-week would gradually increase from 27 hours to 48 hours, depending on the amount of product contained in the company's warehouses.[23]

Similar reductions in the size of the work force and the rate of pay were agreed to by the workers in other enterprises.[24] Overall, employers were able to cut their wage costs and reduce the size of the work force dramatically by the end of 1932. Given the permits to shut down and to reduce the size of the work force, the number of active cotton textile factories at the end of 1932 dropped to 137 from 143 a year earlier. At the same time the number of workers was reduced by 8 percent between 1931 and 1932 (see Table 9.1, above).

Data on profits, dividends, and real stock prices mirror the trend seen in the data on output, physical plant, and the work force. Rate of return on capital stock estimates for CIDOSA, the nation's largest producer, indicate that from 1926 to 1929 the firm more or less broke even, losing money in 1926, making slight profits in 1927 and 1928, and breaking even in 1929. From 1930 to 1932 its losses were sizable, equaling 8 percent of capital stock in 1930, 13 percent in 1931, and 2 percent in 1932. Over the three-year period, total losses equaled 21 percent of capital stock (see Table 9.2). Dividend payments had ceased in 1927, and with their disappearance real stock values plummeted from 350 pesos in 1925 to 91 pesos by 1932 (both in 1940 pesos).[25] Dividend and yield data on other textile companies reveal a similar trend. Of the four cotton textile companies on which it was possible to gather data (CIDOSA, CIVSA, San Antonio Abad, and Compañía Industrial de Atlixco), only CIVSA managed to pay fairly regular dividends after 1925. The others either ceased paying dividends entirely or paid on an extremely irregular basis (see

TABLE 9.2

Estimated Rates of Return on Capital Stock, 1926–1932

(Current pesos)

Year	Capital stock	Profit	Rate of return
Fundidora Monterrey			
1926	14,882,534	438,294	3
1927	13,945,042	128,448	1
1928	13,692,659	237,996	2
1929	13,786,911	1,070,699	8
1930	13,935,995	1,627,102	12
1931	13,902,485	−243,568	−2
1932	12,328,097	25,907	0
El Buen Tono			
1928	9,080,603	−887,959	−10
1929	8,301,180	−964,745	−12
1930	7,937,352	−1,060,745	−13
1931	7,682,468	−106,429	−1
1932	8,788,227	−304,459	−3
CIDOSA			
1926	17,600,000[a]	−882,074	−5
1927	18,200,000[a]	671,546	4
1928	18,832,726	586,812	3
1929	19,234,506	−47,597	0
1930	17,566,592	−1,327,600	−8
1931	16,500,000[b]	−2,149,589	−13
1932	15,500,000[b]	−326,466	−2

SOURCES: Estimates for Fundidora Monterrey calculated from *FMIA*, 1926–33. For El Buen Tono, *BFM*, 4 Sept. 1926, p. 1, 29 Mar. 1927, p. 1, 19 Apr. 1929, p. 1, 7 June 1929, p. 1, 3 Apr. 1930, p. 1, 16 June 1931, p. 1, 17 June 1932, p. 1, 1 July 1933, p. 1. For CIDOSA, *BFM*, 28 Mar. 1925, p. 1, 29 Mar. 1927, p. 1, 1 Apr. 1927, p. 1, 26 June 1928, p. 1, 1 July 1929, p. 1, 2 July 1929, p. 1, 24 June 1930, p. 1, 10 Nov. 1931, p. 1, 12 Nov. 1931, p. 2, 24 Nov. 1931, p. 1, 1 July 1932, p. 1, 2 July 1932, p. 8.

NOTE: For a complete discussion of how profits, capital stock, and the rate of return on capital were calculated and a discussion of the method employed in the adjustment of the raw data, see Haber 1985: appendix A.

[a]Estimates calculated from 1924 and 1928 data. Estimates assume that capital stock grew proportionately from 1924 to 1928.

[b]Estimates calculated from 1930 and 1934 data. Estimates assume that capital stock shrank proportionately from 1930 to 1934.

Table 9.3). The price of their stock went in the same direction as CIDOSA's: down. Between 1925 and 1932 the real price of shares in San Antonio Abad fell by 10 percent, in CIVSA by 56 percent, and in Atlixco by 73 percent.[26] Stock price and dividend data on the nation's largest wool textile producer indicate a similar situation. For the period 1926–32 the Compañía Industrial de San Il-defonso paid dividends only in 1929 and 1930. The real price of its stock fell from 52 pesos per share in 1925 to 38 pesos in 1932, a drop of 27 percent.[27]

Data on the cigarette industry indicate that the situation was much the same as in cotton textiles. Data on the work force, for example, point to a substantial drop in employment in 1927. In the entire tobacco industry, which would also include the nation's hundreds of small cigar producers, the number of workers declined by some 8 percent, from 5,501 in 1926 to 5,051 in 1927.[28] No data are available for 1928, but by the end of 1929 employment had fallen an additional 7 percent, to 4,689 workers.[29]

Financial data from El Buen Tono, La Cigarrera Mexicana, and La Tabacalera Mexicana likewise point to a major downturn in the industry. Estimates of the rate of return on capital stock for the largest of the three, El Buen Tono, indicate losses over the five years 1928–32 equal to 39 percent of the value of its capital stock (see Table 9.2). These losses were so large that they forced

TABLE 9.3
Real Dividend Earnings, Selected Manufacturing Companies, 1926–1932
(Earnings per share, 1940 pesos)

Year	Buen Tono	San Ildef	CIDOSA	S.A. Abad	Atlixco	CIVSA
1926	45	0	20	0	0	14
1927	22	0	0	0	8	0
1928	0	0	0	0	0	14
1929	0	4	0	0	0	13
1930	0	5	0	0	0	11
1931	0	0	0	0	0	0
1932	0	0	0	0	0	0

Year	Jabon[a]	San Raf	Fund Mont	Toluca-México	Cig Mex	Cerv Moct	Tab Mex
1926	—	9	0	0	13	15	0
1927	—	9	3	0	5	0	0
1928	—	9	3	0	7	0	0
1929	—	8	7	0	3	0	0
1930	—	3	1	0	0	21	0
1931	—	7	3	0	0	18	0
1932	—	0	3	0	0	0	0

SOURCES: Calculated from *BFM*, 1925–1933.

NOTE: For full names of companies, see Table 7.2, above; "Tab Mex," La Tabacalera Mexicana. Data adjusted to account for stock splits and stock dividends and deflated using index of implicit prices developed in Haber 1985: appendix B.

[a]Company put into liquidation by stockholders in 1924.

the company's accountants to resort to some creative bookkeeping, inventing an item in the financial statement called "negative reserve account," instead of deducting the losses from the value of paid-in capital, which would have alarmed the stockholders.

Dividend and yield data tell much the same story. El Buen Tono's quite healthy dividends during the early part of the 1920's fell precipitously after 1926. From 1928 to 1932 it paid no dividends at all to its shareholders. Similarly, La Tabacalera Mexicana failed to pay out any profits to its shareholders from 1926 to 1932, indicating that at best it was only breaking even, and La Cigarrera Mexicana, which was 50 percent owned by El Buen Tono, managed to pay only small dividends in the years 1926–29, but then failed to pay anything to its shareholders in the next three years (see Table 9.3). Accompanying the disappearance of dividends was a steady and dramatic decline in stock prices. The real (1940) price of stock in El Buen Tono fell nearly 80 percent between 1925 and 1929: from 605 pesos per share to 129 pesos. By 1932 the value of its shares had fallen to 56 pesos, less than 10 percent of its 1925 value. Similar declines occurred in the stock price of La Cigarrera Mexicana and La Tabacalera Mexicana. A share of Cigarrera Mexicana stock traded for 103 pesos in 1925, but was worth only 12 pesos by 1932. La Tabacalera Mexicana's real stock price declined by over 75 percent during the same period, falling from 214 to 50 pesos per share.[30]

Driving the decline in profitability and investor confidence in these three major producers was a new entrant to the market, El Aguila, S.A. Founded in 1924 with a total paid-in capital of 12.8 million pesos and production facilities both in Mexico City and Irapuato, Guanajuato, El Aguila dwarfed its Porfirian rivals. It had the further advantage of employing more-modern machinery than did its older competitors.[31] Thus, by 1932 it was the undisputed leader of the market, garnering 64 percent of the nation's total output of 536 million packs of cigarettes. Its nearest competitor was the El Buen Tono–La Cigarrera Mexicana combination, which now controlled only 8 percent of the market, compared with nearly 50 percent during the Porfiriato. La Tabacalera Mexicana, which had taken roughly 12 percent of the market prior to the Revolution, now captured less than 2 percent. Eighty-five other producers spread throughout the nation divided up the remainder of the market.[32]

The new industry leader, however, had major problems of its own. Its owners doubtless counted on an expanding market for their product. They therefore did what their Porfirian competitors had done in their time; they erected far larger production facilities than required to satisfy the market. The market did indeed grow, increasing from 380 million packs consumed in 1924 to 580 million packs in 1929, falling slightly during the depths of the Depression to 536 million packs in 1932.[33] But even this increase was nowhere near sufficient to accommodate El Aguila's capacity to produce 925 million packs in its two facilities. Even had the firm captured 100 percent of the market, it still would have run at only 60 percent of capacity. In fact, it ran way below this, in 1930 managing to utilize only 33 percent of its installed capacity, and in 1932 only 37 percent.[34] It is therefore unlikely that El Aguila was more profitable than El Buen Tono, La Cigarrera Mexicana, or La Tabacalera Mexicana. Low levels of capacity utilization, coupled with high fixed capital costs, doubtless resulted in high unit costs of production and low profit margins.

The beer industry was also hit hard by the latter part of the Depression. As Table 9.4 indicates, total annual production actually grew by more than one-third between 1924 and 1930. Out-

TABLE 9.4
Beer Production, National and Cervecería Cuauhtemoc,
1924–1932
(000 liters)

Year	National production	Cuauhtemoc sales[a]	Cuauhtemoc market share
1924	52,003	11,564	22.2%
1925	53,673	15,736	29.3
1926	67,925	21,521	31.7
1927	71,613	23,201	32.4
1928	67,911	22,229	32.7
1929	71,973	23,174	32.2
1930	72,065	21,760	30.2
1931	54,711	18,894	34.5
1932	42,470	14,367	33.8

SOURCES: *Mexico* [12]: 958; Cervecería Cuauhtemoc, unpublished sales data.

[a]Used as proxy for annual production under the reasonable assumption that in the beer industry annual production and annual sales are almost identical, owing to the perishability of the product.

put data from the Cervecería Cuauhtemoc, which controlled just over 30 percent of the market, point to a similar jump; its sales doubled between 1924 and 1930. Beginning in 1930, however, the drop in personal incomes forced a serious decline in demand, and by 1932 beer output had fallen below its 1924 level. Total national production dropped from 72 million liters in 1930 to 42 million liters in 1932, while Cuauhtemoc's output decreased from 22 million liters to 14 million.

As was the case in the cigarette industry, an increase in beer output during the latter half of the 1920's did not necessarily correlate with healthy profits for all of the nation's leading firms. Data on dividends and yields for two of the nation's major producers—at this point there were four—indicate that a major shakeup was occurring in the industry with the entry in the early 1920's of two new competitors in the Mexico City market, the Cervecería Modelo and the Cervecería Central, a subsidiary of the Cervecería Cuauhtemoc. The Compañía Cervecera de Toluca y México, the nation's oldest major brewery, which had paid no dividends at all between 1926 and 1929, never paid a dividend again and was bought out by the Cervecería Modelo in 1935. The Cervecería Moctezuma, the Orizaba-based giant, also failed to pay dividends during the 1927–29 period. It then paid dividends in 1930 and 1931, but nothing in 1932 (see Table 9.3, above).

Along with the decrease in dividends came a concomitant drop in real stock prices. Common shares in the Cervecería Moctezuma, which traded for 348 (1940) pesos in 1925, traded at 187 pesos in 1929. By 1932 their value had dropped further to 159 pesos, a decline of more than 50 percent since 1925. For Toluca y México the drop was equally great, the price per share dropping from 19 pesos in 1925 to 11 pesos in 1929, and to 5 pesos in 1932.[35] This was the death knell for the firm, as this price per share was only 10 percent of its par value.

While the consumer goods industry limped through the Depression, the producer goods sector did rather well. This was largely because the Mexican government was beginning to put more emphasis on federally financed public works projects and was therefore placing orders for large amounts of cement and steel, the two most important intermediate goods industries in the nation. In fact, both steel and cement producers were setting records for production, profitability, and capacity utilization, even in the midst of the Depression. In the steel industry, Fundidora Monterrey, the underutilized giant of the Porfiriato, was now able to function at closer to its optimum rate of capacity utilization, averaging 45 percent between 1926 and 1932, a historic record for the firm (see Table 9.5) and almost double the rate it achieved during the periods 1903–10 and 1918–25.

Along with this jump in production came a marked improvement in Fundidora Monterrey's ability to turn profits. In a historic first for the company, it produced profits for five years straight between 1926 and 1930, a year in which its profits amounted to 12 percent of capital stock (see Table 9.2, above). Though the firm had a slight loss in 1931 and broke even in 1932, the seven years of the crisis were still the most profitable that it had experienced up to that point. Over the period 1926–32 Fundidora Monterrey averaged an annual return of 3.4 percent. With the increase in profitability came, for the first time in the company's history, the ability to pay regular dividends. Profits were distributed to the shareholders in every year after 1927 (see Table 9.3, above). Prior to this, the firm had paid out dividends in only three years: 1912, 1920, and 1921.

TABLE 9.5
Utilization of Installed Capacity in the Cement and Steel Industries,
1926–1932

(000 metric tons)

Year	Cement industry			Steel industry[a]		
	Capacity	Output	Utili-zation[b]	Capacity	Output	Utili-zation[b]
1926	222	151	68	110	62	56
1927	222	158	71	110	41	37
1928	246	204	83	110	51	46
1929	291	158	54	110	60	55
1930	291	227	78	110	58	53
1931	375	157	42	110	53	48
1932	405	138	34	110	20	18

SOURCES: Cement industry, calculated from unpublished data from the Cámara Nacional de Cemento. Steel industry, calculated from *FMIA*, 1925–33.

[a]See note *a* to Table 3.1, above.

[b]Production divided by installed capacity, expressed as a percent.

A similar success story is to be told in the cement industry, which, like steel, had historically functioned at very low levels of capacity utilization. Though no profit or financial return figures are available on any of the nation's major cement producers, aggregate data from the Cámara Nacional de Cemento suggest that on the whole the industry was doing quite well. Beginning in 1926 it was producing record amounts of cement, with a 50 percent additional increase by 1930. Production in the next two years dropped by 39 percent, but total tonnage for 1932 was still over twice the amount that the industry had produced during the Porfiriato (see Table 9.5). Along with the increase in output came an increase in the rate of capacity utilization. During the seven years 1926–32 the average rate of utilization was 61 percent, nearly one-third more than during the Porfiriato and two-thirds more than during the first half of the 1920's. This was still a far cry from the optimum rate of plant utilization but was nonetheless a major improvement over the days when the industry typically ran at 20 to 30 percent of capacity.

The data also suggest that the increase in production, and therefore probably likewise in profitability, sparked a wave of investment in new plant and equipment. As Table 9.5 indicates, the productive capacity industry-wide increased substantially. Between 1926 and 1932 installed capacity increased by 82 percent, as new ovens were installed in old plants and new plants were erected in parts of the country that until then had been outside the industry's distribution network.

In terms of new investment the experience of the cement industry was not the norm. In the rest of the manufacturing sector, firms continued to run their old plants into the ground. My estimates of physical plant values, calculated at cost minus depreciation, for the nation's largest steel firm, largest textile firm, and second largest cigarette firm all indicate that the process of disinvestment, begun during the earlier part of the 1920's, continued unabated during the latter part of the decade (see Table 9.6). From 1924 to 1932 the value of the physical plant of Fundidora Monterrey fell by 26 percent, of CIDOSA by 41 percent, and of El Buen Tono by 19 percent. Similarly, the series I have constructed on the value of plant and machinery in the cotton textile industry as a whole indicate that no new investment

TABLE 9.6

Estimated Value of Physical Plant, Fundidora Monterrey, CIDOSA, El Buen Tono, 1924–1932

(Current pesos)

Year	Fund Mont	CIDOSA	Buen Tono
1924	10,340,039	9,653,661	5,624,739
1925	9,871,560	9,151,460	—
1926	9,699,704	8,649,259	—
1927	9,435,952	8,147,058	—
1928	9,173,426	7,644,857	4,201,603
1929	8,678,520	7,191,491	4,444,359
1930	8,649,130	6,689,290	4,686,158
1931	8,124,244	6,187,089	4,693,393
1932	7,625,985	5,684,888	4,538,830

SOURCES: See Table 9.2.
NOTE: See note to Table 8.8, above.

was taking place in this important line of manufacturing. The total investment in machinery, equipment, and buildings, valued at cost minus depreciation, in cotton cloth production declined during the period by 18 percent, falling from 77.6 million pesos in 1925 to 75.9 million pesos in 1929 and to 63.3 million pesos by 1932 (see Table 9.1, above). If the data are adjusted for the number of mills in operation, the drop is even greater, the average investment per mill dropping by 23 percent between 1925 and 1932.

The decline in new investment is consistent with the perceptions of investors about the strength of the firms they held stock in. An analysis of the ratio of capital stock market values to book values for the three companies for which it was possible to put together reliable series indicates that investors were extremely wary of sinking additional resources into the enterprises they owned. As was the case in the discussion of investor behavior after the Revolution, my concern here is not what the ratio was in any particular year, or how the ratios varied from firm to firm, but how this ratio changed over time. For this reason, in Table 9.7 I have reduced the ratios to an index with 1907 equal to 100.

The series presented in Table 9.7 reveal that by 1932 investors in the two consumer goods firms, El Buen Tono and CIDOSA, valued their assets at 6 percent and 12 percent, respectively, of their perceived value in 1907. It made little sense, therefore, for

TABLE 9.7
Capital Stock, Ratio of Market to Book Values,
Fundidora Monterrey, CIDOSA, El Buen Tono, 1926–1932

(1907 = 100)

Year	Fund Mont	CIDOSA	Buen Tono
1926	36	41	—
1927	36	35	—
1928	46	33	26
1929	64	25	18
1930	78	21	12
1931	57	14	9
1932	66	12	6

SOURCES: Market values calculated from *BFM*, 1926–32; book values from
same sources as Table 9.2.
NOTE: See note to Table 8.11.

firms to undertake new investment, because the financial community would value the new capital stock at only a small fraction of its book value. This valuation of the firms' capital stock was even lower than it had been in the years immediately after the Revolution, when the market value / book value ratio was roughly 50 percent of its level during the Porfiriato. In other words, because investors were extremely pessimistic about their investments, they valued them at less than book value.

Fundidora Monterrey investors, on the other hand, were beginning to value their assets closer to book value because the company was finally becoming profitable. Thus, the market value / book value ratio increased throughout the latter part of the 1920's and the early 1930's. By 1932, during the trough of the Depression, investors had doubled their valuation of Fundidora Monterrey's capital stock since 1925, though it was still only two-thirds of the 1907 value.

The low market-valuation of assets was in large part a reflection of the unprofitability of investments in manufacturing during the Depression. Table 9.8 presents estimates of the real rate of return to a portfolio of common stocks in 12 of the nation's largest manufacturing companies. The estimates assume that the investor purchased the stocks at the end of 1925, after all 1925 dividends had been paid, and sold at the end of 1932. Of the 12 firms, only two—the San Ildefonso wool textile company and the Fundidora Monterrey steel company—would have produced financial gains for their shareholders. The losses in other companies ran from a low of 1.0 percent to a high of 20.3 percent per year. On average, an investor holding a portfolio of the stocks listed would have lost 7.8 percent per year between 1926 and 1932, which is to say that he would have lost close to 50 percent of his investment.

In short, the Great Depression hit early and hard in Mexico. A major contraction of the economy was under way by 1926 and intensified until 1932. The rapid decline of the export sector, coupled with a decrease in government spending and a contraction of the monetary base, severely depressed aggregate demand, thereby driving down manufacturing output, employ-

TABLE 9.8
Real Return to Investors, 1926–1932

(1940 pesos)

Company name	1925 stock price	Capital gain[a]	Total dividends 1926–32	Total return[b]	Annual rate of return[c]
San Ildef	52	−1	9	8	2.1%
Buen Tono	605	−549	67	−482	−20.3
San Raf	92	−52	46	−6	−1.0
CIDOSA	350	−259	20	−239	−15.1
Jabon	—	—	—	—	—
Cig Mex	103	−91	27	−64	−13.0
Toluca-México	19	−14	0	−14	−17.3
Atlixco	67	−49	8	−41	−12.6
CIVSA	214	−119	52	−67	−5.2
Fund Mont	39	51	20	71	16.0
S.A. Abad	42	−4	0	−4	−1.4
Cerv Moct	348	−189	54	−135	−6.8
Tab Mex	214	−164	0	−164	−18.8
Average real rate of return to portfolio[d]					−7.8%

SOURCES: Calculated from *BFM*, 1925–32.
[a]Difference in real stock price, 1925–32.
[b]Total real dividends plus real capital gains. Calculations assume that stock purchases were made at end of 1925 after payment of all dividends.
[c]Implicit compound rate of return, 1926–32.
[d]Assumes equal distribution of investor's resources among all stocks within the portfolio.

ment, and profits. New investment, which had slowed during the early 1920's, except in the cement industry, now came to a halt.

In two respects, Mexico's experience during the Great Depression was unusual. In a reversal of the usual pattern, producer goods manufacturers, to judge from the cases of cement and steel, did much better than did consumer goods manufacturers. This was largely the result of government spending on infrastructure projects, which kept demand for construction materials high. In addition, the Depression began earlier and ended earlier than in the United States and in Western Europe. The economy had begun contracting in 1926 and continued to shrink through 1932, by which date economic activity then began to increase.

TEN

Recovery and Growth, 1933-1940

ALTHOUGH MEXICAN manufacturing was hit hard during the period 1926–32, the Great Depression did not wipe it out, nor did the populist program of the Cárdenas government (1934–40) serve to undo Mexico's industrialists and the firms they controlled. In fact, quite the opposite happened. After the trough of the Depression in 1932, industry grew rapidly. Not only did output and profits pick up briskly after the contraction of 1926–32, but investment did likewise. During the mid-1930's a whole new round of industrial investment took place, and manufacturing, for the first time in Mexico's history, came to lead the economy.

There were several factors behind Mexico's early recovery from the Depression. The first had to do with Mexico's social and economic structure. Because a good part of the population still resided in small villages and produced largely for its own subsistence, the nation had a built-in buffer against external shocks. This, of course, did not make the economy grow faster once the recovery began, but it did limit the degree to which the economy could contract under the weight of a collapse of the export sector. Second, the prices of the goods Mexico traded on the international market began to increase by the mid-1930's, thereby increasing aggregate demand through the same channels that decreases in commodities prices had previously reduced it. Here Mexico was helped by the fact that the prices of two of its main exports, oil and silver, recovered faster than did most commodities prices in the 1930's. Finally, changes in government policies played a role; the Mexican government abandoned the orthodox monetary and fiscal policies that historically had served to heighten booms and busts in the nation's economic life. Let us take up each of these factors in detail.

The process of creating a national economy in which capitalist relations of production and exchange predominated, begun during the Porfiriato, was still incomplete by the 1930's. The fact that the peasantry had lost title to its lands during the nineteenth century did not signify that Mexico's agrarian structure was modern or that wage-labor predominated in the countryside. In some measure the Porfirian land-grab was in effect anti-modernizing. Though the distribution of land became highly concentrated, sharecropping and rental arrangements continued on the large estates that were created. The peasantry had lost control of its lands, but it continued to exist.

Thus Mexico in the 1930's was still overwhelmingly rural, and much of rural Mexico continued to be unintegrated into the national economy. As late as 1930, 68.7 percent of the economically active population continued to work in agriculture. Moreover, a good part of this agricultural population still functioned as a peasantry, continuing to live in small villages and producing largely for its own subsistence. Indeed, according to the 1930 population census, 66.5 percent of the population lived in communities of fewer than 2,500 inhabitants; most people were still village dwellers.[1]

Though no data are available on the degree to which this population produced for the market versus for its own consumption, data on language, education, housing, and dress can tell us a good deal about the degree to which it was integrated into the national mainstream.[2] In the nation's rural states, as much as 34 percent of the population spoke only an Indian language and, by implication, operated only in local markets. Most of the rural population was still illiterate, the national educational system being confined almost entirely to the cities. In the rural states of Chiapas, Guerrero, and Oaxaca, for example, less than 20 percent of the population could read or write. Further indication of the pre-capitalist nature of rural Mexico is given by data on dress. Though no data are available for 1930, the 1940 census indicates that in these rural states one-half to three-quarters of the population went barefoot. Finally, data on housing belie the village nature of rural Mexico in the 1930's, where the vast majority of people lived in dwellings without sewerage or running water. In fact, with the exception of the Distrito Federal, where 75 percent of the population had indoor running water, over 80 percent of the population had no sewerage or plumbing in their homes, and in some states only 2–3 percent of houses were so equipped.[3] In short, rural Mexico was not Kansas or Wisconsin, where farm families bought sewing machines, radios, and automobiles on credit, and where dog-eared copies of the Sears Roebuck catalog got more use than the family Bible.

This buffering effect of the disarticulation between a good portion of the agrarian sector and the rest of the economy was probably somewhat increased as a result of the agrarian reform begun in the mid-1920's, though in any event the largest and most important phase of the reform did not get under way until the latter part of the 1930's. In general, the reform encouraged an even greater reliance on subsistence agriculture by returning to some of the peasantry the lands they had lost during the Porfiriato. That it had a salutary effect on the economy apart from this is doubtful; the lack of irrigation, credit, and extension, coupled with the confusion created by the retitling of the land, probably meant that agricultural yields, and therefore rural incomes, fell over the short run. Over the longer term, the existence of the reformed sector of agriculture and the peculiar organization of land tenure and production that it fostered would ultimately come to serve as a drag on the economy and a structural block to continued industrialization—but not until the 1970's.

Mexico was further helped in the crisis by the fact that, as Enrique Cárdenas has noted, Mexico was relatively lucky in the "export commodity lottery." As opposed to countries like Chile or Colombia that relied almost entirely upon a single export, the price of which stayed depressed throughout the 1930's—copper and coffee, respectively—Mexico had a relatively diversified bundle of exports, including staple crops, tropical fruits, coffee, industrial raw materials, precious metals, and petroleum. More important, international demand for two of its major export commodities, silver and oil, was relatively inelastic.[4]

By 1934 the value and volume of Mexican exports were again on the upswing. In that year export earnings increased by 68 percent in dollar terms (73 percent in peso value). Most of this increase was due to the export of oil, gold, and silver, which accounted for 77 percent of the $82 million increase in export earnings between 1932 and 1934. As Enrique Cárdenas has observed, "The somewhat privileged position of Mexico in owning silver and oil made it possible to accelerate the recovery by increasing demand and the capacity to import, thus allowing the purchase of foreign raw materials which, in the face of idle capacity, permitted the quick resumption of production."[5]

Finally, government policy also played a role in the recovery of the Mexican economy. Beginning in the early 1930's, and then accelerating under the government of Lázaro Cárdenas from 1934 to 1940, the nation's monetary and fiscal authorities abandoned orthodoxy and pursued fairly expansionary policies. These were to some extent conscious policy choices. The government decided to put full employment ahead of a balanced budget and a stable peso. We should, however, be careful not to speak of Keynesianism before Keynes; to an equal extent the Mexican government pursued the policies that it did because it had little choice.

In terms of monetary policy, the Mexican government moved from following an essentially pro-cyclical policy to a counter-cyclical one beginning in March 1932. Instead of trying to defend the exchange rate by contracting the money supply, as it had done in the past, the government pursued an expansionary monetary policy and allowed the peso to float. By a combination of increasing the coinage of silver and issuing paper money—created by the Banco de México, which now had the sole right to issue bills—the money supply grew by 31 percent in 1932 and by 15 percent in 1933. This served to drive down interest rates, from 12 percent in 1931 to 8 percent in 1932, and to fuel consumption by enlarging the monetary base.[6] These expansionary policies continued throughout the decade, accelerating in 1936 when the central bank began to engage in inflationary financing of government budget deficits.[7]

Along with the expansion of the money supply came the decision to stop defending the peso, which was allowed to float freely from March 1932 to November 1933. This move resulted in a depreciation of 35 percent against the dollar over the 20-month period. This in turn fueled domestic production by increasing the peso price of foreign goods, thereby creating an implicit import tax. Unlike the decision to expand the money supply, this decision was a forced one: the government had simply run out of reserves and could no longer afford to intervene in currency markets. As soon as it was able—in November 1933—it went back to a fixed exchange rate. However, even this fixed exchange rate policy kept the peso undervalued because the domestic rate of inflation remained practically nil while that in the United States increased. The real exchange rate therefore fell an additional 19 percent between 1933 and 1935.[8]

The Mexican government also pursued an expansionary fiscal policy during the Depression. Instead of contracting expenditures to stay in line with falling tax revenues, it ran deficits between 1936 and 1938 of 5 to 13 percent to keep the level of aggregate demand high.[9] Like the change in exchange rate policies, these deficits were a function of both explicit choices and forced circumstances. On the one hand, the government ran deficits because its actual expenditures were much higher than the Treasury had planned for, thereby creating deficits when the government had not intended to. On the other hand, beginning in 1936 the government began to run deficits as an explicit part of its anti-depression policies. The effect of this deficit spending was of course the same whether the government did it because it planned to or because it was forced to: it kept aggregate demand high.

We should be careful, however, not to overestimate the effects of this expansionary fiscal policy. The Mexican government had not yet reached the mammoth size that it boasts today. It was in fact still quite small, as were most governments of the time, including that of the United States. Government spending during the latter part of the 1930's accounted for only 7 percent of GDP. For this reason, the deficits run during the Depression, though large in relation to total government spending, were extremely small in relation to the rest of the economy, the largest being barely over 1.3 percent of total GDP.[10]

More important than the actual size of the deficits was the change in the way that the Mexican government allocated expenditures in the latter part of the 1930's. As James Wilkie has shown, the Cárdenas government reallocated the federal budget radically so as to increase the amount of money spent on economic infrastructure and social programs. The amounts of money spent were not large in relation to the total size of the economy, but they had a very high marginal productivity. The expenditure of a few pesos paid off in a big way.

In general, the Cárdenas government reallocated money away from what Wilkie has defined as administrative expenditures, the largest part of which is military spending, and toward economic and social expenditures. Spending on items like rural schools and potable water (classified as social expenditures) and on roads, irrigation facilities, railroads, and electrification (classified as economic expenditures) increased from 36 percent of the federal budget in 1933 to 60 percent in 1936.[11] Because little money had been spent on these items prior to the 1930's, the new programs had a substantial effect on the economy, linking markets through road building, raising agricultural yields on newly irrigated lands, and increasing the productivity of the work force by improving public health. As a measure of the difference that just one of these programs meant, consider that between 1925 and 1928, when the federal government initiated its road-building program, it constructed only 700 kilometers of roadway. By 1930, the national total was 1,426 kilometers. During the Cárdenas years, this figure increased sevenfold to a total of 9,929 kilometers by 1940.[12] Thus, with the expenditure of little money in relation to the overall size of the economy, the government was able to make an impact on national economic life.

The combination of the buffering effect of the agrarian sector, the increase of commodities prices, and a change in government policies produced an economic recovery beginning in 1933. In that year real per capita GDP grew by 9.4 percent and continued growing at better than 5 percent per year until 1937 and 1938, when a minor recession caused the growth of the economy to slow.[13] The engine of growth of this recovery was the nation's industrial sector, which, according to aggregate estimates based on the national industrial census and other official sources, managed to grow 6.1 percent a year on average from 1932 to 1940 (with a slight dip in 1937–38). In fact, manufacturing became the fastest-growing sector of the economy during the 1930's, with manufacturing value added growing 125 percent faster than GDP as a whole.[14]

TABLE 10.1
Utilization of Installed Capacity in the Cement and Steel Industries,
1933–1938

(000 metric tons)

Year	Cement industry			Steel industry[a]		
	Capacity	Output	Utili-zation[b]	Capacity	Output	Utili-zation[b]
1933	405	173	43%	110	54	49%
1934	405	241	60	110	66	60
1935	405	252	62	110	64	58
1936	405	286	71	110	88	80
1937	405	345	85	110	59	54
1938	513	374	73	110	—	—

SOURCES: Cement industry, unpublished data from the Cámara Nacional de Cemento. Steel industry, calculated from *FMIA*, 1933–37.
[a]See note *a* to Table 3.1.
[b]Production divided by installed capacity, expressed as a percent.

Leading the recovery were the producer goods industries. Mexico's steel mills, cement works, and other industries associated with construction boomed under the influence of government spending on infrastructure. The cement industry, for example, was now running at between 60 and 85 percent of capacity, a historic first for what had been one of the most underutilized industries in Mexico. The high rates of capacity utilization are even more impressive when one considers that installed capacity had increased by over 100 percent since the late 1920's. Thus, by the latter part of the 1930's Mexico was using cement in unprecedented amounts (see Table 10.1).

Similar trends were occurring in the steel industry, where Fundidora Monterrey was finally able to take advantage of all the capacity it had installed back in 1903. The rate of utilization of installed capacity was now running at between 54 and 80 percent (see Table 10.1), which meant that what had been one of the most unsuccessful industries in Porfirian Mexico was now one of the most profitable. From 1933 to 1937 the average rate of return on capital stock was over 14 percent per annum (see Table 10.2). For the first time in its history the company was paying out sizable dividends to its stockholders, who since 1903 had listened to the excuses and apologies of the firm's management in innumerable annual meetings (see Table 10.3).

TABLE 10.2
Estimated Rates of Return on Capital Stock, 1933–1937

(Current pesos)

Year	Capital stock	Profit	Rate of return
Fundidora Monterrey			
1933	12,501,456	1,300,653	10
1934	12,301,549	1,877,941	15
1935	12,704,095	3,029,919	24
1936	15,104,104	1,872,643	12
1937	18,341,610	1,941,525	11
El Buen Tono			
1933	8,300,000[a]	−266,718	−3
1934	7,817,149	13,890	0
1935	7,600,000[b]	−19,648	0
1936	7,400,000[b]	−127,308	−2
1937	7,134,413	8,043	0
CIDOSA			
1933	14,500,000[a]	26,565	0
1934	13,425,552	971,069	7
1935	13,562,973	1,192,167	9
1936	19,066,278	1,318,359	7

SOURCES: Fundidora Monterrey, calculated from *FMIA*, 1933–37. El Buen Tono, calculated from *BFM*, 1 July 1933, p. 1, 31 Dec. 1933, p. 17, 10 May 1934, p. 1, 14 May 1935, p. 1, 22 Dec. 1936, p. 1, 31 Dec. 1936, p. 25, 27 July 1937, p. 1, 30 Apr. 1938, p. 1. CIDOSA, calculated from *BFM*, 26 June 1934, p. 1, 27 June 1934, p. 8, 3 May 1935, p. 1, 6 May 1936, p. 1, 8 May 1936, p. 2, 5 Nov. 1936, p. 1, 28 Apr. 1937, p. 1.

NOTE: For a complete discussion of how profits, capital stock, and the rate of return on capital were calculated and a discussion of the method employed in the adjustment of the raw data, see Haber 1985: appendix A.

[a]Estimated based on assumption that capital stock changed proportionately between 1932 and 1934.

[b]Estimated based on assumption that capital stock changed proportionately between 1934 and 1937.

The redynamization of the economy also reached down to the manufacturers of consumer goods, although the effects were more uneven in this sector than in producer goods. In general, the textile and beer industries performed relatively well in comparison with their experiences during the 1920's; other lines of manufacturing lagged behind.

In the beer industry, rising consumer incomes coupled with the further linking of regional markets as a result of government road building caused beer output to nearly quadruple between 1932 and 1940 (see Table 10.4). This is reflected in firm-level data as well, where the output of the Cervecería Cuauhtemoc grew from 14 million liters in 1932 to almost 55 million liters in 1940. Data on dividend payments to shareholders in the Cervecería Moctezuma, which with Cuauhtemoc and the Cervecería Modelo almost totally controlled the national market, also indicate that something of a boom occurred in the industry. From 1932 to 1934 the firm had been unable to pay out a single centavo in dividends, but beginning in 1935 it distributed fairly substantial earnings to its stockholders (see Table 10.3). Only the Compañía Cervecera de Toluca y México, which had not made any money in years, did not benefit from the recovery, and it finally went out of business in 1935. Its failure, like that of many smaller, less efficient breweries throughout the country, was part of the process of the revival of the industry as a whole. The process begun during the Porfiriato—the larger breweries driving the smaller producers to the wall and then buying up their production facili-

TABLE 10.3

Real Dividend Earnings, Selected Manufacturing Companies, 1933–1938

(Earnings per share, 1940 pesos)

Year	Buen Tono	San Ildef	CIDOSA	S.A. Abad	Atlixco	CIVSA
1933	0	0	0	0	0	0
1934	0	4	0	0	2	12
1935	0	0	38	0	1	14
1936	0	0	35	—	1	0
1937	0	4	0	—	1	0
1938	0	3	0	—	0	0

Year	Jabon[a]	San Raf	Fund Mont	Toluca-México	Cig Mex	Cerv Moct	Tab Mex
1933	—	14	13	0	0	0	0
1934	—	11	15	0	0	0	0
1935	—	12	24	0	0	18	4
1936	—	5	25	—	0	16	5
1937	—	0	11	—	0	29	7
1938	—	0	0	—	0	25	0

SOURCES: Calculated from *BFM*, 1933–38.

NOTE: For full names of companies, see Table 7.2 above; "Tab Mex," La Tabacalera Mexicana. Data adjusted to account for stock splits and stock dividends and deflated using index of implicit prices developed in Haber 1985: appendix B.

[a]Company put into liquidation by stockholders in 1924.

TABLE 10.4
Beer Production, National and Cervecería Cuauhtemoc,
1933–1940

(000 liters)

Year	National production	Cuauhtemoc sales[a]	Cuauhtemoc market share
1933	52,991	19,082	36.0%
1934	67,368	24,305	36.1
1935	82,513	29,291	35.5
1936	98,893	36,355	36.8
1937	120,805	44,225	36.6
1938	129,802	43,483	33.5
1939	160,452	49,052	30.6
1940	179,198	54,709	30.5

SOURCES: *Mexico* [12]: 958; Cervecería Cuauhtemoc, unpublished sales data.
[a]Used as proxy for annual production under the reasonable assumption that in the beer industry annual production and annual sales are almost identical, owing to the perishability of the product.

ties—was now being completed. Toluca y México, unable to compete against the combined onslaught of Cuauhtemoc, Moctezuma, and Modelo, was finally forced out and its productive apparatus purchased by Modelo. Other small firms in the beer industry suffered a similar fate.[15]

The cotton textile industry, which had been depressed since the mid-1920's, was also growing and returning to profitability. As Table 10.5 demonstrates, output grew by better than 60 percent between 1932 and 1937, accompanied by an increase in the productivity of labor and capital. Output per worker increased by over 25 percent, while output per active spindle—a proxy for the productivity of capital—grew by a whopping 56 percent. The increase in both output and productivity was accompanied by the recovery of profits. CIDOSA, the nation's largest producer, which had been losing money since 1929, began posting sizable profits by the mid-1930's and, between 1934 and 1936, averaged a rate of return of close to 8 percent per year (see Table 10.2, above). Accordingly, it paid healthy dividends in 1935 and 1936, as did some of the other major producers, like CIVSA.

One of the most interesting things about the textile industry is that several of the major firms, like the Compañía Industrial de

Atlixco and the Compañía Industrial de San Antonio Abad, were still depressed throughout the latter part of the 1930's and therefore paid no dividends to their shareholders (see Table 10.3, above). At the same time, the firms that were paying dividends did not do so on as regular a basis as one might expect, given the increase in productivity and output. Qualitative data, notably the consular reports of U.S. commercial attachés, mirror this judgment, noting a depressed situation in the industry. It appears likely that the 1930's witnessed the entry of a large number of smaller firms that challenged the old Porfirian giants with a good deal of success. The available data indicate that while the larger, older firms were running one or two shifts per day, the newer, smaller enterprises were running three.[16] The general boom in the industry, then, did not necessarily translate into an increase in profits for all of the old producers.

A similar situation, of increasing output without an increase in profitability, was occurring in cigarette production. Output jumped by 67 percent between 1932 and 1937, from 536 million packs to 894 million packs,[17] but profit and dividend data for El Buen Tono, La Cigarrera Mexicana, and La Tabacalera Mexicana

TABLE 10.5
Cotton Textile Industry, Main Economic Indicators, 1933–1940

Year	Operating mills	Active spindles	Active looms	Workers[a]	Cotton (metric tons)[b]	Sales (000 current pesos)	Capital (000 current pesos)[c]
1933	153	860,937	30,981	36,822	41,229	95,245	64,005
1934	160	—	32,605	40,319	—	—	—
1935	179	876,771	32,861	40,321	50,028	—	—
1936	207	875,672	33,971	42,716	53,642	—	—
1937	224	865,356	35,631	43,249	55,803	—	—
1938	221	865,626	34,987	43,299	50,809	—	—
1939	175	—	—	42,603	49,119	—	—
1940	193	—	—	43,698	51,507	—	—

SOURCES: Derived from *Mexico* [54]; de la Peña 1938: 7; *BFM*, 22 June 1933, p. 1; *Mexico* [53]; *Mexico* [30]: 14; *Mexico* [12]: 956.

NOTE: Beginning in 1934 data are from *Mexico* [12], which gives slightly different values for the pre-1934 period than do other sources.

[a]Number of workers employed. Does not include managerial personnel.

[b]Total cotton consumed during the year.

[c]Book value of machinery and plant at end of year. Excludes knitting mills.

do not suggest that the firms were doing well. El Buen Tono either lost money or earned little in every year between 1932 and 1937. The only encouraging sign for its stockholders was that losses were less than they had been during the late 1920's, when losses equaled 10 to 13 percent of capital stock per year (see Table 10.2, above). As might be imagined, the firm paid no dividends in any of these years. Similarly, La Tabacalera Mexicana and La Cigarrera Mexicana failed to produce much in the way of dividend earnings—the former paying only small amounts in 1935, 1936, and 1937, and the latter not paying anything at all (see Table 10.3, above).

The reason that output was able to jump but the financial performance of the firms was weak was the increased competition from El Aguila, which was capturing roughly two-thirds of the market. Though no financial data are available on El Aguila, the fact that output had increased so dramatically since the early 1930's implies that it was most probably able to run its mammoth production facilities closer to their optimum level and that the financial performance of the firm had improved since the 1920's. If we assume that market shares did not change betwen 1932 and 1937, El Aguila would have been operating at 67 percent of capacity in the latter year.[18] Since it is highly likely that it captured a larger percentage of the market in 1937 than it did in 1932, its rate of capacity utilization was probably higher than this.

This does not mean, however, that the three Porfirian giants were being driven out of business. The marked increase in cigarette consumption meant that they faced a much stronger market than they had previously. Though prices were probably depressed because of increased competition, their level of output probably rose, allowing them to utilize their plants efficiently. Stock market data give some credence to this interpretation. The real price of shares in La Tabacalera Mexicana increased by 50 percent between 1932 and 1936, while El Buen Tono's doubled, and La Cigarrera Mexicana's changed not at all. Share prices fell in 1937 when a minor financial panic took place, but still stayed above their 1932 level. Stock prices would not have behaved in this fashion had El Aguila been forcing them out of business.[19]

In general, then, the period from 1933 to 1938 was a relatively good one for Mexican industry and Mexican industrialists. Out-

TABLE 10.6
Real Return to Investors, 1933–1938

(1940 pesos)

Company name	1932 stock price	Capital gain[a]	Total dividends 1933–38	Total return[b]	Annual rate of return[c]
San Ildef	38	−1	11	10	4.0%
Buen Tono	56	1	0	1	0.3
San Raf	40	−22	42	20	7.0
CIDOSA	91	44	73	117	14.8
Jabon	—	—	—	—	—
Cig Mex	12	0[d]	0[d]	0	0[d]
Toluca-México	5	−1[d]	0[d]	−1	−7.1[d]
Atlixco	18	−6	5	−1	−1.0
CIVSA	95	−23	26	3	0.5
Fund Mont	90	21	87	108	14.0
S.A. Abad	38	19[d]	0[d]	19	14.5[d]
Cerv Moct	159	21	89	110	9.2
Tab Mex	50	25[e]	17	42	10.7
Average real rate of return to portfolio[f]					5.6%

SOURCES: Calculated from *BFM*, 1932–38.

[a] Real difference in stock price, 1932–38. Calculations assume that shares purchased at end of 1932 after all 1932 dividends had been paid.

[b] Total real dividends plus real capital gains.

[c] Implicit compound rate of return, 1933–38.

[d] 1932–35. Annual rate of return calculated over three years.

[e] 1932–36. Dividend data are through 1938. Assumed no change in stock price 1936–38.

[f] Assumes equal distribution of investor's resources among all stocks within the portfolio.

put, productivity, and profits were all up. Industrialists were therefore once again achieving sizable real financial returns on their investments. In Table 10.6 I have calculated the possible return on the 12 industrial stocks we looked at for earlier periods. As before, I have assumed that our hypothetical investor purchased the shares at the bottom of the business cycle in 1932 and sold them in 1938, when the market again began to turn downward. The real capital gain or loss on the stocks, as well as the real earnings from all dividends paid between the beginning of 1933 and the end of 1938, were then calculated, and this combined real return was then compared to the 1932 purchase price.

The data indicate that investing in the Mexican stock market in the mid-1930's was a reasonably good way to make money. Investors would have lost a significant amount of money on only one of the 12 companies analyzed, the ill-fated Compañía Cervecera de Toluca y México. Investments in four others—El Buen Tono, La Cigarerra Mexicana, CIVSA, and the Compañía Industrial de Atlixco—would have more or less broken even. In the other seven firms, our investor would have realized substantial returns, varying between 4 and 15 percent per annum. On average, the real return to the 12-firm portfolio would have been a solid 5.6 percent per year.

Accompanying the upsurge in returns to investors was a new wave of investment, the first sector-wide increase in capital spending since the late Porfiriato. Beginning in 1935, investors once again began to sink their resources into manufacturing enterprises. On an aggregate level, real expenditures on private fixed capital formation by 1939 were 167 percent higher than they had been at the trough of the Depression in 1932.[20] In part, this new round of investment in manufacturing enterprises was the result of the reinvestment of earnings from the already established industrial giants, firms like Fundidora Monterrey, CIDOSA, and San Rafael. Doubtless, the select number of firms founded during the early 1920's were undertaking capital modernization projects as well. This new wave of investment was further driven by a new group of smaller industrialists, almost all of them recent arrivals to Mexico, concentrated in new industries like rayon cloth and knitwear. In the years following the Second World War it would be these new industrialists who would come to play a key role in Mexican manufacturing.

In terms of older industries, the available data indicate that a good deal of new investment was taking place. Firms that essentially had not spent any money on new plant and equipment since the latter part of the Porfiriato were now beginning to modernize their factories. Series on the estimated physical-plant values for the important producer in each of the three industries—steel, cotton textile, and cigarettes—indicate that substantial capital spending programs were undertaken in two of the three during the mid-1930's (see Table 10.7). Of the three, only the El Buen Tono cigarette company, which was losing money because of increased competition, did not begin a substantial program of new capital spending. Fundidora Monterrey, on the other hand, began to plow profits back into its steel

TABLE 10.7
Estimated Value of Physical Plant, Fundidora Monterrey, CIDOSA,
El Buen Tono, 1933–37

Year	Fund Mont	CIDOSA	Buen Tono
1933	7,528,179	5,182,687	—
1934	6,530,203	4,680,486	4,442,664
1935	6,881,765	4,225,794	—
1936	7,449,916	9,282,576	—
1937	8,868,257	—	4,238,821

SOURCES: See Table 10.2.
NOTE: See note to Table 8.8, above.

works in 1934, the value of physical plant increasing 36 percent between 1934 and 1937. An even more dramatic investment program took place in CIDOSA, which more than doubled the value of its four cotton-spinning and weaving mills just from 1935 to 1936. Installed capacity data for the cement industry tell a similar story (no data are available on the value of the plant), total capacity having increased by 37 percent from 1931 to 1938 (see Tables 9.5 and 10.1, above).

Firms began new investment programs because shareholders, whose confidence was buoyed by the upsurge in profits, were revaluing the capital stock in the companies they owned. During the 1920's Mexico's industrialists had seriously undervalued their investments, the market value to book value ratio of the three companies all declining from their levels during the Porfiriato.[21] As of 1933 investors began to perceive that their assets were more valuable and therefore pushed stock prices upward, and with them the market value of capital stock. An index of the market value / book value ratio (with 1907 equal to 100) indicates that investors revalued their capital upward by a factor between two and three between 1932 and 1937 (see Table 10.8). Since firms could now coax more capital out of financial markets for each additional unit of capital stock than they could have previously, firms once again began to reinvest.

Of equal significance to the renewed investment program of older industries was the creation of new firms. As might be expected, the new companies did not, generally speaking, enter into competition with the old established giants. They left beer brewing, steel making, paper milling, and the other capital-

TABLE 10.8

Capital Stock, Ratio of Market Values to Book Values,
Fundidora Monterrey, CIDOSA, El Buen Tono, 1932–1937

(1907 = 100)

Year	Fund Mont	CIDOSA	Buen Tono
1932	66	12	6
1933	84	37	9
1934	113	50	18
1935	155	40	14
1936	152	40	17
1937	113	—	17

SOURCES: Market prices calculated from *BFM*, 1932–38; book values from
same sources as in Table 10.2.
NOTE: See note to Table 8.11.

intense, vertically integrated operations to the companies that
had dominated those lines of manufacture since the Porfiriato.
The new firms were basically small operations that concentrated
in activities like the weaving of cotton and rayon knitwear, as
well as the production of high-quality cotton and silk cloth.[22] In-
troducing a whole new array of products, like high-grade cotton
shirtings, cotton velvets, and upholstery fabrics, these enterprises quickly carved out a place in the market for themselves.
Their entry is clearly reflected in Table 10.5, which indicates the
vast increase in the number of active firms in the cotton textile
industry. An analysis of the data indicates that the roughly 70
new firms that entered cotton cloth production in the 1930's
were mostly smaller operations. For this reason the average
number of looms and spindles per cotton factory fell dramatically between 1933 and 1938. The number of looms per mill fell
by 22 percent, from 202 to 158, and the number of spindles fell
by 30 percent, from 5,627 to 3,917.

In other branches of the textile industry the entry of new firms
was even more noticeable. Literally hundreds of small-scale enterprises sprang up during this period, producing goods such as
silk and rayon flat crepes, cotton knitwear, and hosiery. In fact,
of the 692 firms listed in the 1938 tax registry of the textile industry, well over half were involved in the manufacture of these
new products.[23]

Besides being new, these firms had two other interesting attributes. The first was their size. Almost none of them had capital in excess of 100,000 pesos, most had less than 10,000. They survived because there were not significant economies of scale in the products that they manufactured. A second attribute was that, like the Porfirian giants, their owners were for the most part not Mexican. Indeed, the most striking thing about this new group of entrepreneurs was that they were predominantly Eastern European Jews, Lebanese, and Syrians who had come to Mexico in the 1920's fleeing religious persecution—many of the Syrians and Lebanese were Jews and Maronite Christians— and had set themselves up as petty traders in the cloth business. Many started out selling socks, underwear, or similar products door to door. By the 1930's they had amassed sufficient capital that they were able to become the owners of small mills. Thus, by 1938 the tax register for the textile industry is dominated by names of owners like Eli Dwedk, Izzat Nacif, Amade Zidam, León Zakowsky, Jorge David Assef, Jacobo Farji, and Alejandro Kleyff.[24] These were, in fact, the entrepreneurs whom Sanford Mosk dubbed "The New Group"—without identifying their national origins—in his classic work, *Industrial Revolution in Mexico*.[25] It was, of course, this new group that would form the Cámara Nacional de Industrias de Transformación (the National Chamber of Manufacturers) in the 1950's and that would accomplish through the political system essentially what the old Porfirian industrialists had done in their day: pressure the government into giving them the tariff protection, subventions, and subsidies that they needed to compete against foreign goods.

The idea that there was any new investment at all during the Cárdenas years (1934–40) may come as a surprise to some readers. Indeed, Cárdenas is generally seen as hostile to capitalism— the nationalization of the oil industry and the stepping-up of the pace of the agrarian reform being the evidence most scholars point to in making this argument. In fact, it was not so much the fact that Cárdenas was anti-capitalist as that he was an economic nationalist and a shrewd politician. The agrarian reform was carried out in order to ensure social peace. The nationalization of oil was an attack not on private enterprise, but on foreign companies that put themselves above the state. A number of scholars have made much of the conflict between the Cárdenas government and the Garza-Sada interests—which controlled the Cervecería Cuauhtemoc and Vidriera Monterrey—arguing that this is evidence of a generalized conflict between the private sector and the government during the 1930's.[26] The fact is, however, that the conflict between the Garza-Sadas and Cárdenas was a localized dispute that did not involve the industrialist class as a whole. As the present analysis of investor confidence and new capital spending shows, Mexican manufacturers did not perceive the reformist government of Cárdenas as particularly inimical to their interests.

In fact, the only instances in which Cárdenas nationalized any industries involved foreign-dominated cement companies that were throwing Mexican workers out of their jobs, and even here the process of expropriation had gotten under way prior to the beginning of the Cárdenas regime. To cite one example, in 1931 the Cementos Tolteca company purchased the Cementos Cruz Azul works from the Banco National de México, which took over Cruz Azul after it went into receivership during the Revolution. Both companies operated in the state of Hidalgo, and both produced for the Mexico City market. Tolteca's plan was to shut down the rival Cruz Azul in order to attain a regional monopoly. Problems with the government started when Tolteca's Scottish manager fired all the workers at Cruz Azul without compensation, causing the workers to appeal to the government. On May 21, 1931, the factory was expropriated, and in October the company was compensated by the state of Hidalgo for 1.3 million pesos. It was not until 1934 that the workers formed a cooperative in order to run the company, and in 1936 the Cárdenas government transferred ownership to the cooperative.[27]

Three things are notable about this episode. First, the company in question, Cementos Tolteca, was almost 100 percent foreign owned, being controlled by the London-based Portland Cement Co. Ltd.—an ironic twist, since Cementos Tolteca advertised its product as "El Cemento de México." Second, the process of expropriation had begun long before Cárdenas took office; he simply followed through on an action taken earlier. Third, the whole thing would not have happened had

Cementos Tolteca not dismissed Cruz Azul's workers without compensation.

Thus, even with the increased organization of Mexico's working class, and with the various conflicts between some elements of the private sector and the state, Mexican manufacturers did not see Cárdenas as more of a threat to their interests than the other post-revolutionary administrations had been. In fact, they may well have perceived his government as a positive factor, since he was spending substantial sums of money on infrastructure programs that were increasing the integration of the national market. In addition, the fact that he had achieved social peace in Mexico, organizing labor yet keeping it under the control of the state, carrying out an agrarian reform, yet not eliminating the concept of private property, would also have been seen by manufacturers as a measure in their interest. Indeed, by the end of the Cárdenas administration, Mexican manufacturers no longer had to fear the vagaries of an unstable political system. Manufacturers therefore decided to plow back some of their profits into new plant and equipment, believing once again, as they had done during the Porfiriato, that over the long run their investments would be profitable. This time, they turned out to be right.

ELEVEN

Conclusions

IN THE LAST two decades of the nineteenth century Mexico underwent a rapid but unsuccessful process of economic modernization and growth. As capital flowed into the country from Europe and the United States, the obstacles that had held back economic growth since Independence were broken down. Segmented markets began to be connected by the railways; mines were drained and retimbered; and agriculture became increasingly commercialized. At the same time that the nation's productive structures were being reorganized, legal and institutional impediments to growth came under attack; internal tariffs were abolished, banditry and brigandage were brought under control, and the power of the nation's regional caudillos was checked by the expansion of the central government. Along with these changes came new laws, all designed to encourage capital accumulation. Joint-stock companies were now permitted, subsidies and tax holidays for new enterprises were created, and the mining code was rewritten to favor foreign investors.

Mexico's capitalists believed that the process of economic growth would go on forever. Looking out on a rapidly expanding economy and a growing internal market, they perceived that large fortunes could be made in manufacturing. They therefore undertook an ambitious industrialization program, based upon the twin pillars of imported technology and government protection. By the closing years of the Porfiriato Mexico had built an impressive manufacturing plant. In steel, cement, paper, glass, dynamite, soap, beer, cigarettes, and cotton and wool textiles, large factories churned out manufactures at a rate previously unimaginable, driving the nation's artisans to the wall and forcing many imported goods out of the market. Mexico's industrial revolution had begun.

Three factors stand out with respect to this wave of industrialization. The first was the enormous scale of the technology employed. From the start, Mexican manufacturing was characterized by a high degree of horizontal and vertical integration. In many product lines one or two huge firms, employing thousands of workers and controlling every phase of production, took almost the entire market. Why, one asks, did a nation as capital-scarce as Mexico build an industrial plant that required enormous amounts of capital? Why did it not develop small-scale industry, utilizing labor-intensive technology?

To a large extent Mexico utilized capital-intensive methods of production because it imported almost all of its industrial technology from Europe and the United States and these were the methods used in those countries. It made more sense for Mexican entrepreneurs to employ this technology, even though its scale was often inappropriate for Mexico, than to go through the long process of trial and experimentation that would have been necessary to develop their own. Indeed, as Alexander Gerschenkron pointed out with respect to late-developing countries in Europe, the very existence of this backlog of technology served as an impulse to industrialization and allowed the early stages of industrial growth to occur quite quickly.[1]

In addition, a capital-intensive approach to industrialization made sense in light of the fact that there was a shortage of skilled labor accustomed to industrial discipline. Although most of the population lived in a continual state of underemployed misery, there was actually a great dearth of people who knew how to operate industrial machinery. This had two ramifications. It meant, first, that many of the skilled technicians as well as some of the operatives had to be brought from abroad, at relatively high salaries. Second, it meant that it was difficult for Mexican industrialists to control the work force. As had been the case in Europe at the beginning of the Industrial Revolution, in Mexico the workers resisted the routinization of work. The resistance took the form of refusing to work as many machines as the mill owners would have liked—Mexican workers typically operated about half the number of machines that their U.S.

counterparts did—and of overt recalcitrance to heed the call of the factory whistle. There were even occasions when entire shifts of workers simply refused to show up, preferring instead to attend a religious festival or social occasion in their community. Employers therefore had two options, both of which they adopted: use the coercive apparatus of the state to control the working class, and substitute capital for labor.

Finally, Mexico pursued a capital-intensive industrialization strategy because no one thought about doing it any other way. Looking back, it is easy to see the contradictions and problems inherent in the path to industrialization that Mexico followed. At the time, however, the problems were not obvious. The Porfirian ruling class equated foreign ways of doing things with modernity, and modernity with progress. If Mexico was going to become a modern nation, then it needed a modern manufacturing plant such as existed in the United States or England.

The second outstanding feature of this wave of industrial growth was the high degree of concentration of ownership. Not only did a few firms carve up the lion's share of the market in any one product line, but also just a few entrepreneurs controlled the largest and most important enterprises in a variety of undertakings. To a certain extent, technological constraints conditioned the pattern of ownership, just as they conditioned the organization of production. Since fixed capital costs were extremely high, and since the banking system was in its infancy and could not serve as a source of finance, the only entrepreneurs with sufficient liquid capital to bankroll new ventures were the nation's merchant-financiers. Because no individual would risk his entire fortune on any one enterprise, this tightly knit group combined again and again to finance a variety of undertakings. These merchant-financier-industrialists then utilized their entrepreneurial talents to set up a whole variety of anticompetitive structures. From the very beginning of modern Mexican industrialization, manufacturing was characterized by oligopoly and monopoly.

Mexican industry had a noncompetitive structure not in spite of the fact that it was a poor country, but precisely *because* it was ꞏꞏntry. Manufacturing in Mexico at the end of the ninehtury was risky. The market was neither secure nor deep, the threat of foreign competition was strong and the costs of technology high. The reaction of industrialists was therefore both to form oligopolies and monopolies that would reduce the level of risk and uncertainty and to get the government to subsidize and protect these arrangements. To a large extent, Mexican industry was characterized by extremely large firms that could influence the market not because it was in some advanced stage of monopoly capitalism, but because Mexican capitalists were trying to survive in a hazardous, high-risk, low-profit environment.

In addition, a small group of financiers could dominate the country's manufacturing sector because they had the financial and political power to do so. There existed no rival group of entrepreneurs with both experience in manufacturing and capital to finance their enterprises. Thus, the lack of a national capital market and the absence of a banking system that could be called upon to finance new firms kept industry in the hands of the nation's most important merchants and financiers. At the same time that this group controlled the sources of finance, they also controlled the economic apparatus of the state. They were the financial backbone of the government, whether pre- or post-revolutionary. They could therefore count on the government not to interfere even when their anti-competitive arrangements were clearly not in the best interests of long-term national economic growth.

The third notable feature of Mexico's early industrial experience was that it did not set off a process of self-sustaining economic growth. In contrast to what had happened in the United States and in Western Europe, the production of consumer goods did not generate backward and forward linkages into new products and processes. Textile manufacturing, for example, did not spur the development of a textile-machine industry, which then created demand for machine-tool and speciality-steel industries, which in turn spread out into the production of other capital goods, as had happened in the advanced industrial economies. Instead, there was a single wave of intense industrial investment between roughly 1890 and 1907, and then a long period of limited further investment or innovation. The growth that had occurred had to be sustained by government protection and subsidization. Mexico's infant industries never made it to adulthood. In short, what Mexico built during its industrial revolution was underdeveloped industrialization.

In order for self-sustaining industrialization to take place, investors must believe that their investments will yield profits at some time in the foreseeable future. Part of this belief requires entrepreneurs to perceive that the economy will continue to grow, part requires that they perceive the basic configuration of the state as immutable. That is, they must have confidence in the ability of the state to stifle challenges to the existing order effectively, and they must feel secure that the basic rules of the game will not be changed. Neither of these perceptions was widely held by Mexico's industrialists in the period between the close of the Porfiriato and the early 1930's.

In terms of the need for confidence that there will be a substantial return to capital over the medium term, Mexican industrialists found their optimism during the period 1890–1907 dashed. Mexico in the 1890's was not really ready for many of the industries that were erected. That is, Mexico's capitalists misread their situation. Recognizing the highly speculative nature of many of the ventures they founded, they believed that continued economic growth would make these enterprises profitable over the medium term. Like the people who put together Mexico's oil policy in the 1970's, who assumed that the increases in crude oil prices from 1973 to 1979 would continue indefinitely, Mexico's manufacturers believed that the rapid growth of the economy and the impressive transformation of the nation during the early part of the Díaz regime would proceed until Mexico resembled France or the United States. Instead, beginning in 1907, the economy slowed and then stayed depressed until the end of the Revolution. Within a few years another economic contraction hit, this one lasting from 1926 to 1932. It was therefore not until the mid-1930's that Mexican manufacturers could again look out on a fairly healthy economy.

The lack of consistent profits can be expressed in terms of the real financial returns to investors. In Table 11.1, I have calculated the real returns from 1902 to 1938 to a hypothetical industrialist who divided his portfolio among 11 of the 13 companies analyzed in Chapters 7–10. The calculations assume that the stocks

TABLE 11.1
Real Return to Investors, 1902–1938
(1940 pesos)

Company name	1901 stock price	Capital gain[a]	Total dividends 1902–38[b]	Total return[c]	Annual rate of return[d]
San Ildef	295	−258	198	−60	−0.6%
Buen Tono	812	−755	983	228	0.7
San Raf	151	−133	288	155	1.9
CIDOSA	847	−712	868	156	0.5
Jabon[e]	—	—	—	—	—
Cig Mex	228	−216[f]	247[f]	31	0.4[f]
Toluca-México	322	−318[f]	300[f]	−18	−0.2[f]
Atlixco	153	−141	118	−23	−0.4
CIVSA	371	−299	540	241	1.4
Fund Mont	261	−150[g]	125	−25	−0.3
S.A. Abad	79	−22[h]	75	53	1.5
Cerv Moct	560[i]	−380[j]	494	114	0.5
Tab Mex[e]	—	—	—	—	—
Average annual return to portfolio[d]					0.5%

SOURCES: Derived from *EM* 1901–14; *BFM* 1916–38.

[a]Difference in real stock price, 1901–38. Calculations assume that stock purchased after all 1901 dividends were paid.

[b]Total real dividends paid, 1902–38. Does not include dividends paid during 1914–17 because of the lack of a price deflator for these years. However, the results presented here would not be sensitive to the addition of these data since dividends were either negligible or entirely lacking for the firms in question during the Revolution.

[c]Total real dividends plus real capital gains.

[d]Implicit compound rate of return.

[e]Excluded because of incomplete data.

[f]1901–35. Rate of return calculated over 34 years.

[g]1902–38.

[h]1901–35. Dividend data are through 1938. Assumed no change in stock price 1936–38.

[i]In 1908.

[j]1908–38.

were purchased in 1901, after all dividends had been paid, and were sold at the end of 1938.[2] The data indicate that over the long run the real returns to investors were quite small. In fact, our hypothetical investor would have lost money on over one-third of the companies. Of the seven that provided positive real returns to their stockholders only three—CIVSA, the Compañía Industrial de San Antonio Abad, and the Compañía de las Fábricas de Papel de San Rafael y Anexas—would have yielded an average annual return of more than 1 percent, and none produced net real returns of 2 percent or more per annum. Overall, the 11-firm portfolio would have produced an average annual real return of only 0.5 percent. Thus, the vital perception that over the long run profits were going to be consistent and substantial had no empirical foundation.

At the same time that Mexico's nascent industrial entrepreneurs came to realize that their investments were not going to pay off as handsomely as they had expected, they came to perceive that their beliefs about the stability of the political system were also overly optimistic. By the closing years of the Porfiriato, they realized the fallacy of their earlier perception that the working class and the peasantry could be squeezed indefinitely so as to further the process of capital accumulation. Following the Hobbesian dictum that "when all else fails, clubs are trump," the Porfirian ruling class relied on the army and the Rurales to keep the lid on resistance to their program. Yet even in the face of the coercive power of the state, the working class organized and struck, and the peasantry took to arms to defend its lands. By 1907 Mexico's elites were no longer certain of Díaz's ability to maintain political stability. It was for this reason that the Mexican Revolution started out as a movement of the elites and that the Mexican upper class did not defend the Díaz dictatorship against Madero. Here again the ruling groups were overly confident. They believed that they could force Díaz from office without igniting a revolution from below. In this they were all too wrong.

Even though the Revolution actually did little real damage to the nation's manufacturing plant, it did shake the confidence of investors. It was not that the post-revolutionary governments were anti-industrial or anti-business—they were in fact made of businessmen and industrialists—but rather that the rules of the game had been rewritten somewhat by the Revolution and that the fear of a renewed round of violence lurked in the minds of the investment community. That is, though the elites had held on to political power, they had not yet achieved social peace. It was not entirely certain what direction Mexico would follow in the 1920's, whether the Revolution would move to the left toward an attack on private property or to the right in a reaction against the progressive compromises of the Constitution of 1917. It was not until Lázaro Cárdenas found a way to bring all sectors of Mexican society into a unified party, in the 1930's, and accommodated the workers and the peasants by building a welfare state that social peace was attained and investors once again perceived that the political system would be stable over the long term. At this juncture industrialists, both old and new, once again started to invest in manufacturing ventures.

In this way Mexico's early industrial experience conforms to the erratic pattern of massive jumps in investment and output followed by periods of slowed entrepreneurial vigor described by Gerschenkron in regard to late industrializing countries in Europe. Indeed, in many ways his observations about the nature of industrialization in the economically backward countries of the European continent are applicable to Mexico. The emphasis on bigness of firms, the preponderance of heavy industry, the important role of the state, the utilization of capital-intensive methods of production, the unevenness of growth, and the presence of a clearly defined ideology of industrialization that Gerschenkron observed in Eastern and Central Europe were present in Mexico as well.[3]

Over the long run, did any of this make any difference? Did Mexico's pattern of industrialization prior to 1940 in any way affect the outcome of industrial growth in the years after 1940?

Mexico's early industrial experience had basically two ramifications for the period after 1940. The first one was positive. Because the nation already had an impressive and solid industrial base from which to start when the boom of the Second World War hit, it was able to industrialize during the war and afterward much faster than would otherwise have been possible. In fact, had Mexico not had an earlier wave of industrial investment, the war would not have set off a manufacturing revolution because the required capital goods would have been virtually unobtainable. In key industries like steel, for example, where investors wanted to establish new mills and expand old ones, it was not possible to purchase any of the requisite technology until after the war was over. As Clark Reynolds has noted, the rapid growth of output beginning in 1940, which set off a new round of industrial investment and a renewed round of tariff protection and subsidization by the government later in the decade, was mostly the result of running the nation's already installed plant night and day. In addition, the very existence of a significant manufacturing sector meant that by 1940 there was the nucleus of a skilled industrial work force that could serve as a cadre of industrial labor in the following years.

On the other hand, Mexico's early industrial experience had negative effects on the long-run success of the economy. During the early years of Mexican manufacturing, patterns of entrepreneurship and industrial organization evolved that were not conducive to sustained industrial growth. That is, because of the problems and contradictions inherent in the rapid industrialization of a transitional economy like Mexico's in the late nineteenth century, manufacturers did not strive to streamline production methods or to innovate new processes or techniques. Rather, the strategy of firms was to structure the market or manipulate the state so as to preclude competition, either from other domestic manufacturers or from imports. The process of industrialization was therefore as much political as it was economic. By following this strategy, Mexico's entrepreneurs deflected a real modernization of the economy and prevented the development of a manufacturing sector designed to be internationally competitive. Because Mexico's merchant-financier elite was interested in modernizing the state and the economy only to the degree that they themselves could still maintain control, they sidetracked the industrialization process. Mexico's governments, whether pre- or post-revolutionary, basically went along with this because they needed the nation's industrialists as much as the industrialists needed the state. After all, the nation's manufacturers tended also to be the nation's financiers and as such were one of the essential bulwarks of support for whatever government came to power.

For this reason, the patterns of Porfirian manufacturing have persisted up until the present day and are only now being seriously questioned, during a protracted economic decline. The debate—whether Mexican industry will continue to operate the way it has for nearly a century, protected by tariffs and subsidies, not competing in export markets, employing an imported technological base, avoiding domestic competition by price-rigging, cartelization, and monopolies—will set the political agenda for the years to come. In the final analysis, it will not only affect the nation's industrialists and industrial workers, but will shape the nature of work, the structure of society, and the form of political organization for the entire country.

Reference Matter

Notes

Complete authors' names, titles, and publication data are given in the Bibliography, pp. 217–29.

Chapter 1

1. See Stein 1957; Dean 1969.
2. On industrial policy during the Porfiriato, see Cott 1978; on industrial policies during the 1930's: see Cárdenas Sánchez 1982; for a discussion of how the distribution of government expenditures changed throughout this period, see Wilkie 1970. For a discussion of labor during this period, see Anderson 1976; Basurto 1981; González Navarro 1970; Carr 1982; Cardoso, et al. 1980.
3. See Reynolds 1970: 161–68.

Chapter 2

1. Anderson 1976: 19.
2. Cárdenas Sánchez 1981: 16.
3. Coatsworth 1981: 18.
4. Vanderwood 1981: 27.
5. Coatsworth 1981: 19–21.
6. Ibid.: 35.
7. Ibid.: 36, 40.
8. Ibid.: 97–99, 102–3.
9. Anderson 1976: 12.
10. See Randall 1972.
11. Cárdenas Sánchez 1981: 30.
12. Potash 1983: 153.
13. Cárdenas Sánchez 1981: 29.
14. Rosenzweig 1965c: 136–38.
15. Ibid.: 143.
16. Markiewicz 1985.
17. On the relationship between railroads and Indian rebellions, see Coatsworth 1981: 155–68.
18. Coatsworth 1978: 80–100.
19. Vanderwood 1981: 3, 11, 37.
20. Keremetsis 1973: 54.
21. Vanderwood 1981: 11.
22. Ibid.: 32.
23. Kroeber 1983: 29.
24. Cockcroft 1983: 87.
25. Anderson 1976: 34–35.
26. Ibid.: 36.
27. Ibid.: 96.
28. Tenenbaum 1983.

29. Calculated from Rosenzweig 1965c: 172, 199.
30. Vanderwood 1981: 63.
31. Quoted in Anderson 1976: 127.
32. On strikes during the Porfiriato, see González Navarro 1970; and Anderson 1976: chs. 3 and 4.

Chapter 3

1. Calculated from *Mexico* [23]: 252. The figures for 1861 do not include the 1.8 million workers listed under "industrias del petroleo y extractiva," since this category also includes agricultural day laborers, who would have been the vast majority of workers in this category. For purposes of calculation, I have liberally estimated that the number of workers in mining (there was no petroleum industry as yet) in 1861 was the same as in 1895: 88,548 workers.
2. Ibid.: 33.
3. Calculated from Rosenzweig 1965c: 149–50.
4. *EM*, 7 May 1904, p. 114.
5. Molina Enríquez 1978: 318.
6. Wilkie and Wilkins 1981: 577–90.
7. Molina Enríquez 1978: 312.
8. Lamoreaux 1985: 33.
9. See *EM*, 18 Jan. 1902, p. 245, 21 June 1902, p. 203, 5 Sept. 1903 (English ed.), p. 536, 11 July 1908, p. 297; AGNT 1199, La Constancia file; *BFM*, 17 Feb. 1921, p. 1, 13 Apr. 1921, p. 4, 24 Nov. 1921, p. 1, 3 Dec. 1921, p. 8, 16 Feb. 1922, p. 1, 21 Nov. 1922, p. 1, 3 May 1923, p. 1, 1 Apr. 1927, p. 1, 19 June 1931, p. 1; Keremetsis 1973: 172.
10. Clark 1987: 146.
11. For a typical analysis of the productivity of Mexican labor by a Mexican industrialist, see Robredo 1925: 51; for a similar analysis by a foreign observer, see Jenner 1886.
12. Anderson 1976: 94.   13. AGNT 560.6.11.
14. Clark 1987: 151–52.   15. Quoted in ibid.: 168.
16. Quoted in *EM*, 1 July 1899, p. 255.
17. Sada 1981: 47.
18. *EM*, 21 Mar. 1903, p. 540.
19. Vizcaya Canales 1971: 76–79; *EM*, 18 Jan. 1908, p. 307.
20. Clark 1987: 146, 150.
21. *SM*, 4 Apr. 1887, quoted in Tenenbaum 1983: 13.
22. Graham-Clark 1909: 38.
23. Yamada 1965: 49.
24. *EM*, 7 May 1904, pp. 113–16.
25. Ibid.: 114.
26. Quoted in *EM*, 29 June 1901, pp. 256–57.
27. AGNT 731.5, no doc. no.; *Amcham*, Jan. 1924, p. 13; Díaz Dufoo 1918: 157–59.

28. García Ochoa 1971: 36; Cámara Nacional de Cemento, n.d., United Kingdom, n.d.; Rojas Alonso 1967; Patiño Rodríguez 1964.

29. *EM*, 24 Sept. 1904, p. 563.

30. *EM*, 7 May 1904, p. 114.

31. *EM*, 21 Feb. 1903, pp. 442–43; Keremetsis 1973: 172–73.

32. *EM*, 7 May 1904, p. 114.

33. Ibid.: 116.

Chapter 4

1. *Mexico* [36]: doc. 18-2.

2. Ceceña 1973: 87.

3. *MYB 1912*: 114; Torón Villegas 1963: 55; *FMIA* 1902: 46; Realme Rodríguez 1946: 97.

4. *FMIA* 1903: 57; Realme Rodríguez 1946: 97.

5. *Mexico* [3]: 87.

6. *MYB 1909–10*: 414–15; FM 1975: 15–22.

7. *MYB 1908*: 539; *MYB 1909–1910*: 416–17, 425; *MYB 1911*: 287; *MYB 1912*: 113, 126; *MYB 1913*: 93; *MYB 1914*: 103; *SM*, 28 Nov. 1898, pp. 662–63, and 8 Feb. 1904, p. 696; *EM*, 23 Apr. 1904, pp. 75–76; *Amcham*, Aug. 1927, p. 1, and Oct. 1931, pp. 10–11, 24–25; *Mexico* [56]: 8; Bejar Navarro and Casanova Alvarez 1970: 157–59; Lenz and Gómez de Orozco 1940: 80–85; interview with Felipe Moira Robertson, 24 Feb. 1983.

8. Calculated from *MYB 1908*: 539; *MYB 1909–1910*: 416–17, 425; *MYB 1911*: 287; *MYB 1912*: 113, 126; *MYB 1913*: 93; *MYB 1914*: 103; *SM*, 28 Nov. 1898, pp. 662–63, and 8 Feb. 1904, p. 696; *EM*, 23 Apr. 1904, pp. 75–76.

9. *Mexico* [36]: doc. 18-3.

10. Brittingham, n.d.: 59; Sada 1981: 55.

11. Brittingham, n.d.: 1–4, 6–18; *Amcham*, Oct. 1925, p. 16; United Kingdom, n.d.; Graham-Clark 1909: 37; *SM*, 8 Aug. 1898, p. 444; *MYB 1911*: 289.

12. *Mexico* [9]: 123–24.

13. *MYB 1914*: 101.

14. Derived from *BCM*, pp. 288–89; *Mexico* [39]: 47–49; *Mexico* [41]: 140–47; *MYB 1909–1910*: 414–15; *MYB 1911*: 285; *MYB 1912*: 125; *MYB 1913*: 92; *MYB 1914*: 102; *EM*, 19 Jan. 1907, p. 340; Brittingham, n.d.: 12–18; Graham-Clark 1909: 37; Rosenzweig 1960: 282.

15. I estimated the market shares of these two firms using the data from *Mexico* [47], which break production down by state, not by company. I assumed that together the three firms accounted for 100 percent of the production of cigarettes in the state of Veracruz and the Distrito Federal, where the majority of their production facilities were located. The total output of cigarettes of these two states was then divided by total national production.

16. Anderson 1976: 41.

17. *MYB 1908*: 531; *MYB 1911*: 281; *MYB 1914*: 102; *SM*, 4 Dec. 1893, pp. 582–84; *EM*, 12 Mar. 1904, pp. 593–94, 4 Mar. 1905, p. 477, 18 Aug. 1906, p. 421; *MI*, 1 Mar. 1905, p. 8; D'Olwer 1965: 1118.

18. *MYB 1909–10*: 421.

19. *MI*, 1 Mar. 1905, p. 9; *EM*, 23 Aug. 1902, p. 409; *SM*, 15 May 1911, p. 320; *BCM*, pp. 292–93; *MYB 1912*: 126; *MYB 1913*: 91; *MYB 1914*: 102; Rosenzweig 1960: 221.

20. García Ochoa 1971: 36; Cámara Nacional de Cemento, n.d.; United Kingdom, n.d.; Rojas Alonso 1967; Patiño Rodríguez 1964; *MYB 1914*, p. 104.

21. *Mexico* [9]: 113–14.

22. *MYB 1912*, p. 120; Metz 1982: 447–91.

23. AGNT 96.5.49–53; *Mexico* [15]: 238.

24. *EM*, 10 May 1902, p. 103; *Mexico* [18]: 574; Fuentes Mares 1976: 114, 115, 120; Saldaña 1965: 32; unpublished data from the sales department, Cervecería Cuauhtemoc.

25. National production data from *Mexico* [40]: 68; Cervecería Cuauhtemoc production data from unpublished data from its sales department.

26. *BCM*: 294–95; Serrano 1955: 5; Galas de México 1964: 15.

27. Derived from *EM*, 24 Dec. 1898, p. 249; Rosenzweig 1960: 208.

28. *EM*, 27 July 1907, p. 360.

29. Derived from Rosenzweig 1960: 208; and Table 4.3 above.

30. *Mexico* [36]: doc. 18-1.

31. *Mexico* [46]: cuadros de industria.

32. AGNT 5.4.no doc. no. The number of mills and spindles indicated here differs from that presented in Table 8.1, which presents data only on mills in operation; the figures here refer to *all* mills, whether running or not. In addition, the tables in Chap. 8 refer to arithmetic means, the data here to the median.

33. AGNT 5.4.no doc. no.

34. Graham-Clark 1909: 39; *MYB 1912*: 106; *MYB 1913*: 83.

35. AGNT 5.4.no doc. no.; Graham-Clark 1909: 22; Keremetsis 1973: 116, 143; Carden 1890: 18–20; *BCM*: 286–87; *MYB 1908*: 524; *MYB 1909–10*: 423–24; *MYB 1911*: 265; *MYB 1912*: 123; *MYB 1913*: 90; *MYB 1914*: 100; Ceceña 1973: 86; D'Olwer 1965: 1116.

36. AGNT 5.4.no doc. no.; AGNT, 207.43.3–8; D'Olwer 1965: 1116; *MYB 1911*: 289.

37. AGNT 5.4.no doc. no.; D'Olwer 1965: 1117; *MI*, 15 Feb. 1905, p. 13; *MYB 1908*: 525; *MYB 1911*: 280; *MYB 1913*: 90; *MYB 1914*: 100; *BCM*: 312–14.

38. Carden 1890: 18–19; *MYB 1908*: 525; *MYB 1911*: 287; *MYB 1913*: 90; AGNT 5.4.no doc. no.

39. AGNT 5.4.no doc. no.; *MYB 1912*: 122; *MYB 1914*: 101; *SM*, 15 May 1899, p. 275; Carden 1890: 218.

40. *FI*, 15 Oct. 1910, pp. 13–14; AGNT, 5.4.no doc. no.; *SM*, 5 Feb. 1900, p. 79; D'Olwer 1965: 1117.

41. Anderson 1976: 94.

42. Ibid.: 47.

43. See *Mexico* [11]. I estimated value added and capital invested as a percentage of the national total as follows. (1) The industrial categories of textiles, metallurgy, construction materials, chemicals, paper, glass, tobacco, and food products were taken as representative of the sectors that were becoming characterized by large-scale production. With the exception of the food-products category, I did not disaggregate the data any further than by the broad industrial category. In the case of food products, however, I subtracted out all production not attributable to beer brewing, on the grounds that most of the rest of the food processing industry was characterized by large numbers of relatively small firms. (2) Value added was calculated for each industrial category by subtracting from the value of production the costs of raw materials and energy. (3) The overall data for national manufacturing were calculated simply as the sum of all categories listed in the census with the exceptions of petroleum refining and electric energy generation.

44. Lamoreaux 1985: 32.

45. Because the cost of installation of the machinery figured as a large percentage of the total cost of erecting a mill, there was little incentive for firms in the United States or Europe to sell off their used equipment. See Clark 1987: 160.

Chapter 5

1. On the Banco de Avío, see Potash 1983, and Colón Reyes 1982.

2. For a detailed discussion of banking during the Porfiriato, see Batiz and Canudas Sandoval 1980: 405–36, and Sánchez Martínez 1983: 15–94.

3. Stein 1957; Dean 1969.

4. The Société Financière pour l'industrie au Mexique, with a capitalization of 5 million francs (roughly 10 million pesos), was set up in order that French and Swiss capitalists could invest in Mexican companies. It owned large blocks of shares in the Cervecería Moctezuma, CIDOSA, El Palacio de Hierro (Mexico's largest department store), the Compañía Explotadora de las Fuerzas Hidro-eléctricas de San Ildefonso, and the Compañía Nacional Mexicana de Dinamita y Explosivos. Its largest stockholders appear to have been French banks, most notably the Banque de Paris y des Pays Bas. The annual reports of the Société Financière can be found in *SM*, 8 Aug. 1903, p. 428; *EM*, 11 Oct. 1902, p. 26, 6 July 1904, p. 401, 4 Aug. 1904, p. 1010, 21 Oct. 1905, p. 42, 18 Aug. 1906, p. 421.

5. *FMIA* 1902.

6. Mexico's most important financiers operated on an international scale and had connections to the big foreign banks. In fact, a good deal of the financing for Mexico's major commercial banking companies came from abroad. Mexico's first bank, the Banco de Londres y México, was set up in 1864 as a branch of the London Bank of Mexico and South America. The second major commercial bank established in Mexico, the Banco Nacional de México, was established in 1881 by a group of French bankers. It had two boards of directors, one in Mexico City, on which sat such notables as Hugo Scherer, Antonio Basagoiti, and José A. Signoret, and one in Paris, on which sat Eduoard Noetzlin, who was later to be a key actor in the establishment of the Société Financière pour l'industrie au Mexique. Other major banks also obtained capital from abroad. For example, 25 percent of the stock of the Banco Central Mexicano was owned by J. P. Morgan and Company and the Deutsche Bank, and foreign investors controlled the majority of the stock in the Banco Mexicano de Comercio e Industria. Of the 10 million pesos in subscribed capital pertaining to the latter, 3.5 million was owned by the New York banking house of Speyer and Company, and 3.5 million by the Deutsche Bank of Berlin. See *SM*, 17 June 1901, p. 329, 30 June 1906, p. 367, 6 June 1910, p. 301; Sánchez Martínez 1983; Brittingham, n.d.: 22.

7. In fact, this was often a deliberate strategy on the part of some merchants to get hold of particular properties in which they were interested. Interview with Felipe Moira Robertson, 12 Nov. 1982.

8. Information on Antonio Basagoiti derived from *SM*, 8 Jan. 1897, 21 June 1897, p. 336, 27 Sept. 1897, p. 539, 28 Nov. 1898, p. 662, 11 Feb. 1901, p. 69, 29 May 1905, p. 259, 6 June 1910, p. 301, 15 May 1911, 310; *BCM*: 292, 312; *MYB 1909–1910*: 420; *MYB 1912*: 126; *FMIA* 1902–7; Sánchez Martínez 1983: 52; FM 1901; and Peñafiel 1911: 88, 89, 270, 271.

9. *SM*, 4 Jan. 1897.

10. For Indalecio Ibáñez, see *SM*, 4 Jan. 1897, 28 Nov. 1898, p. 662, 11 Feb. 1901, p. 69, 9 May 1904, p. 862, 9 Oct. 1905, p. 497; and also *EM*, 28 Aug. 1902, p. 401; Peñafiel 1911: 220–21.

11. *BCM*: 292; *MYB 1908*: 525; *MYB 1909–1910*: 424.

12. Alcazar 1945: 48, 123–24.

13. Ibid.: 123–24; *SM*, 29 May 1905, p. 259.

14. FM 1901.

15. *FMIA* 1907; FM 1975: 6.

16. For an analysis of the profits and losses of Fundidora Monterrey, as well as of other Mexican manufacturing companies, see Chap. 7.

17. For Sebastian Robert, see AGNT 96.16.8–9; *SM*, 15 July 1912, p. 451; *FI*, 15 Sept. 1910, p. 16; *MYB 1908*: 524; *MYB 1911*: 289; Peñafiel 1911: 204–5, 256–57, 266–67; Díaz Dufoo 1902: 226.

18. *SM*, 19 Aug. 1907, p. 449.

19. For Hugo Scherer, see *SM*, 28 Oct. 1895, p. 506, 17 June 1901, p. 329, 10 Apr. 1905, p. 177, 19 Feb. 1906, p. 139, 18 Feb. 1907, p. 91, 19

Oct. 1908, p. 583, 6 June 1910, p. 301, 15 July 1912, p. 453. See also *EM*, 4 Mar. 1905, p. 477; *FI*, 15 Oct. 1910, p. 13; *FMIA* 1907–12; Peñafiel 1911: 56–57, 84–85, 132–33, 242–43; *MYB 1909–10*: 420; *MYB 1911*: 282, 284; *MYB 1912*: 120, 124, 125, 140; *MYB 1913*: 103; Sánchez Martínez 1983: 52, 56; Rippy 1948: 3–16.

20. García Díaz 1981: 16–19.

21. *Amcham*, Aug. 1922, p. 14; Peñafiel 1911: 46–47.

22. For a detailed discussion of the activities of these banks, see Sánchez Martínez 1983.

23. *EM*, 5 Feb. 1887, p. 8, 1 Nov. 1888, p. 156, 22 March 1890, p. 91; D'Olwer, 1965: 1118.

24. Keremetsis 1973: 134; *SM*, 3 May 1897, p. 217; Yamada 1965: 55.

25. FM 1901.

26. Keremetsis 1973: 134; Genin 1922: 567.

27. Keremetsis 1973: 172–73.

28. Collado Herrera 1983: 12–19.

29. Ibid.: 69–71.

30. Keremetsis 1973: 132–33; *SM*, 28 Feb. 1898, p. 124, 17 June 1901, p. 329.

31. Keremetsis 1973: 132–33; *FMIA* 1902–5.

32. Collado Herrera 1983: 40, 78.

33. See Brading 1971.

34. See Cerutti 1981a; Cerutti 1981b: 231–66; Cerutti 1982: 81–118; Cerutti 1983.

35. For a general overview of the transformation of Monterrey during this period, see Montemayor Hernández 1971; and Viscaya Canales 1971.

36. Information on Garza from FM 1901; *Trabajo y ahorro*, Nov. 1980; and *El abanderado*, Nov. 1970 (official journals of the Cervecería Cuauhtemoc).

37. *Mexico* [18]: 167; *MYB 1909–1910*: 420; *MYB 1911*: 280; *MYB 1912*: 122; FM 1901; *FMIA* 1909–1913; Saldaña 1965: 37.

Chapter 6

1. *Mexico* [3]: 87.

2. *MYB 1909–10*: 414–15; FM 1975: 15–22.

3. *Mexico* [9]: 13; Díaz Dufoo 1902: 157.

4. *BCM*: 294–95; Serrano 1955: 5; Galas de México 1969: 15.

5. Brittingham, n.d.: 1–4.

6. Ibid.: 6–12.

7. Ibid.: 12–13.

8. Ibid.: 6–11; *Amcham*, Oct. 1925, p. 16; United Kingdom, n.d.

9. Brittingham, n.d.: 11.

10. Ibid.: 12–18; Graham-Clark 1909: 37.

11. *SM*, 8 Aug. 1898, p. 444.

12. Graham-Clark 1909: 37; *MYB 1911*: 289; *MYB 1914*: 101; *Amcham*, Oct. 1925, p. 16.

13. Brittingham, n.d.: 59.

14. Sada 1981: 55; Brittingham, n.d.: 59.

15. *Amcham*, Aug. 1923, p. 20.

16. Hamilton 1982: 210.

17. *BCM*: 288–89; *Mexico* [39]: 47–49; *Mexico* [41]: 140–47; *EM*, 1 Feb. 1902, p. 284; Wasserman 1979: 18.

18. For a discussion of the concession, see *BCM*: 288–89; also *Mexico* citations in n. 17, above, and *EM*, 4 Jan. 1902, p. 217. Dynamite import prices calculated from *MYB 1909–1910*: 414–15.

19. *MYB 1909–10*: 414–15; *MYB 1911*: 285; *MYB 1912*: 125; *MYB 1913*: 92; *MYB 1914*: 102.

20. Derived from Rosenzweig 1960: 282; *EM*, 19 Jan. 1907, p. 340; and *MYB* citations in n. 19, above.

21. Wasserman 1979: 18.

22. *Amcham*, Nov. 1925, p. 24.

23. Calculated from AGNT 5.4.no doc. no.

24. *Amcham*, July 1922, pp. 19–20.

25. On the Compañía Industrial de Parras, see *La compañía industrial de Parras* 1949.

26. D'Olwer 1965: 1117; *BCM*: 296–97; *SM*, 3 May 1897, p. 247; *MYB 1909–10*: 425; *MYB 1912*: 124; *MYB 1913*: 90; *MYB 1914*: 100; Bejar Navarro and Casanova Alvarez 1970: 159.

27. *MYB 1909–10*: 421.

28. Lamoreaux 1985: 141.

29. For a historical summary of the paper industry, see Lenz and Gómez de Orozco 1940.

30. United Kingdom, n.d.; Lenz and Gómez de Orozco 1940: 83.

31. Lamoreaux 1985: 126–27.

32. Lenz and Gómez de Orozco 1940: 80–85; *MYB 1908*: 539; *MYB 1909–10*: 416–17, 425; *MYB 1911*: 287; *MYB 1912*: 113, 126; *MYB 1913*: 93; *MYB 1914*: 103; *SM*, 28 Nov. 1898, pp. 662–63, 8 Feb. 1904, p. 696; *EM*, 23 Apr. 1904, pp. 75–76; *Amcham*, Aug. 1927, p. 1, Oct. 1931, pp. 10–11, 24–25; Bejar Navarro and Casanova Alvarez 1970: 157–59; *Mexico* [56]: 8; interview with Felipe Moira Robertson, 24 Feb. 1983.

33. *MYB 1908*: 531; *MYB 1911*: 281; *MYB 1914*: 102; D'Olwer 1965: 1118; *SM*, 4 Dec. 1893, pp. 582–84; *EM*, 12 Mar. 1904, pp. 593–94, 4 Mar. 1905, p. 477, 18 Aug. 1906, p. 421; *MI*, 1 Mar. 1905, p. 8.

34. *MYB 1909–10*: 421.

35. *MI*, 1 Mar. 1905, p. 9; *EM*, 23 Aug. 1902, p. 409; *SM*, 15 May 1911, p. 320; *BCM*: 292–93; *MYB 1912*: 126; *MYB 1913*: 91; *MYB 1914*: 102.

36. Rosenzweig 1960: 221.

37. Lamoreaux 1985: 141.

38. For a discussion of the circumstances leading up to the great merger movement in the United States, see ibid.: ch. 2.

39. Ibid.: 103.

Chapter 7

1. Yet another conceptualization of profit, the social rate of profit, is not based upon the methodology of cost accounting. Social rates of profit, which derive from the Marxian concept of profits, analyze profits in their entire social context. This line of analysis argues that what appear as costs of production for any individual firm are, in their larger context, the congealed wages and profits of some prior stage of production. That is, profits are shared from sector to sector, and it is the combined profits of all sectors of the economy that constitute the actual rate of profit. For example, unlike accounting rates of profit, which treat interest payments on outstanding debts as costs of production, social rates of profit treat them as profits shared with the financial sector. The interest payment is not a cost of production, but is a hidden profit transferred to another firm. Because of the incomplete nature of the data available, it has been possible to calculate only the accounting rates of profit.

2. An attempt to fit values for the years in which observations were not available, using the yield on common stock as a proxy, was not satisfactory because the correlation between stock yields and the rate of return on capital was too low. However, the analysis of the two variables does indicate an important relationship between them. One would expect that dividends would go up as the rate of return on capital stock increases. As the latter climbs, however, so does the price of the stock, with the result that the ratio dividends / price of stock might or might not increase proportionately.

To take the El Buen Tono data as an example, for 11 years (1902, 1903, 1904, 1907, 1908, 1909, 1910, 1918, 1919, 1923, and 1924) we can use data for both variables, rate of return on capital stock (x) and dividends divided by the price of the stock (y). A linear regression of y on x generated an r^2 of 0.101, with $a = 1.679$ and $b = 0.230$. To take into account the fact that the price of stocks increases along with the increase in the rate of return, we can use log y in the equation, and the r^2 increases to 0.143 with $a = 1.318$ and $b = 0.058$.

One might expect that both dividends and the price of the stock are more closely correlated to the previous year's rate of return on capital stock, so that we can use the $n + 1$ data for y, which is to say, for every year's rate of return data we use the following year's dividend / price of stock ratio. Staying with x against log y, we find an r^2 of 0.31, three times higher than the initial r^2 of 0.101, and $a = 1.090$ and $b = 0.058$.

Although none of the r^2's are extremely significant in and of themselves, it is interesting to note that we obtain a higher correlation coefficient as we move from a linear regression to the linear-log and lagged regression. This would suggest that the dividend / price ratio increases along with the rate of return on capital stock, but proportionately less so, which in turn suggests the importance of the stock price / rate of return on capital stock relationship.

3. The two price indices that cover the Porfiriato differ in the rate of inflation from one year to the next, but they agree that the overall rate from 1902 to 1910 was almost exactly 4 percent. For an index of wholesale prices in Mexico City, see Rosenzweig 1965c: 172. For an index of implicit prices, see Haber 1985: appendix B.

4. The three bonds analyzed—the Bonos de la Deuda Interior, the Bonos de la Deuda Consolidada, and the Emprestito of 1899—were chosen because they were traded on the Mexico City stock exchange (as opposed to the many other government bonds traded only in Europe) and because it was possible to gather information about their nominal interest rate and repayment schedule. Their average yields were calculated as follows. Yearly averages of each bond's market price were obtained by averaging their price at the end of each month. The average annual prices were then used to derive the effective yield of each bond by dividing the nominal interest rate by the bond's market price. The yields were then averaged in order to obtain the average yield for the three bonds. Data for the Emprestito of 1899 run only to 1907. For 1908–10 the average is therefore only for the other two bonds. The yields of these three bonds were so close, however, that the results are not sensitive to this change in coverage.

Chapter 8

1. Womack 1978: 92–93.   2. Ibid.: 86–89.
3. Ibid.: 81.   4. *SM*, 17 Mar. 1913, p. 161.
5. Calculated from *MYB 1912*: 123; *EM*, 26 Apr. 1912, p. 51; *EM*, 23 May 1914, p. 77. No table is included on the profits of CIVSA because it was not possible to construct reliable series for the years after 1913.

6. Fuentes Mares 1976: 123; García Naranjo 1955: 48–52.

7. AGNT 173.25.1–3, 207.30.4–6; interview with Felipe Moira Robertson, 24 Feb. 1983.

8. Compañía Industrial de Parras 1949: 53.

9. Brittingham, n.d.: 120–22.

10. For examples of destruction by direct action during the Revolution, see AGNT 174.1.108, 106.14.1, 134.50.1.

11. Interview with Carlos Prieto, 7 Jan. 1983; Saldaña 1965: 43; AGNT 92.1.no doc. no.; Womack 1978: 84.

12. AGNT 46.3.1–5, 52.12.1–3, 90.17.1, 91.21.1–2, 96.5.49–53, 96.9.45, 107.16.1, 107.22.2, 110.28.1, 173.23.1.

13. Cámara Nacional de Cemento, n.d.: 5; Rojas Alonso 1967: 37;

Amcham, Sept. 1919, p. 9; García Ochoa 1971: 36; Patiño Rodríguez 1964: 22.

14. *BFM*, 29 Apr. 1919, p. 8, 30 Apr. 1919, p. 8, 1 May 1919, p. 5.

15. Interview with Hanz Lenz, 15 Jan. 1983.

16. *Mexico* [27]: 82, 263.

17. Ibid.: 72, 76.

18. Quoted in Meyer and Sherman 1979: 544.

19. *Mexico* [27]: 177, 181.

20. Ibid.: 35.

21. Nominal book values are used because it is not possible to calculate the real value of a company's physical plant without knowing the vintage of the machinery.

22. Series on both nominal and real stock prices can be found in Haber 1985: ch. 5.

23. Sterrett and Davis 1928: 190.

Chapter 9

1. Calculated from *Mexico* [54]; *Mexico* [10]: 134. Nominal wages deflated with wholesale price index for consumption goods, in *Mexico* [23]: 750.

2. *Mexico* [26]: 64.

3. Kindleberger 1984: 316.

4. Fitzgerald 1984: 245. Sterrett and Davis (1928: 190) in their report to the Committee of Bankers in 1928 noted the price of silver as falling from 69 cents to 56 cents.

5. Fitzgerald 1984: 246.

6. *Mexico* [26]: 335.

7. Cárdenas Sánchez 1982: 37, 39.

8. Fitzgerald 1984: 254. The absolute figures on unemployment reported by the Dirección General de Estadística were 1.7 percent in 1930, 6 percent in 1932, and 1 percent in 1934. Fitzgerald quite correctly notes that these figures are much too low.

9. Calculated from Table 9.1.

10. For a complete discussion of the deportation of Mexican workers during the Great Depression, see Carreras de Velasco 1974.

11. Calculated from *Mexico* [54]; *Mexico* [10]: 134. Nominal wages deflated with wholesale price index for consumption goods, in *Mexico* [23]: 750.

12. Sterrett and Davis 1928: 132; Krauze 1977: 247.

13. Calculated from *Mexico* [26]: 306.

14. For a complete discussion on government monetary and fiscal policy, see Cárdenas Sánchez 1982: chs. 3 and 4.

15. Ibid.: 131. 16. Ibid.: 128.

17. Ibid.: 67. 18. Ibid.: 68, 70.

19. Calculated from *Mexico* [23]: 311.

20. *Amcham*, Mar. 1928, p. 20; AGNT 1460.3.1–2; Sherwell 1929: 110.
21. *Amcham*, June 1928, pp. 19, 26.
22. Ibid.
23. *Mexico* [64]: 221–34.
24. *Mexico* [63]: 204; *Mexico* [64]: 236–37.
25. For annual nominal and real stock prices, see Haber 1985: ch. 5.
26. See n. 25, above.
27. See n. 25, above.
28. Derived from *Mexico* [61]: 61–62; *Mexico* [7]: 29–30.
29. *Mexico* [11]: chs. 64 and 65.
30. See n. 25, above.
31. *Mexico* [35]: 45–66.
32. Calculated from ibid.: unpaginated output table; *Mexico* [12]: 959.
33. *Mexico* [12]: 959.
34. Calculated from *Mexico* [35]: 90 and unpaginated output table.
35. See n. 25, above.

Chapter 10

1. Cárdenas Sánchez 1982: 13.
2. Haber 1983: 633–54.
3. Wilkie 1970: 208, 212, 223, 230.
4. Cárdenas Sánchez 1984: 230–31.
5. Ibid.: 230.
6. Cárdenas Sánchez: 1982: 72–73.
7. Ibid.: 65–66.
8. Ibid.: 76.
9. Ibid.: 131.
10. Ibid.: 138.
11. Wilkie 1970: 62, 69, 78.
12. *Mexico* [23]: 566.
13. Derived from ibid.: 311.
14. Cárdenas Sánchez: 1982: 6, 47.
15. Serrano 1955: 6–8.
16. See, for example, the reports reprinted in *Amcham*, Apr. 1934, p. 6, July 1934, p. 10, Jan. 1935, p. 12, Mar. 1935, p. 5, Apr. 1935, p. 24, June 1935, p. 8, July 1935, p. 25, Aug. 1935, p. 23, Sept. 1935, p. 23, Jan. 1936, p. 28, May 1936, p. 12, July 1936, p. 23, Sept. 1937, p. 13, Oct. 1937, p. 12, Feb. 1939, p. 32, Apr. 1939, p. 21.
17. *Mexico* [12]: 959.
18. Calculated from ibid.; and *Mexico* [35]: unpaginated output table.
19. Data for 1936 are used because no data are available for some firms after that date. For series on real and nominal stock prices from the Porfiriato until 1938, see Haber 1985: ch. 5.
20. Derived from Cárdenas Sánchez 1982: 210.
21. See ch. 8, above, for a more complete discussion of the market value / book value ratio and how it was calculated.
22. *Amcham*, Apr. 1934, p. 6.
23. *Mexico* [52].
24. Ibid.
25. Mosk 1950.

26. See, for example, Hamilton 1982.
27. García Ochoa 1971: 100–101.

Chapter 11

1. For a more complete discussion of his ideas about late industrialization, see Gerschenkron 1962: ch. 1.

2. These calculations do not include dividends paid during 1914–17 because of the lack of a price deflator for those years. However, the results presented here would not be sensitive to the addition of these data since dividends for the firms in question during the Revolution were either negligible or altogether lacking.

3. Gerschenkron 1962: ch. 1.

Bibliography

Agraz García del Alba, Gabriel. 1963. *Historia de la Industria Sauza: tres generaciones y una tradición.* Guadalajara, Mexico.

Alanís Patiño, Emilio. 1952. "La productividad de la industria textil algodonera de México." Thesis, Universidad Nacional Autónoma de México.

Alcázar, Ricardo de. 1945. *Don Adolfo Prieto y Alvarez de las Vallines o el caballero español, 1867–1945.* Mexico City.

Alejo López, Francisco Javier. 1969. "La estrategia del desarrollo económico de México en 1920–1970." Thesis, Universidad Nacional Autónoma de México.

Alejo López, Jaime. 1969. "La industria textil y el desarrollo económico de México: el caso del algodón." Thesis, Universidad Nacional Autónoma de México.

Anderson, Rodney O. 1976. *Outcasts in Their Own Land: Mexican Industrial Workers, 1906–1911.* Dekalb, Ill.

Antuñano, Estevan de. 1955. *La industria del algodón en México, 1833.* Mexico City.

Arias, Patricia. 1983. *Fuentes para el estudio de la industrialización en Jalisco: siglo XIX.* Mexico City.

———. 1985. *Guadalajara: la gran ciudad de la pequena industria.* Zamora, Michoacán.

Aubey, Robert T. 1979. "Capital Mobilization and Patterns of Business Ownership and Control in Latin America: The Case of Mexico." In Sidney Greenfield, Arnold Strickon, and Robert T. Aubey, eds., *Entrepreneurs in a Cultural Context.* Albuquerque, N.M.

Banco Central Mexicano. 1908. *Las sociedades anónimas de Mexico, año I.* Mexico City. Cited as *BCM.*

Banco de Comercio. 1975a. *La economía del estado de Nuevo León.* Mexico City.

———. 1975b. *La economía del estado de Puebla.* Mexico City.

———. 1977. *La economía del Distrito Federal.* Mexico City.

Banco Nacional de México. 1978. *Exámen de la situación económica de México, 1925–1975.* Mexico City.

Barajas Manzano, Javier. 1959. "Aspectos de la industria textil de algodón en México." Thesis, Universidad Nacional Autónoma de México.

Basáñez, Manuel. 1981. *La lucha por la hegemonía en México*. Mexico City.

Basurto, Jorge. 1981. *El proletariado industrial en México (1850–1930)*. Mexico City.

Batíz, José Antonio, and Enrique Canudas Sandoval. 1980. "Aspectos financieros y monetarios (1880–1910)." In Ciro Cardoso, ed., *México en el siglo XIX: historia económica y de la estructura social*, 405–36. Mexico City.

Bazant, Jan. 1962. "Estudio sobre la productividad de la industria algodonera mexicana en 1843–1845." In Luis Chavez Orozco, ed., *La industria nacional y el comercio exterior, 1842–51*, 29–85. Mexico City.

———. 1964a. "Evolución de la industria textil poblana (1544–1845)." *Historia Mexicana* 13(4): 473–516.

———. 1964b. "La industria algodonera poblana de 1800 a 1843 en números." *Historia Mexicana* 14(1): 131–42.

Beato, Guillermo. 1981. "La casa Martínez del Río: del comercio colonial a la industria fabril, 1829–1864." In Ciro Cardoso, ed., *Formación y desarrollo de la burguesía en México, siglo XIX*. Mexico City.

Becerril Benítez, Joel Luis. 1961. "La industria del cemento en México." Thesis, Universidad Nacional Autónoma de México.

Bejar Navarro, Raúl, and Francisco Casanova Alvarez. 1970. *Historia de la industrialización del estado de México*. Mexico City.

Boletín Financiero y Minero. 1916–38. Mexico City. Cited as BFM.

Bonaparte, Roland Napoleon. 1904. *Mexico at the Beginning of the 20th Century*. St. Louis.

Bortz, Jeffrey L. 1987. *Industrial Wages in Mexico City, 1939–1975*. New York.

Brading, David. 1971. *Miners and Merchants of Bourbon Mexico, 1763–1810*. London.

Brittingham, Albert A. N.d. *Juan F. Brittingham, 1859–1940*. Los Angeles.

Calderón, Francisco R. 1955. *Historia moderna de México: la república restaurada, la vida económica*. Mexico City.

Calderón, Miguel Angel. 1982. *El impacto de la crisis de 1929 en México*. Mexico City.

Calderón de la Barca, Frances. 1920. *La vida en México*. Mexico City.

Cámara Nacional de Cemento. N.d. *Medio siglo de cemento en México*. Mexico City.

Carden, Lionel. 1890. "Report on the Cotton Manufacturing Industry in Mexico." British Diplomatic and Consular Reports, Misc. series no. 453. London.

Cárdenas Sánchez, Enrique. 1981. "Some Issues on Mexico's 19th Century Depression." Mimeo.

———. 1982. "Mexico's Industrialization During the Great Depression: Public Policy and Private Response." Ph.D. diss., Yale University.

———. 1984. "The Great Depression and Industrialization: The Case of

Mexico." In Rosemary Thorp, ed., *Latin America in the 1930s: The Role of the Periphery in World Crisis*, 222–41. New York.

Cardoso, Ciro. 1980. "Las industrias de transformación, 1821–1880." In Ciro Cardoso, ed., *México en el siglo XIX (1821–1910): historia económica y de la estructura social*, 142–66. Mexico City.

Cardoso, Ciro, Francisco G. Hermosillo, and Salvador Hernández. 1980. *La clase obrera en la historia de México: de la dictadura porfirista a los tiempos libertarios*. Mexico City.

Cardoso, Ciro, and Carmen Reyna. 1980. "Las industrias de transformación (1880–1910)." In Ciro Cardoso, ed., *México en el siglo XIX (1821–1910): historia económica y estructura social*, 381–99. Mexico City.

Carr, Barry. 1982. *El movimiento obrero y la política en México, 1910–1929*. Mexico City.

Carreras de Velasco, Mercedes. 1974. *Los mexicanos que devolvió la crisis, 1929–1932*. Mexico City.

Ceceña, José Luis. 1973. *México en la órbita imperial*. Mexico City.

Cementos Tolteca, Compañía de Cemento Portland, S.A. 1969. *Sesenta años, 1909–1969*. Mexico City.

Cerutti, Mario. 1981a. "Frontera, burguesía regional, y desarrollo capitalista: el caso de Monterrey—reflexiones sobre el periodo 1860–1910." In Roque González Salazar, ed., *La frontera del norte: integración y desarrollo*, 196–234. Mexico City.

———. 1981b. "Patricio Milmo: empresario regiomontano del siglo XIX." In Ciro Cardoso, ed., *Formación y desarrollo de la burguesía en México: siglo XIX*, 231–66. Mexico City.

———. 1982. "La formación de capital pre-industrial en Monterrey (1850–1890)." *Revista Mexicana de Sociología* 44(1): 81–118.

———. 1983. *Burguesía y capitalismo en Monterrey, 1850–1910*. Mexico City.

Cervecería Cuauhtemoc. 1970. *El Abanderado* (Nov.). Company journal.

———. 1980. *Trabajo y Ahorro* (Nov.). Company journal.

Chandler, Alfred D., Jr. 1977. *The Visible Hand: The Managerial Revolution in American Business*. Cambridge, Mass.

Chandler, Alfred D., Jr., and Herman Daems, eds. 1980. *Managerial Hierarchies: Comparative Perspectives on the Rise of the Modern Industrial Enterprise*. Cambridge, Mass.

Chavez Orozco, Luis. 1933. "La industria de hilados y tejidos en México, 1829–1842." In Luis Chavez Orozco, ed., *Documentos para la historia económica de México*, 1: 1–144. Mexico City.

———. 1962. "La industria de transformación mexicana, 1821–1867." In Luis Chavez Orozco, ed., *La industria nacional y el comercio exterior*. Mexico City.

Chavez Orozco, Luis, and Enrique Florescano. 1965. *Agricultura y industria textil de Veracruz, siglo XIX*. Xalapa, Veracruz.

Clark, Gregory. 1987. "Why Isn't the Whole World Developed? Lessons from the Cotton Mills." *Journal of Economic History* 47(1): 141–74.

Clark, Marjorie Ruth. 1979. *La organización obrera en México*. Mexico City.

Cleland, Robert Glass. 1921. *The Mexico Yearbook, 1920–21*. Los Angeles.
———. 1924. *The Mexico Yearbook, 1922–1924*. Los Angeles.
Coatsworth, John H. 1978. "Obstacles to Economic Growth in Nineteenth Century Mexico." *American Historical Review* 83(1): 80–100.
———. 1981. *Growth Against Development: The Economic Impact of Railroads in Porfirian Mexico*. Dekalb, Ill.
Cockcroft, James D. 1968. *Intellectual Precursors of the Mexican Revolution*. Austin, Texas.
———. 1983. *Mexico: Class Formation, Capital Accumulation, and the State*. New York.
Cole, William E. 1967. *Steel and Economic Growth in Mexico*. Austin, Texas.
Collado Herrera, María del Carmen. 1983. "Los Braniff y la creación de su imperío en México: 1865–1920." Mimeo.
Colón Reyes, Linda Ivette. 1982. *Los orígenes de la burguesía y el Banco de Avío*. Mexico City.
Compañía de las Fábricas de Papel de San Rafael y Anexas, S.A. 1931. *Homenaje de la Compañía de las Fábricas de Papel de San Rafael y Anexas, S.A. al Congreso Mundial de la Prensa*. Monterrey.
Compañía Fundidora de Fierro y Acero de Monterrey, S.A. 1900–37. "Informe anual, 1900 to 1937." Corporate annual reports, available in Library of the Banco de México. Cited as *FMIA*.
———. 1901. "Actas constitutivas, estatutos y recopilación de los informes." Available in Library of the Banco de México.
———. 1975. *Memoria Fundidora Monterrey*. Mexico City.
Compañía Industrial de Parras, S.A. 1949. *Quincuagésimo aniversario de su fundación, 1899–1949*. Parras, Coahuila.
Conkling, Alfred R. 1895. *Appleton's Guide to Mexico*. New York.
Contreras, Mario, and Jesús Tamayo, eds. 1975. *México en el siglo XX: textos y documentos*. Mexico City.
Convención Industrial. 1912. "Tarifa mínima, uniforme en toda la república: tarifa para preparación de hilados." Resolution passed by the convention.
Cordova, Arnaldo. 1973. *La ideología de la Revolución Mexicana: la formación del nuevo regimen*. Mexico City.
———. 1980. *La clase obrera en la historia de México: en una época de crisis, 1928–1934*. Mexico City.
Cott, Kennett S. 1978. "Porfirian Investment Policies 1876–1910." Ph.D. diss., University of New Mexico.
Cue Canovas, Agustín. 1959. *La industria en México, 1521–1845*. Mexico City.
Davis, Keith A. 1972. "Tendencias demográficas urbanas durante el siglo XIX en México." *Historia Mexicana* 21(3): 481–519.
Davis, Lance E., and Robert A. Huttenback, with the assistance of Susan Gray Davis. 1986. *Mammon and the Pursuit of Empire: The Political Economy of British Imperialism, 1860–1912*. Cambridge, Eng.
Dean, Warren. 1969. *The Industrialization of Sao Paulo*. Austin, Texas.

de la Peña, Moisés T. 1938. *La industria textil del algodón: crises—salarios contratación.* Mexico City.
de la Peña, Sergio. 1975. *La formación del capitalismo en México.* Mexico City.
Derossi, Flavia. 1977. *El empresario mexicano.* Mexico City.
Díaz Dufoo, Carlos. 1902. *México: Its Social Evolution.* Mexico City.
———. 1918. *México y los capitales extranjeros.* Mexico City.
———. 1935. *La vida económica: hechos y doctrinas 1916–1934.* Mexico City.
D'Olwer, Luis Nicolau. 1965. "Las inversiones extranjeras." In Daniel Cosío Villegas, ed., *Historia moderna de México: el Porfiriato, la vida económica,* 973–1185. Mexico City.
El Economista Mexicano. 1896–1914. Mexico City. Cited as *EM.*
Fitzgerald, E. V. K. 1984. "Restructuring Through the Depression: The State and Capital Accumulation in Mexico, 1925–1940." In Rosemary Thorp, ed., *Latin America in the 1930s: The Role of the Periphery in World Crisis,* 242–65. New York.
Fitzgerrell, J. J. 1906. *Fitzgerrell's Guide to Mexico.* Mexico City.
El Fomento Industrial. 1909–10. Mexico City. Cited as *FI.*
Franco, Luis G. 1945. *Glosa del periodo del gobierno del C. General y Ingeniero Pascual Ortíz Rubio, 1930–1932: industria, comercio y trabajo (informe presidencial, 1930–1932).* Mexico City.
Fuentes Mares, José. 1976. *Monterrey: una ciudad creadora y sus capitanes.* Mexico City.
Galas de México. 1969. *La cerveza y la industria cervecera mexicana.* Mexico City.
Gamboa Ojeda, Leticia. 1985. *Los empresarios de ayer: el grupo dominante en la industria textil de Puebla, 1906–1929.* Puebla.
García, D. Rafael. 1901. *El presente y el porvenir económico de la república: colección de artículos económicos políticos escritos y publicados en el Universal y la Gaceta Comercial.* Mexico City.
García Beraza, Felipe, ed. 1973. *Liber amicorum: tributo de admiración y de afecto a Don Carlos Prieto.* Mexico City.
García Cubas, Antonio. 1885. *Cuadro geográfico, estadístico, e histórico.* Mexico City.
———. 1893. *México: Its Industry, Trade, and Commerce.* Mexico City.
García Díaz, Bernardo. 1981. *Un pueblo fabril del Porfiriato: Santa Rosa, Veracruz.* Mexico City.
García Naranjo, Nemesio. 1955. *Una industria en marcha.* Monterrey.
García Ochoa, Jaime Salvador. 1971. "La industria del cemento y las sociedades cooperativas." Thesis, Universidad Nacional Autónoma de México.
García Vargas, Benito. 1967. "La industria cervecera en la integración económica de México." Thesis, Universidad Nacional Autónoma de México.
Garza, Virgilio. 1969. "Brief Sketch of the Industrial Development of Monterrey." In *Basic Industries in Texas and Northern Mexico.* New York.

Garza Villarreal, Gustavo. 1980. *Industrialización de las principales ciudades de México: hacia una estrategia espacio-sectorial de descentralización industrial.* Mexico City.

———. 1985. *El proceso de industrialización en la ciudad de México, 1821–1970.* Mexico City.

Genin, Auguste. 1922. *México contemporáneo, 1921.* Mexico City.

———. 1924. *La cerveza entre los antiguos mexicanos y en la actualidad.* Mexico City.

Gerschenkron, Alexander. 1962. *Economic Backwardness in Historical Perspective: A Book of Essays.* Cambridge, Mass.

Gilly, Adolfo. 1971. *La revolución interrumpida: México, 1910–1920, una guerra campesina por la tierra y el poder.* Mexico City.

González López, Alejandro A. 1950. "Estudio en la Compañía Fundidora de Fierro y Acero de Monterrey." Thesis, Universidad Nacional Autónoma de México.

González Navarro, Moisés. 1956. "Las huelgas textiles en el Porfiriato." *Historia Mexicana* 6(2): 201–16.

———. 1957. "La huelga de Río Blanco." *Historia Mexicana* 6(4): 510–33.

———. 1970. *Las huelgas textiles del Porfiriato.* Puebla.

———. 1977. *Anatomía del poder en México, 1848–53.* Mexico City.

Graham-Clark, William A. 1909. "Cuba, Mexico, and Central America." Part 1 of *Cotton Goods in Latin America.* Washington, D.C.

Guadarrama, Rocío. 1981. *Los sindicatos y la política en México: la CROM, 1918–1928.* Mexico City.

Haber, Stephen H. 1983. "Modernization and Change in Mexican Communities, 1930–1970." In James W. Wilkie and Stephen H. Haber, eds., *Statistical Abstract of Latin America* 22: 633–54. Los Angeles.

———. 1985. "The Industrialization of Mexico, 1890 to 1940: The Structure and Growth of Manufacturing in an Underdeveloped Economy." Ph.D. diss., University of California, Los Angeles.

Hamilton, Nora. 1982. *The Limits of State Autonomy: Post-Revolutionary Mexico.* Princeton, N.J.

Hansen, Roger D. 1982. *La política del desarrollo mexicano.* Mexico City.

Heath Constable, Hilaria Joy. 1982. *Lucha de clases: la industria textil en Tlaxcala.* Mexico City.

Hernández, Ana María. 1940. *La mujer mexicana en la industria textil.* Mexico City.

Hernández Elizando, Roberto C. 1981. "Comercio e industria textil en Nuevo León, 1852–1890." In Ciro Cardoso, ed., *Formación y desarrollo de la burguesía en México, siglo XIX,* 267–86. Mexico City.

Herrera Canales, Ines. 1980. "La circulación: transporte y comercio." In Ciro Cardoso, ed., *México en el siglo XIX (1821–1910): historia económica y de la estructura social,* 193–226. Mexico City.

Jenner, G. 1886. "Informe de Mr. G. Jenner sobre la inversión del capital inglés en México." *Informes y documentos relativos a comercio interior, mes de septiembre 1886.* Mexico City.

Journal of the American Chamber of Commerce of Mexico. 1918–24. Mexico City. Succeeded by *Mexican Commerce* (1925) and *Mexican Commerce and Industry* (1926–40). Cited as *Amcham.*

Katz, Friedrich. 1980. *La servidumbre agraria en México en la epoca porfiriana.* Mexico City.

Keesing, Donald B. 1969. "Structural Change Early in Development: Mexico's Changing Industrial and Occupational Structures from 1895 to 1950." *Journal of Economic History* 29(4): 716–38.

Kemmerer, Edwin. 1940. *Inflation and Revolution: Mexico's Experience of 1912–1917.* Princeton, N.J.

Keremetsis, Dawn. 1973. *La industria textil mexicana en el siglo XIX.* Mexico City.

Kindleberger, Charles P. 1984. "The 1929 World Depression in Latin America—from the Outside." In Rosemary Thorp, ed., *Latin America in the 1930s: The Role of the Periphery in World Crisis*, 315–30. New York.

Krauze, Enrique. 1977. *Historia de la Revolución Mexicana, 1924–1928: la reconstrucción económica.* Mexico City.

Kroeber, Clifton. 1983. *Man, Land, and Water: Mexico's Farmlands Irrigation Policies, 1885–1911.* Berkeley, Calif.

Lamoreaux, Naomi. 1985. *The Great Merger Movement in American Business, 1895–1904.* Cambridge, Eng.

Lenz, Hans, and Federico Gómez de Orozco. 1940. *La industria papelera en México.* Mexico City.

Lewis, William Arthur. 1978. *Growth and Fluctuations, 1870 to 1913.* London.

López Cámara, Francisco. 1967. *La estructura económica y social de México en la época de la Reforma.* Mexico City.

López Rosado, Diego G. 1965. *Ensayos sobre historia económica de México.* Mexico City.

Macedo, Pablo. 1905. *La evolución mercantil, communicaciones y obras públicas, la hacienda pública: tres monografías que dan idea de una parte de la evolución económica de México.* Mexico City.

Manero, Antonio. 1957. *La revolución bancaria en México.* Mexico City.

Markiewicz, Dana. 1985. "Mexico's Agrarian Reform." Unpublished manuscript.

Martínez del Campo, Manuel. 1985. *Industrialización en México: hacia un análisis crítico.* Mexico City.

Martínez López, Luis. 1924. *Hilados y tejidos: colección de todas las disposiciones vigentes.* Mexico City.

Masuoka Kashiwamoto, Isomi. 1971. "La industria cervecera mexicana." Thesis, Universidad Nacional Autónoma de México.

Mauro, Frederic. N.d. "El desarrollo económico de Monterrey, 1890–1960." Mimeo. Available in library at AGENL.

Metz, Brigida von, Verena Rudkau, Beatriz Scharrer, and Guillermo

224 *Bibliography*

Turner. 1982. *Los pioneros del imperialismo alemán en México.* Mexico City.

The Mexican Yearbook. 1908–1914. London. Annual. Cited as *MYB.*

Mexico, Official Publications and Reports:

[1] Banco de México. 1981. "Datos sobre los diferentes agregados de México, 1895 a 1979." Mimeo.

[2] ———. Departamento de Investigaciones Industriales. 1961. "La industria siderúgica de México." Mimeo.

[3] ———. Departamento de Investigaciones Industriales, Comité de Estudios Siderúgicos. 1955. "Informe preliminar sobre algunos aspectos de la industria siderúgica." Mimeo.

[4] Banco Nacional de Comercio Exterior. 1959. *Los industriales mexicanos y el comercio exterior: 1848–1852.* Mexico City.

[5] Departamento de la Estadística Nacional. 1924. *El progreso de México: estudio económico estadístico del Departamento de la Estadística Nacional.* Mexico City.

[6] ———. 1926. *Anuario estadístico, 1923–1924.* Mexico City.

[7] ———. 1929. *Algunos cuadros sintéticos de estadísticas de México.* Mexico City.

[8] Departamento de Trabajo. 1936–40. *Memoria, 1935–1940.* Mexico City.

[9] Dirección General de Estadística. 1903. *Estadística industrial formada por la Dirección General de Estadística a cargo del Dr. Antonio Peñafiel, 1902.* Mexico City.

[10] ———. 1926. *Anuario estadístico de la República Mexicana, 1924.* Mexico City.

[11] ———. 1934. *Primer censo industrial de 1930.* Mexico City.

[12] ———. 1948. *Anuario estadístico de la República Mexicana, 1942.* Mexico City.

[13] Distrito Federal. 1901–13. *Boletín de estadística del Distrito Federal 1901–1913.*

[14] Ferrocarriles Nacionales de México. 1932. *México-económico, 1928–1930: Anuario estadístico de la oficina de estadísticas económicas de los Ferrocarriles Nacionales de México.* Mexico City.

[15] Gobierno del Estado de México. 1911. *Concentración de los datos estadísticos del estado de México en el año 1910.* Toluca.

[16] Gobierno del Estado de Nuevo León. 1895. *Memoria del estado, 1891–1895.* Monterrey.

[17] ———. 1899. *Memoria del estado de Nuevo León, 1895–1899.* Monterrey.

[18] ———. 1903. *Memoria del Gobernador Bernardo Reyes, 1899–1903.* Monterrey.

[19] Gobierno del Estado de Puebla. 1901. *Memoria.* Puebla.

[20] ———. 1903. *Memoria.* Puebla.

[21] ———. 1905–11. *Boletín de estadísticas del estado de Puebla.* Puebla.

[22] ———. 1907. *Memoria.* Puebla.

[23] Instituto Nacional de Estadística, Geografía, e Informática. 1985. *Estadísticas históricas de México.* Mexico City.

[24] Ministerio de Fomento. 1866. *Memoria 1865.* Mexico City.

[25] Ministerio de Hacienda. 1880. *Report of the Secretary of Finance of the United States of Mexico of the 15th of January 1897, on the Actual Condition of Mexico and the Increase of Commerce with the United States, Rectifying the Report of the Hon. John W. Foster, Envoy Extraordinary and Minister Plenipotentiary of the United States in Mexico, the 9th of October, 1878 to Mr. Carlisle Mason, President of the Manufacturers' Association of the City of Chicago, in the State of Illinois, of the United States of America.* New York.

[26] Nacional Financiera. 1981. *La económica mexicana en cifras.* Mexico City.

[27] Primer Congreso Nacional de Industriales. 1918. *Reseña y memorias del primer congreso nacional de industriales reunido en la Ciudad de México bajo el patroncinio de la Secretaría de Industria, Comercio, y Trabajo.* Mexico City.

[28] Secretaría de la Economía. 1956. *Estadísticas sociales del Porfiriato, 1877–1910.* Mexico City.

[29] Secretaría de la Economía Nacional. 1932. *Memoria, 1932.*

[30] ———. 1934a. *La industria textil en México: el problema obrero y los problemas económicos.* Mexico City.

[31] ———. 1934b. *Memoria, 1934.*

[32] ———. 1938. *Memoria, 1938.*

[33] ———. 1940a. *Memoria, 1940.*

[34] ———. 1940b. *Geografía económica del estado de Hidalgo, 1939.* Mexico City.

[35] Secretaría de la Economía Nacional: Departamento de Industria. 1934. "Monografía económico-industrial sobre la industria cigarrera en la República Mexicana." Mimeo.

[36] Secretaría del Estado. 1857. *Memoria de la Secretaría del Estado y del Despacho de Fomento, Colonización, Industria y Comercio de la República Mexicana, 1857.* Mexico City.

[37] Secretaría de Fomento, Colonización e Industria. 1885. *Memoria, 1883–1885.*

[38] ———. 1896. *Memoria, 1892–1896.*

[39] ———. 1900. *Memoria, 1897–1900.*

[40] ———. 1901. *Cuadro sinóptico y estadístico de la República Mexicana formado por la Dirección General de Estadística a cargo del Dr. Antonio Peñafiel, año de 1900.* Mexico City.

[41] ———. 1904. *Memoria, 1901–1904.*

[42] ———. 1907. *Memoria, 1905–1907.*

[43] ———. 1909. *Memoria, 1908–1909.*

[44] ———. 1910. *Cuadro sinóptico informativo.* Mexico City.

[45] ———. 1912. *Memoria, 1910–1911.*

[46] Secretaría de Hacienda. 1880. *Estadística de la República Mexicana.* Mexico City.

[47] ———. 1894–1915. *Boletín de estadística fiscal.* Mexico City.

[48] Secretaría de Hacienda y Crédito Público. 1915–32. *Boletín de la Secretaría de Hacienda y Crédito Público.* Mexico City.

[49] ———. 1921. *Anuario de estadística fiscal, 1918.* Mexico City.

[50] ———. 1922. *Anuario de estadística fiscal, 1919.* Mexico City.

[51] ———. 1933. *La crisis económica en México y la nueva legislación sobre la moneda y el crédito.* Mexico City.

[52] ———. 1938. "Directorio de las fábricas de hilados y tejidos registrados." Mimeo, available in Biblioteca Miguel Lerdo de Tejada.

[53] ———. 1943. "La industria de hilados y tejidos en Mexico." Mimeo, available in Biblioteca Miguel Lerdo de Tejada.

[54] ———, Departamento de Impuestos Especiales. 1925–33. "Estadística del ramo de hilados y tejidos de algodón y de lana, 1925–1933." Mimeo, available in Library of the Banco de México.

[55] ———, ———. 1930. *Hilados y tejidos—leyes, reglamentos, decretos circulares, y ademas dispocisiones que en materia fiscal se encuentra vigentes.* Mexico City.

[56] ———, Departamento Técnico Fiscal. 1936. *El problema actual de la industria papelera en México.* Mexico City.

[57] ———, Dirección de Estudio Financieros. 1942. "Cooperativa de Cemento Cruz Azul, S.C.L." Mimeo, available in Library of Banco de México.

[58] Secretaría de Industria, Comercio y Trabajo. 1918. *Directorio de los principales manufactureros y productores de materias primas de México, diciembre de 1918.* Mexico City.

[59] ———. 1918–22. *Boletín de industria, comercio y trabajo.* Mexico City.

[60] ———. 1928. *La industria, el comercio, y el trabajo en México, 1925–1927.* Mexico City.

[61] ———. 1929. *Monografía sobre el estado actual de la industria en México.* Mexico City.

[62] ———. 1929. *Memoria, 1928–29.*

[63] ———. 1931. *Memoria, 1931.*

[64] ———. 1932. *Memoria, 1932.*

[65] ———. 1933. *Memoria, 1933.*

[66] Secretaría de Industria y Comercio. 1967. *Información estadística sobre la industria textil en México.* Mexico City.

México Industrial. 1905–6. Mexico City. Cited as *MI.*

Meyer, Michael C., and William L. Sherman. 1979. *The Course of Mexican History.* New York.

Middleton, Philip Harvey. 1919. *Industrial Mexico, 1919: Fact and Figures.* New York.

Molina Enríquez, Andrés. 1978. *Los grandes problemas nacionales [1909] [y otros textos, 1911–1919].* Mexico City.

Montemayor Hernández, Andrés. 1971. *Historia de Monterrey.* Monterrey.

Mosk, Sanford. 1950. *Industrial Revolution in Mexico.* Berkeley, Calif.

Muller, Wolfgang. 1978. "El financiamiento de la industrialización: el caso de la industria poblana, 1830–1910." *Comunicaciones* 15: 35–41.

Nuncio, Abraham. 1982. *El Grupo Monterrey*. Mexico City.

Ortiz Hernán, Sergio. 1974. *Los ferrocarriles de México: una visión social y económica*. Mexico City.

Patiño Rodríguez, Raúl. 1964. "La industria de cemento en México." Mimeo, Banco de México.

Peñafiel, Antonio. 1911. *Noticias del movimiento de sociedades mineras y mercantiles, 1886–1910*. Mexico City.

Pérez Hernández, José María. 1862. *Estadística de la República Mejicana*. Guadalajara.

Pérez Herrero, Pedro. 1981. "Algunas hipótesis de trabajo sobre la imigración española a México: los comerciantes." In Clara E. Lida, ed., *Tres aspectos de la presencia española en México durante el Porfiriato*, 103–73. Mexico City.

Pombo, Luis. 1893. *México: 1876–1892*. Mexico City.

Potash, Robert A. 1983. *The Mexican Government and Industrial Development in the Early Republic: The Banco de Avío*. Amherst, Mass.

Quintana, Miguel A. 1957. *Estevan de Antuñano: fundador de la industria textil*. Mexico City.

Ramírez Brun, Ricardo. 1980. *Estado y acumulación de capital en México, 1929–1979*. Mexico City.

Randall, Robert W. 1972. *Real del Monte: A British Mining Venture in Mexico*. Austin, Texas.

Realme Rodríguez, Oscar. 1946. "La industria siderúgica nacional." Thesis, Universidad Nacional Autónoma de México.

Renaud, Ellen. 1987. "Banco Nacional de México, 1886–1910." M.A. thesis, Columbia University.

Reynolds, Clark W. 1970. *The Mexican Economy: Twentieth-Century Structure and Growth*. New Haven, Conn.

Rippy, J. Fred. 1948. "French Investment in Mexico." *Inter-American Economic Affairs* 2(3): 3–16.

Robles, Gonzalo. 1982. *Ensayos sobre el desarrollo de México*. Mexico City.

Robredo, José. 1925. *Punto de vista de los industriales de hilados y tejidos de la republica sobre los asuntos puestos a discusión en la convención industrial obrera del ramo textil reunida en México el día 6 de octubre 1925*. Mexico City.

Rojas, Javier. N.d. *Antecedentes históricos del movimiento obrero en Monterrey: el mutualismo*. Monterrey.

Rojas Alonso, Angel. 1967. "Aspectos económicos de la industria del cemento en México." Thesis, Universidad Nacional Autónoma de México.

Romero, Matías. 1953. "Los jornales en México." *Revista Jornadas Industriales*, January: 35–51.

Rosenzweig, Fernando. 1960. *Comercio exterior de México, 1877–1911: estadísticas económicas del Porfiriato*. Mexico City.

———. 1963. "La economía novohispana al comienzo del siglo XIX." *Ciencias Políticas y Sociales* 33: 465–94.

———. 1965a. "La industria." In Daniel Cosío Villegas, ed., *Historia moderna de México: el Porfiriato, la vida económica*, 311–482. Mexico City.

———. 1965b. "El desarrollo económico de México de 1877 a 1911." *El Trimestre Económico* 32(3): 404–54.

———. 1965c. *Estadísticas económicas del Porfiriato: fuerza de trabajo y actividad económica por sectores.* Mexico City.

Sada, Roberto G. 1981. *Ensayos sobre la historia de una industria.* Monterrey.

Salazar, Roberto G. 1978. "Los franceses en la formación de la burguesía industrial durante el Porfiriato." Mimeo, Centro de Estudios Sociológicos, El Colegio de México.

Saldaña, José P. 1965. *Apuntes históricos sobre la industrialización de Monterrey.* Monterrey.

Salinas, Miguel. 1965. *Datos para la historia de Toluca.* Mexico City.

Sánchez Martínez, Hilda. 1983. "El sistema monetario y financiero mexicano bajo una perspectiva histórica: el Porfiriato." *La banca, pasado y presente: ensayos del CIDE*, 15–94. Mexico City.

Saragoza, Alex. 1978. "The Formation of a Mexican Elite: The Industrialization of Monterrey, Nuevo León, 1880 to 1920." Ph.D. diss., University of California, San Diego.

La Semana Mercantil. 1894–1913. Mexico City. Cited as *SM*.

Serrano, Alberto. 1955. "La industria de la cerveza en México." Mimeo. Banco de México, Departamento de Investigaciones Industriales.

Sherwell, G. Butler. 1929. *Mexico's Capacity to Pay: A General Analysis of the Present International Economic Position of Mexico.* Washington, D.C.

Sokoloff, Kenneth L. 1984. "Investment in Fixed and Working Capital During Early Industrialization: Evidence from U.S. Manufacturing Firms." *Journal of Economic History* 44(2): 545–56.

Stein, Stanley J. 1957. *The Brazilian Cotton Textile Manufacture: Textile Enterprise in an Underdeveloped Area, 1850–1950.* Cambridge, Mass.

Sterrett, Joseph Edmund, and Joseph Stancliffe Davis. 1928. *The Fiscal and Economic Condition of Mexico.* Report submitted to the International Committee of Bankers in Mexico, May 1928.

Ten Kate, Adriaan, et al. 1979. *La política de protección en el desarrollo económico de México.* Mexico City.

Tenenbaum, Barbara A. 1983. "Planning for Mexican Industrial Development: The Liberal Nation State, Tariff Policy, and Nationalism, 1867 to 1910." Paper presented at the Conference of the American Historical Association, December 28.

———. 1985. *México en la época de los agiotistas, 1821–1857.* Mexico City.

Theisen, Gerald. 1972. "La mexicanización de la industria en la época de Porfirio Díaz." *Foro Internacional* 12(4): 497–506.

Torón Villegas, Luis. 1963. *La industria siderúgica pesada del norte de México y su abestecimiento de materias primas.* Mexico City.

Torres Gaytan, Ricardo. 1982. *Un siglo de devaluaciones del peso mexicano.* Mexico City.

Unger, Kurt. 1985. *Competencia monopólica y tecnologia en la industria mexicana.* Mexico City.

United Kingdom, Mexican Embassy. N.d. *The First One Hundred Years: British Industry and Commerce in Mexico, 1821–1921.* Mexico City.

United States, Department of State: Bureau of Foreign Commerce. 1903. *Commercial Relations of the United States with Foreign Countries During the Year 1902.* Washington, D.C.

Vanderwood, Paul J. 1981. *Disorder and Progress: Bandits, Police, and Mexican Development.* Lincoln, Neb.

Velázquez Cruz, Ernesto. 1965. "La industria papelera nacional." Thesis, Universidad Nacional Autónoma de México.

Vellinga, Menno. 1979. *Industrialización, burguesía y clase obrera en México.* Mexico City.

Villarreal, René. 1976. *El desequilibrio externo en la industrialización de México (1929–1975): un enfoque estructuralista.* Mexico City.

Villaseñor, Eduardo. 1934. *Nuestra industria textil del algodón.* Mexico City.

Viscaya Canales, Isidro. 1971. *Los orígenes de la industrialización en Monterrey (1867–1920).* Monterrey.

Walker, David W. 1986. *Kinship, Business, and Politics: The Martinez del Rio Family in Mexico, 1823–1867.* Austin, Texas.

Wasserman, Mark. 1979. "Foreign Investment in Mexico, 1876–1910: A Case Study of the Role of Regional Elites." *Americas* 36 (July): 3–21.

———. 1984. *Capitalists, Caciques and Revolution: The Native Elite and Foreign Enterprise in Chihuahua, Mexico, 1854–1911.* Chapel Hill, N.C.

Wilkie, James W. 1970. *The Mexican Revolution: Federal Expenditure and Social Change Since 1910.* Berkeley, Calif.

Wilkie, James W., and Paul D. Wilkins. 1981. "Quantifying the Class Structure of Mexico, 1895–1970." In James W. Wilkie and Stephen Haber, eds., *Statistical Abstract of Latin America* 21: 577–90. Los Angeles.

Womack, John. 1978. "The Mexican Economy During the Revolution, 1910–1920: Historiography and Analysis." *Marxist Perspectives* 1(4): 80–123.

Yamada, Matsuo. 1965. "The Cotton Textile Industry in Orizaba: A Case Study of Mexican Labor and Industrialization During the Diaz Regime." M.A. thesis, University of Florida.

Zabladowsky, Jaime. 1980. "La política económica en México durante la gran depresión." Mimeo.

———. 1983. "Mexican Exports in the 1890s." Mimeo.

Zaremba, Charles W. 1883. *The Merchants' and Tourists' Guide to Mexico.* Chicago.

Index

In this index an "f" after a number indicates a separate reference on the next page, and an "ff" indicates separate references on the next two pages. A continuous discussion over two or more pages is indicated by a span of page numbers, e.g., "57–59." *Passim* is used for a cluster of references in close but not consecutive sequence.

Agrarian reform, 151, 173, 187
Agriculture, 6, 18, 172, 190
Agujita coal company, 73
Ahedo, Andrés, 97
Ahedo y Compañía, 97
Alcabala, 21, 24, 27, 190
Al Puerto de Veracruz, 74
Alvarez, Eugenio, 70
American Smelting and Refining Company, 17
Anderson, Rodney, 23
Arias Prieto, Santiago, 80
Army, 22, 25, 93, 196
Artisans, 7, 30, 47, 50, 58, 61, 123, 190
Assef, Jorge David, 187
Avisador Comercial de Havana, 40
Aztecs, 13

Backward linkages, 60–61, 193
Banco Central Mexicano, 73 f
Banco de Avío, 55, 64
Banco de Londres y México, 74, 77
Banco de México, 104, 155, 174
Banco Hispano de Madrid, 71
Banco Internacional Hipotecario, 73, 77
Banco Nacional de México, 69, 72, 116–18, 136, 188
Bancos Refaccionarios, 65
Banditry, 21 f, 24, 27, 190
Banking system, 64–66, 192 f

Barcelonette, France, 74
Barroso Arias, Luis, 70
Basagoiti y Arteta, Antonio, 69–80 *passim*, 100, 140
Batopilas, 17
Beato, Guillermo, 97 n
Beer industry: market structure, 4, 85–86, 144, 164, 185–86; focus of study on, 11, 104; technology, 30; workers, 37, 53; connection with glass industry, 47, 82; growth of, 52–54, 190; entry costs, 64; during Revolution, 124, 126, 135–41 *passim*; during Great Depression, 163–64, 178–80
Belem paper factory, 97
Bessemer converters, 32
Boletín Financiero y Minero, 104, 112
Boots, *see* Leather working
Braniff, Thomas, 76–79, 97, 99
Brazil, 9, 38, 42, 68
Brigandage, 21 f, 24, 27, 190
Brittingham, John, 87–90, 133
Bureau of Foreign and Domestic Commerce (U.S.), 36

Caciques, 12
Caja de Prestamos para Obras de Irrigación y Fomento de la Agricultura, 73
Calderón, José, 81–82

Calles, Plutarco Elías, 157
Cámara Nacional de Cemento, 166
Cámara Nacional de Industrias de
    Transformación, 187
Canals, *see* Water transport
Cantú Treviño, Manuel, 82
Capacity utilization: and exports, 4,
    44; cement industry, 31, 40 f, 52,
    126 f, 136, 140–41, 165–66, 177,
    185; steel industry, 31, 126–27,
    136, 140–41, 165, 177; textile in-
    dustry, 33–34, 109; cigarette indus-
    try, 109, 163, 182
Capital flight, 149
Capital formation, 184
Capital gains, 111
Capital goods: cost of, 5, 63; lack of,
    8, 30, 60–61, 156, 197
Capital markets, 68, 86, 96–101 *pas-
    sim*, 192
Cárdenas, Lazaro, 171–76 *passim*,
    187–89, 197
Cárdenas Sanchez, Enrique, 173 f
Casa Calderón merchant house,
    81–82
Catholic Church, 19
Caudillos, 21
Cement industry: production meth-
    ods, 8, 30; focus of study on, 11,
    104; capacity utilization, 31, 40 f,
    52, 126 f, 136, 140–41, 165–66, 177,
    185; workers, 37; market structure,
    44, 51, 85, 143–44, 190; entry costs,
    64; during Revolution, 126–27,
    136, 139 ff; during Great Depres-
    sion, 156, 164–67 *passim*, 188–89;
    new investment, 165–70 *passim*
Cementos Cruz Azul, 51–52, 86, 136,
    188–89
Cementos Hidalgo, 51–52, 86, 136,
    143
Cementos Mexicanos, 143–44
Cementos Monterrey, 143–44
Cementos Tolteca, 51–52, 86, 136,
    188–89
Census: industrial, 9, 59, 176; popula-
    tion, 172–73
Cerritos textile factory, 56
Cervecería Central, 164
Cervecería Chihuahua, 90
Cervecería Cuauhtemoc: control of
    beer market, 4, 85–86; founding

of, 52 ff, 82; and glass industry,
    90–91; during Revolution, 126,
    132–38 *passim*; during Great De-
    pression, 163–64, 179–80, 188
Cervecería Moctezuma: control of
    beer market, 4, 52 ff, 85–86, 104,
    179; financing of, 75; profits,
    113–20 *passim*, 145 f, 161, 164, 169,
    179, 183, 195
Cervecería Modelo, 4, 52, 144, 164,
    180
Chile, 173
CIDOSA, *see* Compañía Industrial de
    Orizaba
Científicos, 23, 122
Cigarette industry: focus of study on,
    11, 104; market structure, 44,
    48–51, 96, 99–100, 144, 182, 190;
    productivity growth, 49–50; entry
    costs, 64; capacity utilization, 109,
    163, 182; during Great Depression,
    161–63, 181–82
Cigar industry, 50, 59
Civil War, U.S., 81
CIVSA, *see* Compañía Industrial
    Veracruzana
Clark, Gregory, 34 f, 37
Coatsworth, John, 16, 20
Cocolapam textile factory, 55 f
Coffee, 173
Collado Herrera, Maria del Carmen,
    78 n, 79 n
Colombia, 173
Comisión de Cambios y Monedas, 69,
    73, 79
Compañía Bancaria de Fomento y
    Bienes Raíces de México, 72–73
Compañía Bancaria de Paris y Mexí-
    co, 74
Compañía Cervecera de Toluca y
    México: founding of, 52 ff, 65–66;
    market control, 85–86, 104; use of
    glass bottles, 91; profits, 113–20
    passim, 129, 131, 139, 145 f, 161,
    169, 183, 195; bankruptcy, 144, 164,
    179–80, 184
Compañía Compresora de Algodón, 73
Compañía de las Fábricas de Papel de
    San Rafael y Anexas: founding of,
    46–47, 64, 96–99; vertical integra-
    tion of, 60; investors in, 78 f; prof-
    its, 113–20 *passim*, 129, 131, 145 f,

161, 169, 179, 183, 195; control of market, 96, 104; during Revolution, 136, 144; during Great Depression, 184

Compañía de Marmoles Mexicanos, 79

Compañía Eléctrica de Lerdo a Torreón, 76

Compañía Explotadora de Concessiones de Muzquiz, 45

Compañía Ferrocarril Mexicana, 77

Compañía Fundidora de Fierro y Acero de México, *see* Fundidora Monterrey

Compañía Industrial de Atlixco: size, 57, 104; founding of, 65–66; investors, 82, 95, 97; profits, 112–20 *passim*, 129, 131, 145 f, 159–61, 169, 179–84 *passim*, 195

Compañía Industrial de Guadalajara, 57

Compañía Industrial de Orizaba: size, 45, 56, 94, 104; founding of, 56; machinery of, 62; financing of, 65–68 *passim*, 75–79 *passim*, 95; profits, 106–20 *passim*, 126–31 *passim*, 137 ff, 145 f, 159–61, 169, 178–83 *passim*, 195; asset value, 141–42, 147–48, 166–68, 184–86; during Great Depression, 158–59

Compañía Industrial de Parras, 94–95, 132–33

Compañía Industrial de San Antonio Abad: size of, 57, 104; investors, 71, 95, 97; profits, 113–20 *passim*, 129, 131, 139, 145 f, 159–61, 169, 179–83 *passim*, 195; during Revolution, 132, 144–45

Compañía Industrial de San Ildefonso: founding of, 65–66; financing of, 75, 79, 95; size of, 104; profits, 112–20 *passim*, 129, 131, 137, 145 f, 161, 169, 179, 183, 195

Compañía Industrial Jabonera de la Laguna: history of, 47–48, 87–91 *passim*, 95, 104; profits, 113–20 *passim*, 129, 131, 145 f; during Revolution, 133

Compañía Industrial Manufacturers, 57, 73

Compañía Industrial Veracruzana: size of, 57, 94, 104; founding of, 65–66; financing of, 95; profits, 106–20 *passim*, 126–31 *passim*, 145 f, 159–61, 169, 179, 183 f, 195

Compañía Jabonera La Unión, 89

Compañía Maderera de la Sierra de Durango, 73

Compañía Manufacturera El Buen Tono: control of market, 48–51, 96, 104, 106, 106 n, 144; founding of, 65, 99–100; investors in, 73, 79; profits, 106–12 *passim*, 127–31 *passim*, 137 ff, 145 f, 160 ff, 163, 169, 178, 180–84 *passim*, 195; asset value, 141–42, 147–48, 166–68, 184–86

Compañía Nacional Mexicana de Dinamita y Explosivos, 48, 73, 91–95 *passim*, 143

Company store, 122

Comte, Auguste, 23

Confederación Obrera de las Fábricas del Valle de México, 23

Confederación Regional de Obreros Mexicanos, 151

Consolidated Rolling Mills and Foundries Company, 46, 85

Constitution of 1917, 123, 139, 141, 152, 197

Cotton plantations, 18

Cottonseed, 87 ff, 133

Cotton textiles: focus of study on, 7, 11, 104; fine weaves, 8, 44, 55 ff, 94, 186; production costs, 17, 34, 37, 63; consumer demand for, 28, 156; automatic machinery in, 33–34, 55–60 *passim*; capacity utilization, 33–34, 109; during Revolution, 34, 124 ff, 135–41 *passim*; workers, 37, 56 f, 151–59 *passim*; labor productivity, 37, 180; market structure, 44, 55–58, 93–95; growth of, 54–58; transfer pricing, 108; capital spending, 143; sales, 156–57; during Great Depression, 180–81; machine industry, 193

Creel, Enrique, 93

Cristero Rebellion, 151

Cuba, 43

Currency, 134

Davis, Joseph, 149

Dean, Warren, 68

234 *Index*

Debt-equity ratios, 65–67
Departmento de Trabajo, 133, 135
Depreciation, 107, 107n, 111n
Díaz, Porfirio: government of, 12, 15,
    20–25 *passim*, 38, 76–82 *passim*,
    91 ff, 109, 120, 122, 194; overthrow
    of, 6, 122–26 *passim*, 196
Díaz, Porfirio, Jr., 92–93, 100
Donkeys, 134
Dos Estrellas mining company, 73
Dumping, 41
Du Pont de Nemours, 143
Dwedk, Eli, 187
Dynamite industry: production meth-
    ods, 8; focus of study on, 11, 104;
    workers, 37, 93; monopolization,
    44, 48, 87, 91–93

Eastern Europeans, 187
Economies of scale, 32, 37, 39, 59, 86,
    187
Economies of speed, 32–39 *passim*,
    59f, 86, 98
Education, 172, 176
El Aguila cigarette company, 144,
    162–63, 182
El Boleo mining company, 17
El Buen Tono, *see* Compañía Manu-
    facturera El Buen Tono
El Centro Mercantil, 72
El Economista Mexicano, 42, 104, 112,
    137
Electrification, 176
El Progreso Industrial paper mill, 71,
    97f, 136
Explosives, *see* Dynamite industry

Fábrica de Curtiduría la Velocitán, 79
Fábrica de Vidrios y Cristales, 37, 90
Factory system, 7
Farji, Jacobo, 187
Ferrocarriles Nacionales de México,
    73
Financial panic of 1907–8, 6–7
Financial returns to investors, 103,
    118–21, 140, 144–47 *passim*, 169,
    183–84, 194–96
First World War, 137, 152
Fiscal policy, 154, 171, 174–75
Food processing, 59
Ford Motors, 143

Foreign investment, 12–24 *passim*, 29,
    143, 190
Forward linkages, 60–61, 193
Freight rates, *see* Transport costs
French Intervention, 13
Fundidora Monterrey: liquidation of,
    4; capacity utilization, 32f, 45, 109,
    127, 136, 165, 177; competitors,
    40f, 46, 104; workers, 45; founding
    of, 45 ff, 62–67 *passim*; vertical inte-
    gration, 60; investors, 68, 73–82
    passim; profits, 71, 85, 104–20 *pas-
    sim*, 126–31 *passim*, 136, 139, 145f,
    160f, 165, 169, 177ff, 183, 195; as-
    set value, 142, 147–48, 166–68,
    184–86

Garza, Isaac, 81–82
Garza-Sada interests, 188
General Electric Company, 101n
Geneva stock exchange, 59, 68
Genín, Augusto, 91
Gerschenkron, Alexander, 191, 197
Glass industry: focus of study on, 11,
    104; bottle industry, 30, 36f, 47, 61,
    82, 89–91, 136f, 156; workers,
    37, 47; monopolization of, 44, 47,
    89–91; entry costs, 64
Glycerine industry: 8, 11, 104, 133.
    See also Soap industry
González, Manuel, 6n
González, Pablo, 132, 135
González Cosío, Manuel, 100
Government bonds, 116ff
Government revenues, 24, 154,
    175
Government spending, 175–76
Graham-Clark, W. A., 36
Great merger movement, 96, 101
Gross Domestic Product, 156, 176
Gross National Product, 1, 20
Grupo Vitro, *see* Vidriera Monterrey
Guadalajara Tramways, Light, and
    Power Company, 73
Guggenheim family, 17, 81

Hacienda Encinas, 35
Hacienda Santa Catarina, 98
Hacienda Zavaleta, 98
Highways, 13, 24, 156, 176
Hobbes, Thomas, 196

Honnorat, León, 74f
Hoover, Herbert, 153
Hosiery, 186
Hugo Scherer y Compañía, *see*
  Scherer, Hugo
Hydroelectric power, 46, 56–59 *passim*, 95, 98

Ibáñez, Indalecio, 70f
Ibáñez, Manuel, 70
Ibáñez y Prieto (banking and brokerage house), 71, 78
Income tax, 108
Indian languages, 172
Indian rebellions, 20
Inflation, 109, 119, 136, 174
Interest rates, 2, 41, 174
International Committee of Bankers, 149
International Paper Company, 98–99
Irrigation, 173, 176

Jabonera La Unión, 48
J. H. Robertson and Company, 96
Jobbers, 60f, 93–94
Joint stock companies, 7
Juárez, Benito, 19, 24

Kelly, Eugene, 75
Kleyff, Alejandro, 187
Knitwear, 184–87 *passim*
Kroeber, Clifton, 22

La Agencia de Tlalmanaco paper factory, 97
Labor: productivity of, 5, 34–38, 49–50, 191; costs of, 37, 63. *See also* Workers
La Cigarrera Mexicana: control of market, 48–51, 100, 104, 144; profits, 129, 131, 145f, 161ff, 169, 179–84 *passim*, 195
La Consolidada, 46, 85
La Esperanza soap factory, 87–88
La Estrella textile factory, 132
La Hormiga cotton textile mill, 72
La Independencia (Mexico City newspaper), 21f
La Laguna, 18, 133
Lamoreaux, Naomi, 101
La National soap factory, 87

Land tenure, 19f
La Owens de Mexico glass company, 90
La Planta de Zavaleta paper factory, 97
La Semana Mercantil, 104, 137
La Tabacalera Mexicana: control of market, 48–51, 100, 104, 144; founding of, 71; profits, 104, 129ff, 137, 145f, 161ff, 169, 179–83 *passim*, 195
La Unión (Monterrey newspaper), 36
La Valenciana, 72
La Victoria wool textile mill, 71, 95
Leather working, 11, 30, 59
Lebanese, 187
Limantour, José Y., 23
Limantour, Julio, 93
López de Santa Ana, Antonio, 21
López Portillo, José, 1
Loreto paper factory, 97, 136

Macedo, Pablo, 100
Machine tool industry, 30
Machine tools, 61, 193
Madero, Francisco I., 123f, 132, 196
Madero family, 95, 122
Maison d'Achats, 72
Managers, 7
Manta, 55
Marendes, Agustín, 52
Meiggs, Henry, 76
Merchant marine, 39–40
Mexican Mining and Industrial Company, 73
Mexican Yearbook, 112
Mexico City stock exchange, 59, 104, 121, 144, 184–85
Mill agents, 60f
Milmo, Patricio, 75
Minas del Fierro del Pacífico, 73
Minimum wage, 28
Mining, 6, 16ff, 30, 93, 152, 155, 190
Miraflores textile mill, 97n, 132
Molina Enríquez, Andrés, 28f
Monetary policy, 155, 171, 174–75
Mosk, Sanford, 187
Mules, 13, 15, 134
Mullins, Patrick, *see* Milmo, Patricio

Nacif, Izzat, 187
National Conference of Industrialists, 139–40

National Congress of Tobacco Workers, 25
New Group, 187
Newsprint, *see under* Paper
New York Stock Exchange, 149
N. M. Rothschild and Sons, 96
Nuñez, Roberto, 93, 100

Occupational structure, 29
Oil, *see* Petroleum
Owens patents, 90

Palmolive company, 143
Paper: newsprint industry, 8, 20, 34, 46, 136ff, 156; focus of study on, 11, 104; monopolization, 44, 96–99, 185–86, 190; imports, 46–47. *See also* Compañía de las Fábricas de Papel de San Rafael y Anexas
Paris stock exchange, 59, 68
Partido Revolucionario Institucional, 8
Patent rights, 89–90, 101 *n*
Peasantry, 18ff, 28, 122f, 141, 150–51, 172–73, 196f
Peña Pobre paper factory, 97, 136–37
Petroleum, 1, 18, 30, 150–54 *passim*, 171–74 *passim*, 187–88
Pig iron, *see under* Fundidora Monterrey
PIPSA, 99
Porfiriato, 6f, 20f
Portland Cement Company, 188
Positivism, 22f, 25
PRI, 8
Price–earnings ratio, 111
Prieto, Carlos, 80
Prieto y Alvarez, Adolfo, 69–80 *passim*, 140
Pugibet, Ernest, 95, 99
Pulque, 35, 54

Railroads: track laid, 15, 28; transport costs, 16f, 40; and economy, 19, 25, 27, 190; movement of army on, 24; engineering of, 30, 76; and San Rafael y Atlixco Railway, 46, 60, 98; and Revolution, 132, 134; refurbishment, 156, 176
Rate of return on capital stock, 103–11 *passim*, 126–27, 139f, 159–60, 165

Rayon, 184–87 *passim*
Real del Monte Company, 17
Rebozos, 58
Restored Republic, 13
Retained earnings, 66, 115
Revolution, 10, 122–49
Reyes Retana, Tomás, 91
Reynolds, Clark, 9, 197–98
Rio Blanco textile factory, 25, 55f
Risk premium, 117–18, 147
Robert, Sebastian, 72
Robertson, Felipe, 97 *n*
Robertson, J. H., 96, 97 *n*
Romero, Matías, 23
Roux, Eugenio, 77
Rurales, *see* Rural Guard
Rural Guard, 24f, 196

Sada, Consuelo, 82
San Antonio Abad textile mill, 35
Sánchez Ramos, José, 97
San Cristobal sugar hacienda, 71
San Lorenzo textile mill, 35, 56, 77
San Rafael, Fábricas de Papel, *see* Compañía de las Fábricas de Papel de San Rafael y Anexas
Santa Maria de la Paz mining company, 73
Santa Teresa paper factory, 97
Sauto, Saturnino, 91
Scherer, Hugo, 72–73, 77, 99
Scherer, Hugo, Jr., 72–73, 79
Schnaider, Joseph F., 82
Scientific managers, 68
Second World War, 7, 9f, 184, 197f
Secretaría de Industria, Comercio, y Trabajo, 157
Sewerage, 172–73
Shoes, *see* Leather working
Sidermex, 4
Sierra, Justo, 25
Sierra Mojada, 17
Signoret, León, 28, 42, 74–77 *passim*
Signoret Honnorat y Compañía, 74–76
Silk, 186
Silva Herzog, Jesús, 1
Silver, 16ff, 152–55 *passim*, 171–74 *passim*
Sisal, 18
Smith-Knight Company, 76

Soap industry, 44–48 *passim*, 87–89, 104, 133. *See also* Compañía Industrial Jabonera de la Laguna
Social Darwinism, 22 f
Société Central de Dynamite de Paris, 91
Société Financière pour l'industrie au Mexique, 68, 73, 91
Spencer, Herbert, 23
S. Robert y Compañía, 72
Steel industry, 8, 30–37 *passim*, 44 f, 85, 141, 177, 185, 193, 197. *See also* Fundidora Monterrey
Stein, Stanley, 68
Sterrett, Joseph, 149
Syrians, 187

Tariffs, 23, 38–42 *passim*, 56, 64, 96, 140, 158, 187, 190, 198
Terms of trade, 152 f
Terrazas, Juan, 87
Textiles, *see* Cotton textiles; Wool textiles
Tobin's *q*, 147
Toledo Glass Company, 90
Trade mission of 1902, 39–43
Transfer pricing, 108
Transport costs, 16 f, 40, 46, 50–51, 57, 86. *See also* Railroads
Tron, Henri, 77, 99–100

United States Steel Company, 40 f, 101 n

Vanderwood, Paul, 21 f, 24
Veracruz: occupation of, 134
Vidriera Monterrey, 3, 47, 82, 89–91, 137, 188
Villa, Francisco, 123, 133

Wagon transport, *see* Transport costs
Walker, David, 97 n
Water transport, 13, 39–40
Watson Phillips and Company, 96
Westinghouse Company, 101 n
Wilkie, James W., 29, 175 f
Wilkins, Paul D., 29
Womack, John, 123–24
Wool textiles, 11, 64, 95, 104. *See also* Compañía Industrial de San Ildefonso
Workers: organization of, 24 f, 122 f, 141, 150–51, 189, 197; distribution of, 27; diet of, 28; foreign, 34, 36–37, 63; skilled, 36, 38, 54, 59, 191; wages, 151, 159, 196; unemployed, 153. *See also* Labor

Yaqui Indians, 20
Yield on common stock, 103, 111–18, 127–32, 140, 144, 147, 159–61

Zakowsky, León, 187
Zaldo Hermanos y Compañía, 71, 100
Zapata, Emiliano, 123, 132, 136
Zapatistas, *see* Zapata, Emiliano
Zidam, Amade, 187
Zollverein, 21

Library of Congress Cataloging-in-Publication Data

Haber, Stephen H., 1957–
  Industry and underdevelopment.

  Bibliography: p.
  Includes index.
    1. Mexico—Industries—History—19th century.
  2. Mexico—Industries—History—20th century.
  I. Title.
  HC135.H17 1989   338.0972   88-24863
  ISBN 0-8047-1487-8 (alk. paper)

DATE DUE